# By the Way

# By the Way . . .

## A lifetime of experiences
*Autobiographical Anecdotes*

Written by Leslie Herman

**Gotham Books**

30 N Gould St.
Ste. 20820, Sheridan, WY 82801
https://gothambooksinc.com/

Phone: 1 (307) 464-7800

© 2024 *Leslie Herman*. All rights reserved.

No part of this book may be reproduced, stored in a retrieval system, or transmitted by any means without the written permission of the author.

Published by Gotham Books (September 11, 2024)

ISBN: 979-8-3303-7684-1 (H)
ISBN: 979-8-3303-3825-2 (P)
ISBN: 979-8-3303-3826-9 (E)

Because of the dynamic nature of the Internet, any web addresses or links contained in this book may have changed since publication and may no longer be valid.

The views expressed in this work are solely those of the author and do not necessarily reflect the views of the publisher, and the publisher hereby disclaims any responsibility for them.

*Reviving Leslie Herman: A Labor of Love by the children of the author: Paul Herman, Janet Rostovsky, Susan Greenberg, Edwin Herman, and Derek Herman*

*In loving memory of Leslie Herman, we, Paul Herman, Janet Rostovsky, Susan Greenberg, Edwin Herman, and Derek Herman, have come together to relaunch his cherished work. This book is a celebration of his life and the profound impact he had on us and countless others. We hope his words will continue to inspire and resonate with you.*

**Old writers**

*do not die*

*they only fade away*

*leaving their tales behind them*

Leslie Herman

# What Is Home

When away, and completely comfortable with your surroundings, you refer to wherever you might be as a home away from home. But, to be home in the real sense, means it is a part of you, and you are a part of it. Home could be:

    Your native land could well be your home.

    Rupert Brook, during the First World War, penned from his hospital bed words that concisely described this thinking.

    If I should die

    Think only this of me

    That a corner of a foreign field

    Will remain forever England.

Home might refer to another human being who shares your abode.

    One with whom you share your life,

    Whom you love and cherish,

    Through health and happiness, sickness and sorrow;

    The person who is always there to rejoice when you succeed

    To ease your sorrow with understanding when you fail;

    The place where you are happy to be,

    Where you can escape

    When affairs from outside are pressing.

    That is your home.

# Contents

## PART 1

Vera, Do You Remember ................................................................3
A Long While Ago ........................................................................11
Hello Mr. Macintosh ....................................................................17
The Song of the Cobbler ..............................................................20
Luck or Fate .................................................................................23
University of Life A Retrospect of My First Two Years ............30
Take Me Back to Blighty .............................................................35
Book Wanted ................................................................................39
The Mantelpiece ...........................................................................42
People in Glass Houses . . ...........................................................47
Banbury Cross ..............................................................................50
My Battle of Trafalgar .................................................................53
Off With His Head .......................................................................58
The Curious Case Concerning a Cruel Canard ...........................60
A Walk on the Wilde Side ...........................................................62

## PART II

Efficiency From the Ridiculous to the Sublime ..........................67
On Our Way ..................................................................................71
How Embarrassed Can One Get? ................................................77
Pagel's Circus ...............................................................................80

Import Trouble ............................................................................. 83
Buy South African First ............................................................. 85
Capitulate ................................................................................... 87
The Strike .................................................................................. 91
Doctor Livingston I Presume .................................................... 94
Lion Trouble .............................................................................. 97
Namibian Venture .................................................................... 100
The Greeks Had a Word for It ................................................. 105
Overnight Stay ......................................................................... 107
There Came a Big Spider ........................................................ 109
A Ring in the Dark .................................................................. 112
The Tin Temple ....................................................................... 116
Black Tie and Candles ............................................................. 119
Late for Dinner ........................................................................ 122
Decisions ................................................................................. 125
Pat Farley ................................................................................. 128
Graham Daniels ....................................................................... 130
Leo Jacobs ............................................................................... 133
A Train of Evidence ................................................................ 136
A War Time Story Never Told ................................................ 140
Shoulder Arms ......................................................................... 145
Invisible ................................................................................... 148

## PART III

Hong Kong ............................................................................... 153

My First Time in Italy ................................................................159

Sanctions May Not Be Fire Resistant ........................................163

Alpine Wonderland ..................................................................168

"Parlez Vous Francais" ............................................................172

A Visit to Vancouver ................................................................175

Out of the Blue ........................................................................179

## PART IV

The Policeman's Story ..............................................................185

Gone With the Wind ................................................................187

The Fifth Sunday A woman for all Sundays ............................190

Life Class ................................................................................195

First Time in America ..............................................................198

The Sound and the Fury ...........................................................201

I Don't Understand Art, But I Know What I Like ...................204

A Day in Tacoma .....................................................................207

The Puget Sound ......................................................................210

The Race at Nisqually ..............................................................214

## PART V

Dining Out ...............................................................................219

Don't Tell Susan ......................................................................222

Twice One Are Two .................................................................227

Twice One Are Two (continued) ..............................................231

Sentimental Journey .................................................................235

Henochsberg Saga ....................................................................241

# PART VI

African Flight .................................................................... 247
Dinner on the Plane .......................................................... 250
Edinburgh Castle .............................................................. 254
A Flying Start ................................................................... 256
Honest .............................................................................. 259
Incidents I Would Rather Forget ...................................... 261
The Insect World .............................................................. 264
A Lone Voice ................................................................... 267
The Missing Link ............................................................. 272
Money for Jam ................................................................. 275
Order Please A lighthearted look at the eating scene ...... 278
Out of Touch .................................................................... 281
The Pictures on My Wall ................................................. 284
Silence .............................................................................. 287
Smoke and Mirrors .......................................................... 290
Tangled Emotions ............................................................ 294
Uncertain Times ............................................................... 296
The Wedding Present ....................................................... 298
Spiders and Achilles ........................................................ 303
You Can't Alter Malta ...................................................... 305
Go to Blazes .................................................................... 307
Neighbors ......................................................................... 309
Next-Door Neighbors ...................................................... 313

Prejudice ................................................................................317
The All Blacks ......................................................................320

# PART 1

# English Landscape

# 1

## *Vera, Do You Remember*

*Of course* you remember 103 High Street Harlesdon, where we were both born. We lived above our father's Picture Palace. Dad's mother Hannah, and father Hyman, lived there, too, on a lower floor than we. Grandma, always called Ma, was the most loving of grandmas anybody could have had, but grandpa died just after you were born. Everybody went to his funeral, but Jack, you, and I were left behind with mother. All the mirrors were turned to face the wall and the curtains were all drawn. I remember him though, a jolly round man with a comfortable lap that I snuggled into while he told me stories of long ago.

Dad managed the Picture Palace, and Dad's sister, our Aunt Jessie, sat up high in front, to the right of the screen playing on the piano the music that came with each film. What fast, exciting sounds she played when Red Indians attacked the trains and loud thunderous banging on the keys when there was a storm.

For children it was just one penny to go to the cinema in the mornings and we were handed a folded newspaper in shape of a cone filled with sweets for the same price. I remember the serial with Pearl White in The Clutching Hand. Each episode ended with her in dire straits, such as being strapped down to a track with a train approaching, or in a canoe being drawn to the edge of a waterfall, only to be miraculously rescued in the next episode.

In the attic there were several pinball machines and a milk shake machine. This was a gadget that had holders for a number of glasses. When milk and ice cream were put in them, a handle was turned to spin the glasses around at a fast speed, to thoroughly shake their contents up. These items were evidentially the remnants left over when Aunt Jessie and her husband Moss spent several summers with their own stall in the fun fair at Blackpool.

Blackpool was where the action was in those days. The cotton mill hands spent their time and money on their yearly holidays called Wakes. Jack used to boast to us that he had been taken there one year, and enlarged on the wonders we had missed.

On rainy days we wound up the gramophone with its large brass horn and would play and replay the few records we had, over and over again. The records had a picture on them of a dog listening to the sounds coming out of the horn. "His Master's Voice" was the name of the company that made them.

We lived near the Willesdon Clock Tower, a paved area with several water troughs around it. Carters let their horses drink there and put nose bags full of hay on them to feed.

Our nurse used to take us to Clissold Park where she joined her friends, and sat with them around the fountain holding onto their perambulators keeping an eye on the toddlers running around, while flirting with the soldiers and sailors who soon surrounded them. War had started, and women were issuing white feathers to anyone not in uniform, to shame them for not joining up. We hated it because Dad had already joined up and Mummy was upset about it. After Grandpa had died, his bakery shops closed. Father sold his cinema and enrolled in Seventh Middlesex Regiment.

It was an unsettling time as Mother and the three of us followed from military camp to military camp with other soldiers' families. The first one was at Sewardston, a small village on the river Lea in Essex. We played with the local children around the village green, who were surprised that we did not know the local superstitions.

Dad took us for a country walk along a road about to be mettled (stones to form a foundation.) Jack tried to jump over a heap of stones at the side of the road and fell on a pointed bit of flint, which went right through his knee. At a nearby farm Dad, the farmer and his wife pried it out with pliers and filled the gaping hole with iodine. Jack bore the scar for the rest of his of his life.

The last camp was at Southampton, from where the regiment eventually sailed. With a number of other wives and children we stayed at a boarding house. You slept with mother, but Jack and I shared a double bed with a much bigger boy named Robert. We did not like him but all the mothers adored him. He was choirboy with a voice of an angel.

While there we all went to the Isle of Wight, but mother and we children were stopped at the gangway and prevented from going on the boat. That is until dad arrived wearing his uniform. They apologized saying they thought mother looked like a French woman, though why that should have mattered, France being an ally. Dad thought it must have been because of the perky hats she always wore.

We then moved to 50 Kyverdale Road in Stoke Newington. There we stayed for the whole period of the war. Dad's sister, Aunt Jess and husband Moss owned it. There were eight of us living there: Aunt Jess, Uncle Moss, Grandma, Mother and Rosie, dad's younger sister, and we three children. Bertha Welch was the daily who, apart from her multifarious other duties, used to bathe us in a galvanized tub in front of the fireplace on Friday nights. One day when she was hanging up the washing in the garden, there was a large rumbling explosion that continued for some time. A lot of windows in the house were blown in. Bertha came running in shouting that the Germans were here. Actually, we found out that a huge ammunition dump had exploded at Silverton 16 miles away.

What with that, and a German bomb dropping on a house in a nearby street and Dad being pronounced missing by the War Office, Mother was in such a state that one day on the spur of the moment she packed us all in a cab to go to Charing Cross station. There she bought single tickets to Tunbridge Wells, a town she had heard had not been bombed.

We were dragged all round town looking for accommodation without success. Once, we were left in a tearoom to be looked after by a waitress, while she looked up and down street after street on her own. Eventually, on the outskirts of the town, worn out, we flopped on to the grass verge and ate the blackberries that were plentiful on the bushes at that time of the year.

A policeman seeing our berry stained, and crying group took us to the Chapman's house and asked if they would put us up for the night. We stayed with them for six months. Mr. and Mrs. Chapman were very kind and made us feel at home.

During that time Jack's asthma got so bad that mother took him to see a doctor in London. While there, he went with Aunt Jess to see Chu Chin Chow, the big musical show in those days. He never let us forget the wonders of the show, and still feels sorry that we had not been privileged to see it.

To make matters worse, while the Chapman children were away at school, the three of us spent a lot of time with Mr. Chapman in his shoe repair shop at the bottom of the garden. He gave us scraps of leather to cut into one-inch squares that he said he needed, but I really think it was just to keep us busy. What annoyed us though, was that he and Jack sat cross-legged together on the counter singing the big hit from "Chu Chin Chow."

Do you remember that I broke my collarbone, jumping over a log in a timber yard? I had my arm strapped firmly to my body for six weeks. I'll never forget that when at the hospital they eventually took the strapping off, my skin my skin came with it. It was much more painful than the break. During that time I walked one armed with my empty right sleeve dangling down. It was not particularly unusual because at that time, there were a lots of wounded soldiers about, with limbs missing.

When we returned back to Kyverdale Road, we found that the park at the bottom of the road had been partitioned into allotments. Every house had an area allotted to it in which to grow vegetables. Milk in bottles was delivered early every morning and the baker's van brought cottage shaped bread loaves later on. The streetlight man came every evening with a short ladder over his shoulder, and rested it against an arm that projected from the light-post and lit the gas mantle. An organ grinder with a monkey on his shoulder used to come around and grind out crackly opera music, receiving payment mostly from people wanting him to go away.

Our next-door neighbor was a bank manager, a superior job in those days. A strictly religious man, he openly denounced sinners. He had two sons whom he suspected were stealing from the candy jar. One day he filled it with black sweets but put two red ones on top. When he found the red ones gone, he whipped the boys with his leather belt on which was a heavy metal buckle. The noise when this punishment was being administered was terrible. The boys nearly died in agony and people in the surrounding houses summoned the police.

Aunt Rosie, dad's youngest sister, was a civil servant who worked in the filing department of parliament. We did not see much of her because she usually worked late. If a minister required a document that was not immediately available she had to work to all hours until it was found.

An Australian soldier named Isadore Weiss, courted her, during which time he found I could not swim. He said he would teach me to swim the Australian method. When we got to the Hackney swimming bath he pushed me into the deep end, and watched me struggle to keep my head above water. Unfortunately, I only learned to dog paddle, not the Australian crawl.

After they married, they went with thousands of other Australian soldiers and their new brides to Perth in Western Australia. They gave me as a parting gift a Nuttalls dictionary, signed by both of them, dated November 1918.

Mother, as a young woman, had worked for a German man who sold some kind of musical instrument. He evidently thought the world of her and kept in touch after the war was over. One day a van arrived at 50 Kyverdale Road and unloaded a huge case addressed to her. It contained the biggest wooden doll's house we had ever seen, complete with toy furniture for each room. Naturally it was for you, Vera. Jack and I each got one dozen pencils with our names on them, in handsome leather cases. We never met him because he never came back to England.

Dad's pre-war friend was a Mr. Stevens, I have forgotten his first name. We were great friends of the Stevens family. They had three children about our ages; Pinny, a boy, and two girls, Goldie and Rose. I mention them because we had a great laugh when you came back from Rose's birthday party. When mother asked you what they had given you to eat, you insisted just hundreds and thousands and nothing else.

Rose came to live in Johannesburg and married a doctor, while Goldie married a realtor in San Francisco. When Goldie came to Johannesburg to see her sister, Jack and I had lunch with her at the Automobile Club, Pinny, the brother, we never saw again.

We always kept Christmas as children. We always had a Christmas Tree with presents under it and hung up stockings on the mantle piece, and enjoyed it all. Mostly as children we used to go to mother's parents' house in Brondesbury for Christmas. Jack and I slept in the attic, adjoining an area in which were odd pipes and water tanks that fed the baths, toilets and kitchen sinks. All sorts of noises, gurgles and rumbles emanated from there from time to time. I was sent up to bed before Jack, because I was younger. But I was frightened of all the queer noises, so they sent you up with me to keep the bogeyman away. You did not have a nerve in your body at that time.

I am sure that we all remember the only toilet in that Brondesbury house. It was on a landing on its own. Its door had colored leaded light glass windows, and the toilet, a large Victorian ceramic museum piece was set up on a pedestal like a throne.

Then there was the time when I had been taken with terrible stomach pains, which I suffered with over a long weekend. On the Tuesday, I went to see Dr. Joe Schwartz who suggested that instead of going to the General Hospital and be operated by an unknown surgeon he would do it himself. By the time I arrived there next morning, my temperature was so high that I was rushed into the operating theater immediately. On being opened up, he found my appendix had burst, and peritonitis had set in. The infection was spreading and he dared not touch the appendix. Penicillin or any kind of antibiotic had not yet been invented, there was nothing to combat the infection. I was unconscious, in a coma and did not know anything for many weeks.

The family called in Dr. Lurie, one of Johannesburg's best-known surgeons. He asked Dr. Macgregor, the head surgeon of the Chamber of Mines, to come in as a second consultant. Whatever they did, I do not know, but I lived through it. When I eventually came round, I found that while I had been in a coma, Mother had been diagnosed with appendicitis also, the family insisted that Dr. Lurie do the operation, not Dr. Schwartz.

A day or two later you found that you needed your appendix removed as well. So, although I knew nothing about it, the three of us were in hospital at the same time. Three appendices in the same family was naturally the talk of Johannesburg. Joe Schwartz's medical practice was immediately affected. You knew this and, against the families' advice, insisted on letting Joe Swartz operate. It was the bravest thing you could have done at the time, and it certainly kept his practice together when a number of his patients were wavering.

# 2
## *A Long While Ago*

***Perhaps, I should*** recall some memories of my youth, in the early days of the twentieth century, before they disappear into an unforgiving past.

Toys were simpler and less varied when we were children. Girls of course had dolls, baby prams and doll's houses to keep them busy, while boys played endlessly with clockwork trains and Mecanno, with its many holed metal strips that could be attached together with nuts and bolts into imaginative designs. Of course wooden building blocks sometimes pasted with printed-paper on their six sides were a basic toy. With playing cards, we started off playing beat your neighbors out of doors, then moved on to more complicated ones as we got older. Board games such as ludo and snakes and ladders were character builders that taught us to take losing in our stride.

Schooling started at age five, with two years of grade school. Junior school continued with standards one, two and three. In standard four, boys and girls were separated. The boys moved to the third floor to be taught by schoolmasters. The girls went to the second floor. The junior school remained at ground level. Even the playgrounds were separate.

School uniforms were mandatory. Blazers and caps bore the school emblem. White shirts with a knitted tie, and woolen socks that folded back under the knee to display the school colors. Navy blue shorts exposed our bare knees to the elements, winter and summer. Long trousers were not worn until you were thirteen or fourteen.

An American boy was jeered and made fun of when he arrived at our school from New York in 1922. Not only did he wear knickerbockers buttoning below the knee, unheard of in those days, but, even worse, he wore a jersey bearing the name Babe Ruth across the front. That a boy should wear a baby girl's name on his clothing was inconceivable. Of course we had never heard of baseball and its heroes. We only knew about cricket and football. Our heroes were Jack Hobbs and Herbert Sutcliffe, and the only Ruth we knew was a woman mentioned in the Bible.

On our arrival in the standard four classroom, Mr. Whittaker, our first schoolmaster, introduced himself. The First World War had just ended and he won our hearts by telling us that he was a gunner in the artillery team that had fired the first salvo in the Battle of Ypres. He further endeared himself to us by marking and naming the positions of all the fielders in a cricket team on the board.

But, we soon found out that school life was not to be all beer and skittles. For homework he told us to write a composition on our 'summer holiday' using all the longest words in our vocabulary. This we did, using any dictionary and encyclopedia that we could lay our hands on. After reading our work, he said, "Now that you have got all those long words off your chests, if you ever use them again I'll cane the lot of you."

Playground games varied with the season. Marbles and its variations were played all summer. The idea was to accumulate more of them, by rolling your marble along the ground and knocking your opponent's marble out of the ring. Other than that, one sat against a wall holding a cardboard shoe box in which three different sized arched holes had been made. We then challenged other boys to roll their marbles into the holes and win several marbles for each successful shot.

"Conkers" was the big game in the winter. A conker was a horse chestnut in which a hole had been bored, and then roasted to the correct amount of hardness. A string was put through it and knotted, leaving about twenty inches of string protruding. You held it suspended while your opponent, similarly armed, swung his conker at it. When a conker remained unsmashed, its value increased by the number of times it had won.

Cigarette cards were collected avidly, year round. They pictured cricketers mostly and there was much bargaining to collect all the members of your favorite team.

Winter warmers kept our hands warm when walking to and from school, on cold days. These were closed empty jam tins with holes pierced in them at each end. Old rags were stuffed inside. Then the rags were set alight. These warmers were eventually banned, when one was left still alight in an overcoat pocket. My brother Jack became the school hero when he saw flames coming from the cloakroom and rang a fire alarm bell, which was close at hand. The school's much practiced fire drill worked like a charm. The children trooped out of the building in an orderly fashion and in record time. If he had waited to report it, valuable time would have been lost that might have proved fatal.

Public indoor swimming baths had three separate pools, first, second and third class. The price to use them was three pence, six pence and twelve pence (one shilling). The first class pool was filtered continuously; the second class one was filtered once a week while the third class was filtered only at the end of the season. The water was dark green by then. There was no mixed bathing, separate hours were set aside for men and women.

We sent secret messages to one another by scratching them on the soft back of a laurel leaf. The message showed up, only when baked in an oven. Of course, we played a lot of schoolboy pranks as well. One was the disappearing ten-shilling note. Having collected ten shillings together with some of our pocket money, we attached a length of thread to it. We placed the note on the sidewalk, and hid. When a passerby stooped to pick it up, we pulled the note sharply away, enjoying their aggravation.

We read the Boy's Own Paper, a monthly and also a weekly that recounted the incredible sporting feats of a boy named Nelson Lee. Besides these rather more accepted schoolboy publications, we could hardly wait for the more juvenile comics that came out every Friday.

Bicycles ridden at night had to have lighted oil lamps back and front. One evening, I was stopped by an over zealous policeman who refused to let me carry on because my red rear lamp was not alight. He insisted on walking with me to an oil shop where he woke the owner to put oil into my lamp. After lighting the wick himself, he allowed me to continue.

In those days all vans were horse drawn and, riding a bicycle up a long hill, I used to hold on to the back of the van to be pulled along. I had to give this up, however, because it was common practice then for every urchin on the sidewalks to cry out, "Whip behind Guv'nor" and the van driver invariably would do just that.

A harmless little Jewish boy, Fatty Bernstein was vindictively harassed by a group of boys. Every day as he left school, they chased him to his home striking him with knotted handkerchiefs as he ran. The teachers did nothing about it although they must have known it was happening. Eventually Philip Cohen, a big boy, suggested that both of us challenge two of them to a fight. My father, home from the war in 1919, had shown me a few moves of the noble art. Having put them to good use on one or two occasions, I agreed.

Philip challenged the leader, who proved to be a coward. After Philip had hit him once or twice, he gave in. My opponent made more of a fight of it, but in a scrimmage I must have banged his nose. With his nose bleeding profusely he decided he'd had enough. Fatty Bernstein was now able to get home without being followed. We never heard any more about it.

Wireless (Radio) called crystal sets had just come in. High outside aerials were needed to pick up the low powered sound waves being broadcast. On an insulated Bakelite base, a thin wire, called a cat's whisker, had to be maneuvered to connect to a particular spot on a small crystal. The sound was very faint and could only be heard with earphones by one person at a time. The rest of us in the room were continually being told to shush.

A year later, an electric valve was added, which amplified the sound sufficiently to be played through a speaker. Our schoolteacher brought this new, one valve contraption to our classroom one day. We collectively listened to music arriving seemly from nowhere. It was Mendelssohn's Spring Song. We sat transfixed. It was a miracle, as though an orchestra of angels was playing on cloud nine.

The turntables of these early gramophones were activated by turning an attached handle and unwinding a tightly wound spring. The main record company of that time was "His Master's Voice." Its trademark (RCA) was a dog listening to sounds coming out of a big brass horn.

We had only two records at home, the first had Signor Caruso on one side and Madam Melba on the other. The other record was The Overture from Tannhauser and The Ride of the Valkyries. On rainy days we played them continuously though boring it drowned out the noise of the passing trams.

Perhaps the biggest lesson I learned at school was at the 'Prize Giving' in my final year there. A great number of assorted books were placed on a long table in the school hall. The whole school was assembled and the prizewinners were to choose their own book when their name was called out.

As head boy and top of the class that year, mine was the first name to be called. I walked straight up to the table, and chose a handsome book, bound in green leather with gilt-edged pages. I think it was about Greek Mythology, something in which I had not the slightest interest, but it certainly looked more like a first prize than anything else there.

After we were dismissed, the Headmaster called me to his office and said, "You have sorely disappointed me, I thought better of you. You obviously chose the book because of its good looking cover, without a care for its contents." He continued, "Let this be a lesson to you. In future never judge anything by its appearance. Take your time to weigh all its pros and cons, before you make a decision."

# 3

## *Hello Mr. Macintosh*

*My father* was demobilized in 1919. The army awarded him a lump sum, as compensation for having contracted tuberculosis during the war. He had been trained as a baker and confectioner having had first-class training in his own father's business. He rented suitable premises in an excellent position, and purchased and installed the bakery ovens and shop fitting equipment that were required.

Before the war "Herrmann the Baker" had been a well-known and expanding business. As a new shop was opened, a uniformed brass band marched from the Town Hall bearing a large sign.

"Follow us to the grand opening of a new Herrmann's Bakery and get free buns and pastries all day." The Pied Piper could not have had a bigger following than was had, those days.

War broke out in 1914. Any name that sounded German was suspect. The windows of his bakeries were broken, and the contents looted. His father, my grandfather died of a heart attack, after which the business was closed. The family decided to drop the double R and double N from the name and we became Herman.

But now, just before his promising new venture started, the health department revoked the license they had previously granted, on account of his having TB. On top of this a large bakery conglomerate objected to the premises being sold as a bakery. They said the council had given them the sole rights to operate a confectionary business in the immediate area. Consequently, he got next to nothing for his equipment or the lease on the premises when he sold them.

Left with little capital after this setback he had to look for a job.

He had been Regimental Quartermaster Sergeant in the army, and I remember going with him to purchase a second-hand officer's tunic and a Sam Browne belt, hoping that wearing it would help. He did get various jobs from time to time such as managing a billiard saloon, then a bicycle shop and for a considerable time he managed a theater. But, the fact that he could not lift heavy packages and occasionally had to go for weeks at a time for treatment to military sanatoriums precluded him from being kept on in any of them.

He had heard of what appeared to be a suitable position in the nearby town of Reading. He applied by letter and was given an appointment to be interviewed the next day. He got to Reading an hour or two before his appointment, not wanting to be late. Walking down the main street he met Bill Johnson an army friend who greeted him warmly and after a short talk mentioned he was employed by the manufacturers of Mackintoshes Toffee. He said that his photo had featured prominently in the local newspaper and stated that anybody who recognized him and said out loud "Hello Mr. Mackintosh" would receive one hundred pounds.

The trouble was that Bill together with the advertising firm's photographer had walked around for two hours, without anybody recognizing him. He told dad that his photographer has just gone across the road to have a rest and a quick cup of tea. I don't want him to see us talking, so quickly walk round the block and come back with a newspaper under your arm, and in a loud voice say "Hello Mr. Mackintosh." The toffee firm will give you one hundred pounds right away and the Reading Daily News will send you a check for a further fifty.

When my father returned, he said his piece, and everything worked like a charm. The photographer made a big to-do of taking pictures while a big crowd gathered. The toffee people and the newspaper were given the publicity they hoped for. Bill in the meantime handed out packets of toffee to all and sundry, to make sure they would remember it.

My father, who had been for some time short of money, had let his clothes get shabby. He went into the nearest outfitters, bought a new suit and shirt and changed into them there and then. Feeling more assured he went on confidently to the interview. It was just as well, because it was a senior position that dealt with the public. The firm were obviously impressed with his appearance because they offered him the job right away.

It proved to be a position that suited him; his old confidence that had been badly shaken by his unfortunate recent job experiences, returned. The family were delighted that he was more like his old self. "Good old Mr. Mackintosh" became the family's rallying cry for years.

# 4

## *The Song of the Cobbler*

***During the First World War***, a bomb was dropped in the North London suburb in which we lived. The next day my worried mother took the three of us children to Tunbridge Wells, a town someone had told her had never had an air-raid. Failing all day to find accommodation, she eventually appealed to a policeman, who marched us to the house of a family friend. Here the lady, moved by our tear-stained, worn-out plight, agreed to put us up for the night. She was Mrs. Chapman ("Call me Mrs. C") whose husband, the local shoemaker, had his workshop on the premises.

Next day, the Chapmans insisted that we look no further. We could stay with them for as long as we liked. "After all," said Mrs. C., "Your husband is fighting the Kaiser for us and it's the least we can do."

Unable to attend school until the beginning of next term, Jack, aged eight, myself, six, and my sister Vera, two years younger, were left very much to our own resources. Jack, I suppose, like most older brothers, was inclined to boast about places that he had been taken to or other things he was allowed to do because he was the eldest. Having no one else to play with we rather got on one another's nerves. That was until, by a stroke of luck while playing in a lumberyard next door, I broke my collarbone. With my arm tightly strapped to my body for six weeks, I was able to play the then all too common role of a wounded soldier to good effect.

My time in the spotlight was short lived, as my mother took Jack, who suffered from asthma, to see a doctor in London for a few days.

She left my sister and me in the very capable hands of Mrs. C. On their return from London, we tried to no avail, to relate all the exciting treats the Chapmans had given us.

Jack shrugged off all our stories with the astounding news that he had been taken to a real theater with a stage and an orchestra. He had watched a golden curtain go up to reveal the breathtaking heaven that had arrived on earth, called Chu Chin Chow. The wondrous stage, the lights and the music were beyond mere mortals' powers of description. Besides which he had not gone to bed until twelve o'clock that night!

Embellished versions of his story were related for our benefit every day until we were heartily sick of them. To make matters worse, Mr. Chapman, as a shoemaker, knew one of the songs, and together with Jack, they would sit cross-legged in his workshop and sing the main hit of the show "I sit and cobble all day long." Whatever happened to me for a long time to come, no matter how exciting, Jack would patronizingly say, "Not bad, but of course when I saw Chu Chin Chow..." and he would then hum a bar or two of the Cobbler's song to boot.

For a long time afterwards it seemed to me that my world was divided into two distinct parts: BCCC (Before the Chu Chin Chow) era, and, ACCC (After the Chu Chin Chow) period. These intimidating three C's were not the only experiences that Jack had had that I was considered too young for. For him such wonderful things seemed to happen all the time. His constant relating of them became more annoying as time went on.

Even after he left school and got his first job, Jack would cap any tale that I had about my own day at school by saying it was nothing to what had happened in the City. Everything was Bigger, Smaller, Hotter or Colder in the City.

Eventually, however, when I started work myself, I was able to discuss what happened in the City on equal terms. But, to my one regret, to this day, I have never managed to see that breathtaking vision of heaven on earth, called "Chu Chin Chow."

# 5
## *Luck or Fate*

***On looking back***, I do not know whether it was luck or fate that followed me all my life, but whichever it was, I am extremely grateful.

At the elementary school that I attended in northeast London we were walked in file to the Hackney swimming baths for the weekly swimming lesson. After changing, I was standing on the springboard when I saw a boy lying on the tiles at the bottom. I dived in and, as we had been taught, held his shoulders and on my back brought him to the surface and got him to the side. Immediately we were pulled up on the bank. To my surprise, the Headmaster in the school assembly hall next morning, acclaimed me as a hero. I was even more embarrassed when the boy, whom I did not know, brought me a shining red apple with a letter of thanks from his mother.

On the strength of that, and probably because of doing fairly well in class, I was appointed Head-Boy. By a strange coincidence, the chief perk of the title was that every morning when I came out of the house the head of the girls school passed by at the same time and allowed me to walk her to school, something I would never have had the presumption to do myself.

At that time in 1922, an early effort was being made to establish a method to determine I.Q's. The same fifty questions on arithmetic, spelling and general knowledge were set for every standard in every school in London. Later, my father was called to the school and told that I had come third in the whole of London. The Headmaster said I should go to a Grammar school and then on to University. My father said he was paying for a private school for my brother who suffered from asthma, and could not afford to pay for another school for me. I had no alternative but to leave school at the age of fourteen.

The Headmaster insisted that I attend a night school. Not just the one for boys who had just left school, but the adult one where students had to be at least eighteen years of age. The head mistress of this adult night school was reluctant to have me. She insisted on my passing tests in several subjects before I would be allowed to attend. Fortunately, this night school took place in the same elementary school building that I had attended for years. I could write the tests on my own in any classroom that was empty. Naturally I wrote the geography test in the room with maps on the wall and went into the history classroom for the history paper, and so on, and passed easily.

I was fifteen, when I was employed with a coal tar products broker in the city. In May 1926, a General Strike was declared. All industrial firms would close, no trains or buses would run and newspapers would not be published. At the same time Mr. Gelpke, the boss, got private news that the largest producer of cresylic acid had an explosion in their plant and would be out of action for some time.

Everybody was told they need not come to work if they heeded the government's appeal to keep the economy running. Mr. Gelpke got into a hotel nearby, and next day I weaved in and around the stalled traffic on my bike.

He and I were the only ones to get to the office. Over the next few days I got all the suppliers of cresylic acid on the phone. A long and tedious job in those days when each call had to go through several operators. He managed at a very high price to buy most of the gaslight and coke companies' entire output of cresylic acid for the next few months, telling them to hold it in tankers at his expense until he gave delivery instructions. Fortunately the strike only lasted one week but he had cornered the market and made a lot of money. I was lucky to be there with him and got a raise. I daresay I would have got a considerable promotion if I had stayed on, but it did not matter to me, as I was soon to emigrate to South Africa and start a new life.

My brother and I had booked on the SS Dunluce Castle on the sixth of September 1926. It sailed from Tilbury Docks at the mouth of the Thames. It happened to be Rosh Hashanah the first day of the Jewish New Year.

Reverend Bronkhorst our Hebrew teacher said, when we questioned our going on that date, "What better beginning to a new life could you have than to go at the start of a New Year."

My father and my maternal grandfather came to see us off on the boat. My father's tuberculosis prevented him from coming then, but my grandfather Maurice Henochsberg who had been in South Africa many years before said, "It's a great country, but don't try and win back the money I lost at the Turffontein Race Track." So with Rabbinic blessing, and advice to keep away from horse racing, how could we go wrong.

Joe Emmanuel, a South African uncle who had promised me a job as a linotype operator when I arrived in Johannesburg, was on Johannesburg station to meet me as I arrived, to say the job was no longer available. After a strike at the Star Newspaper where he worked, it had been agreed that no apprentices would be taken on for two years. Since I had no idea know what a linotype operator was anyway, it did not worry me. Having just arrived, it was just as well that the job was not available. It turned out to be my first bit of luck in this new country.

My grandfather's brother, Henry Henochsberg, had a clothing factory but when I went to see him, he told me that he hadn't any vacancy but I could work in his packing room until I got a job. When I was offered a job with The Castle Wine and Brandy Company to start at the end of the month, Mr. Henochsberg asked me what my duties would be there. I told him that I had to take the inventories every week in the company's bottle stores. He said, "You will become a drunkard, you had better stay here." That was my second bit of luck.

In 1930 he called the factory manager, the cutting room manager and me into his office. He told us that his accountant and lawyer had advised him to put the factory building into a trust for his family, and a private company named H. J. Henochsberg Propriety Ltd would be formed with a capital of 10,000 one-pound shares. This new company would own the business and pay rent for the building, to the trust. He intended to give 3300 hundred shares in this new company to Mr. Battersby the company manager, who had originally been brought out from Lancashire, one thousand shares to each of his two sons, Dudley and Alfred. And magnanimously one hundred shares, to each of the three of us.

Fred Kilmartin, the cutting manager, and Abe Pam the factory foreman, told me that they had no intention of taking the 100 shares offered them. It would make them shareholders. If the firm did not declare a dividend, they would not get the annual bonus that was part of their yearly salary. What is more, it was essential that I refuse it too. Without a thought, I said, "I haven't any intention of refusing the shares, no matter what both of you do." They threatened me with dire consequences if I insisted on taking my 100 shares, but I held my ground.

In 1931 H. J. Henochsberg Pty Ltd came into existence. Unfortunately, Henry Henochsberg, who had started the company in 1887, died after a cataract operation. In those days patients had to lie on their backs for four days without moving their heads. As he was a heavily built man he got pneumonia, which proved fatal.

When it came to issuing the shares in this new company the family decided that they had no intention of registering the 100 shares in my name, as their father had never discussed it with them. However, the lawyer involved showed them Mr. Henochserg's original notes saying he wanted me to have the 100 shares. The family's response was, "It can't possibly matter one way or the other," and so I became the owner of the 100 shares. It turned out to be most fortunate, and definitely it was my third bit of luck.

For some years I had been studying accounting subjects at nighttime, one subject was company law. Consequently I knew that the shares of a public company (Ltd) can be bought and sold to any one at any time. Whereas, a private company (Pty Ltd), which Henochsberg was, cannot have more than fifty shareholders, none of whose shares can to be sold until they have first been offered to all the other shareholders in the company and refused.

Working there happily, I was naive enough to think that with my ownership of 100 shares, I owned a 100$^{th}$ part of the company. With 240 pennies to the pound, 12 pence in the shilling and 20 shillings in the pound, my share for every 1000 pounds of business sold, my share was 2.24 pence. Every day I added up every one of 2.24 pence earned to the previous days total. So, remembering the old nursery rhyme, "See Saw, Margery Daw, he shall work for a penny a day, as Johnny can't work any faster," I did my arithmetic and worked as fast as I could.

Dudley, one of the sons who did not work for the company, offered his 1000 shares for sale, but nobody in the family had any faith in the firm, with Mr. Henochsberg not there to run it, except me. I borrowed the money from the Netherlands Bank on collateral provided I lodged the shares with them. After I received the money, the bank manager phoned me to say that he had notice from head office that owing to the depression he cannot lend any money on collateral. In my case it was too late for him to cancel. That was my fourth bit of luck.

In those days we delivered the completed uniforms to the defense stores in Pretoria by packing them in large wicker skips locked with a padlock. The defense stores had duplicate keys. If they ever complained of a shortage or of some garments not coming up to specification, I had to motor over to Pretoria to settle the problem. Since I had done this for years, I had become friendly with all the corporals sergeants and lieutenants there.

When War broke out in September 1939, there were only five thousand men altogether in both our standing army and air force. All these permanent force men were instantly promoted. A sergeant became a lieutenant a captain a major and so on. Naturally I remained personally friendly with most of these now senior officers.

This position was the same with the government buyers. I had attended the opening of uniform tenders in Visagie Street Pretoria for years, and usually lunched with the clerks and buyers, mostly Afrikaners, while the tenders were being opened. They all became senior officials in due course. Over the years I was on a first name basis with many of them, which I would not have been if I had gone to High School or University. My close personal relationship with the staff of both the defense stores and the government buyers turned out to be my fifth bit of luck.

In 1944 after the war, when Mr. Battersby, the managing director, had serious heart trouble, I had to take over the firm in his place. He died a year later. The firm's auditor, Mr. Mockford of Mockford and Allen, must have suggested to Mrs. Battersby that she was now the biggest shareholder, and since her son had no interest in going into the business, it would be in her best interest to sell the company if possible.

One evening Eli Wunsch of Dugsons, a high quality men's suit manufacturer, phoned me to say that they had been given the option to buy Henochsberg without any mention of me. Eli, an old friend, thought that I ought to know. It was my sixth bit of luck.

I telephoned Claude Leon, an uncle of my wife and head of the Elephant Trading Company. I found that he was on vacation at his house in Kalk Bay near Capetown, and telephoned him. At his suggestion, I flew down taking our balance sheets with me. He agreed we should make an offer to buy the firm of Henochsberg ourselves. The only condition was that his company the Elephant Trading insisted on having fifty-one percent. I certainly did not have the money to do it on my own, and willingly accepted the deal. It was my seventh bit of luck.

I ran the firm entirely on my own for the next thirty years, with little or no interference from the major shareholder. But the Elephant Trading Company, in partnership with the OK Bazaars, floated it into a public company called the Affiliated Exporters Ltd, which was eventually bought by the Castle Brewery Corporation, a large industrial conglomerate.

For a time, I was a co-director of Henochsberg with the Castle Brewery management. When they told me they intended to sell all their textile interests. I retired. Fifty-five years was enough. Was it luck or fate that eight happened to be my lucky number?

# 6

## *University of Life*
## *A Retrospect of My First Two Years*

***In 1924***, I was fourteen years of age, in my last year of school. That year every grade in every school in London was given three sets of the same fifty questions over a three-day period. The subjects were arithmetic, spelling and general knowledge. In those days, before I.Q. ratings these three simple tests were in the nature of an experiment. I found them very easy and never gave them another thought.

One day without any explanation the headmaster asked me to bring my father to see him. I waited outside the door while they talked and wondered what I had done wrong. It appeared I had come third in the whole of London. The head master urged my father to be sure that I get further education. My father explained that he could not afford it at that time. I started applying for jobs advertised in the newspapers.

My first job, with the Esperanto Association in Bloomsbury, was as office boy at fifteen shillings per week. The hours were nine to six and until one on Saturdays. I helped Maggie, a young typist, fold, wrap and mail several thousand of the monthly Esperanto Magazine.

Most of my lunch hours were spent at the British Museum, just across the road, The Elgin Marbles were the featured exhibit at that time. Lord Elgin had brought whole sections of the pediment of the Parthenon and it's supporting Corinthian columns, together with many sculptures by Phidias, from the Acropolis. This was before the Greek authorities realized what a national treasure they were.

I also found myself also immersed in the wonders of ancient Egypt. King Tut's tomb had recently been opened and many of its artifacts were on view.

I left the Esperanto Association thinking that it would be better to work in a commercial firm. Perhaps the fact that I was expected to learn Esperanto had something to do with my decision.

I took a job at Falk Stadelman, agents for Veritas gas mantles and all forms of street lighting. They occupied a large number of warehouses at the bottom of Ludgate Hill, a very rough area. The only place nearby to eat, was Lockhart's, a cheap eating house, which catered to carters and van drivers whose language consisted mainly of four letters words. To eat, you sat twelve to a side on wooden benches alongside plain deal tables. They were rough types, but they called me "young-un" and were very helpful and considerate. I got a mug of hot tea and something filling to eat for two-pence ha'penny. I learned many things from them that I would not have learned in college.

At this new job I and six other boys had to slit open the post and extract that day's orders many of which were for multiple items. The order department manager would then sort them into seven piles. After counting them, he would write down the number of orders were in each pile and hand one pile to each of us to take them to whichever departments were involved. While he laboriously counted, I counted them in my head. I then told him how many there were in each pile. He checked my figures against his, and without saying a word, sent us off.

The first department I arrived at sent me to the ledger room to check the buyer's credit. Eighteen men stood at slanting desks entering sales and receipt details on lengthily hand-written ledgers.

I had to go to the ledger keeper that dealt with this customer, to authorize his credit. I then returned the order to the department.

That afternoon in the restroom, the six boys set on me and gave me the hiding of my life. They said I had made them look bad. My father took my battered self-back to complain. I was offered a job in another department, but decided not to go back. I had been too clever for my own good.

My next job was at Boss & Co, a glass beveling firm, a supplier of mirrored glass to the furniture trade. There were three brothers in the firm. Mark Boss, the oldest brother, was a despot whose slightest wish was a command. At ten-thirty every morning I walked to a tobacconist shop about half a mile away, and fetched him a Corona cigar, taken freshly out of a humidor. I had to do the same thing again at two o'clock every afternoon.

They were Boss by name and boss by nature. No sooner did one tell me to do something than another would tell me to do something else. It was mind shaking. I had managed to stay there for six months, but it wasn't to last.

A Belgian glassmaker had sent Mark Boss a dozen unbreakable drinking glasses, which Mark used as a gimmick to impress important customers. Using me as a sacrificial lamb, he would call me to climb up on the counter and reach up to the top shelf for a glass, and accidentally drop it. It would remain unbroken. One fatal day I slipped, my elbow knocked the whole dozen off the shelf with some force. They caught the metal edge of the glass counter as they fell, smashing most of them to smithereens. Mark didn't blame me at the time but he did not take to losing face well. It was obvious that my sojourn there was nearing an end.

My next job was with the firm of H. Gelpke, a coal-tar products broker. The office was in the heart of the City. I spent my lunch hours absorbing the sights and sounds of what was to me, the center of the world, with two thousand years of history behind it.

Mr. Adams the shipping clerk took it upon himself to steer me away from paths he had trodden. "Never be talked into learning shorthand and typing, my boy. You will find yourself doing routine jobs all your life if you do." "Thanks, Mr. Adams," I agreed, only too pleased not to bother to learn something that might prove to be detrimental.

One day I was sent up to Mr. Gelpke's office for the first time. He asked me what I was studying at night school. "Bookkeeping and French, sir." I said proudly.

"Very good, but make sure you learn shorthand and typewriting as well."

"Right sir," I replied not having the slightest intention of putting my whole future in jeopardy. Thank goodness I had been warned.

On the third of May 1926, the Trade Union Congress had called a General Strike to take place immediately. No trains or buses would run. Newspapers would not be published and production of all industrial firms would be stopped. Mr. Baldwin the Prime Minister, appealed for volunteers to keep essential services running. Mr. Gelpke told us that whoever volunteered to answer the government's call need not come to work until the strike was over.

Next day all roads leading into the city were jammed with every conceivable vehicle and traffic was stalled for hours. I managed to ride my bike in and out of the stalled traffic. I fought a crowd, endeavoring to buy a newspaper from a street corner seller, only to find when I got to the office that it was several days old.

Apart from Mr. Gelpke, I was the only one who managed to get in. The strike lasted for one week only, thank goodness. He insisted on my taking notes of all his telephone conversations. I held my notebook close to my chest so that he could not see that my hieroglyphics bore no trace of Mr. Pitman's influence. When the strike was over, he congratulated me on my shorthand and gave me a raise in salary. But I was soon to leave for what I hoped would be a promising future in South Africa and would celebrate my sixteenth birthday on the boat.

It was obviously the end of a period in my life. But my exposure to what was hoped to be an international language, as well as my study of the ancient cultures at the British Museum, had done me no harm.

What had I done in the two years since I left school? I had not studied trigonometry, algebra or calculus. Instead, I had suffered the harsh reality of the consequences of being too clever in the wrong place at the wrong time at Falk Stadelman; I appreciated the genuine kindness shown me by the toughest of tough van-drivers while eating at Lockhart's. They had taught me a lot.

I had handled the tricky situations with kid gloves every day at the Boss brothers; I had also avoided putting my career in jeopardy by not learning shorthand and typewriting.

And, I now knew that the by-products of coal comprised chemicals used in the manufacture of dyestuffs, fertilizers and explosives.

**My two years in the University of Life in the long run may not have been entirely wasted. I will see what happens to me in South Africa before I make up my mind.**

# 7

## *Take Me Back to Blighty*

***During the depression*** years, money was in short supply, but with the proceeds of a saving certificate that had matured, I took a two-month vacation back to England. In those days, one full month was needed for the round trip: two days each way on the train to Capetown, and two weeks each way on the boat.

As sales manager of a Johannesburg firm manufacturing uniforms, I had been asked by the Legion of Frontiersmen, a patriotic, quasi-Masonic group of ex-servicemen, to get the specification of their new uniform while in London. Legion headquarters in Britain had approved a new style that, it was hoped, would be accepted on May 7 at the annual general meeting. It was the very day that I was due to arrive. They enrolled me as an associate legionnaire and I was appointed to be their South African representative at the legion's general meeting.

The train journey to Capetown entailed sleeping two nights, and spending one long dreary day of travel mostly through the Karoo Desert. In Capetown I went aboard the S.S Edinburgh Castle that was to be my home for the next two weeks. I found that I had been placed in a five-berth cabin in the stern directly underneath the screws. However, I was young enough in those days not to mind.

There was no such thing as air-conditioning then, so we slept on deck right through the tropics, only waking up when the sailors arrived to swab the deck. The days passed all too quickly, with organized games during the day and dancing at night. There were daily sweepstakes on the ship's mileage, and when we crossed the equator, Father Neptune ducked all and sundry in the swimming bath. Of course, over all there was much romance. Somehow, before we realized it, we found that we had arrived at Madeira.

Surrounded by boats hawking goods for sale, we were besieged by young boys willing to dive from the highest deck to retrieve coins thrown into the sea below. We could hardly tear ourselves away from the boat because so much was going on. After touring the island, we made our way back to the dock to join the boat.

The stalls on the dockside displayed a magnificent assortment of the famed embroidered linens and were besieged with buyers. I very cleverly held back and was one of the last to start the buying process, which involved selection and much bargaining. As the last launch was preparing to leave, it was obvious that the sellers were lowering their prices. Wanting a present for my Grandmother I made a ridiculously low offer for a beautifully embroidered tablecloth, complete with twelve napkins. The seller refused to accept it, but on my insistence, looked back at the owner of the stall who, shrugging his shoulders, glanced at his watch and nodded a regretful acceptance. The sailor in charge of the last launch shouted that he was about to go without me, so paying hurriedly, I snatched the parcel and scrambled aboard.

The last few days of the trip were rather an anticlimax, especially as the crossing of the Bay of Biscay was so rough that most people were seasick. Luckily, bright sunshine greeted us in Southampton and I traveled up to London on the boat train.

The Legion of Frontiersmen meeting was scheduled for 2 PM, so I left my luggage in the cloakroom at the station, had an early lunch and tried to get reoriented to a London that I had not seen for seven years. I took a bus to Buckingham Palace Road, where I did not find anything that looked like the headquarters of such an important organization. Nobody seemed to have heard of it. So I did what I should have done earlier—I asked a policeman. He lifted his helmet to scratch his head while he pondered the address I gave him. Then, with a broad smile appearing on his face, he said, "Why, that's the Boozer." across the road.

Only a back door was open, I went up the stairs and found a mass of uniformed Legionnaires in a large hall, noisily swapping old soldier talk. I signed in. Surprised that I did not look like a veteran, who had served in the last War, if not in the Boer War as well like most of them, they nevertheless welcomed me warmly. As a guest from abroad I was led to the main table and given the seat of honor on the right hand side of the chair that the Officer Commanding was to occupy when he arrived. They all had large mugs of beer with them as they took their places at the tables. An officer then brought me a beer and, after chatting a while, he very thoughtfully put a glass of whisky on the table as well. Not aware that it was the only glass of whisky served, I drank it as he went off to meet the Colonel at the front door.

The Colonel arrived, a towering impressive figure with fierce beetled eyebrows and waxed cavalry mustache. The ribbons on his chest reflected every engagement of the British forces over the last fifty years. After I was introduced to him, he called the meeting to order, and asked us to rise for the Toast to the King. Standing to attention, our mugs held high, nothing happened!! There were several unbearable seconds of complete silence, a silence eventually shattered by a loud explosive roar, from the Colonel, "Where's my bloody, blankety blank whisky!"

A murderous look spread over the colonel's face, a look that must have struck terror into many a foreign foe in the past. Everybody was aghast. Sure enough, there was only an empty glass where his whisky was supposed to be. A hundred pairs of eyes focused on me. I wished that the floor would open and allow me to escape the horror of the moment. Remembering the unwritten law of my military training "Never to volunteer or admit guilt," I held my ground and tried to look as horrified as everyone else. A new glass arrived and a newly opened bottle of whisky was put before him. Much shaken, we now drank to the King's health and when the Colonel sat, we sat. I was still alive, but it was a near thing.

A big welcome awaited me when I arrived at my Grandmother's home that same evening. She had cooked a dinner that included everything she remembered as having been a favorite of mine. All the family were there and we talked non-stop until midnight. Then I remembered the parcel from Madeira, which I had not yet unpacked. So I went to my bedroom, got out her present and gave it her.

After carefully undoing the string, she proceeded to roll it up into a ball, ready for some future use. An old habit of hers. Then she undid layer after layer of paper, only to discover a brick wrapped in some old rags.

What a fool I had been to fall for such an old trick. I could have kicked myself, but eventually the humor of it was too much for us, and my grandmother, God bless her, wiping tears of laughter from her eyes, said it was the best present that she had ever received.

But what a day! I still bear the scars. If you ever have a drink in a bar with me, and see me peer to my left and right before I touch it, or are in a shop when I tell the counter-hand not to parcel it, you will understand.

# 8
## *Book Wanted*

***When a friend*** asked me to join him to buy a book that had been highly recommended, I agreed to go with him. The name of the book he said was "The Heel of Achilles." The shop we went into had never heard of it. They looked up their book list and asked him if a new book just published, named "The Five Fingers of Cicero," could be the one he meant. He, very apologetically, said it was. He bought a copy and thanked them for their help.

It reminded me of a book called "The First Two Hundred Million Years" that I had read and enjoyed as a young man in 1927. I remembered that I had been fascinated by a number of past civilizations that it recorded as having ruled the world over the centuries.

I decided to read it again some twenty odd years later. Nobody had ever heard of it, so I went to the Johannesburg Main Library to borrow a copy. They had it listed as being in their basement book reserve, but could not find it. They said they had not recorded the name of the author but he had been a lecturer at Leeds University and it was first published in 1920.

As I was going to London the following year, I thought I would have no trouble in finding a copy in one of the many bookshops in Charring Cross Road. The Second World War was just over, and most of the bookshops for which the road had been famous, were still there. Unfortunately, "84 Charring Cross Road," the bookshop that was the title of a charming book by a very literary New York young woman, had closed. The people than had been the friendly characters with whom she had corresponded, and written about over so many years, had died.

I first went to Foyles, just off Oxford road. It was the largest and most well-known. Miss Foyle, who had inherited the firm, said they had not go a copy of the book but thought I would be sure to get it in one of shops down the road. I eventually reached Cecil Court that housed twelve specialist bookshops at the Trafalgar Square end of the road, but still with no luck.

I was advised to wait until Saturday to go to Portobello Road. It is the street market whose shops contain myriad stalls, which sell out of print books, silver, china, stamps and anything and everything that is unobtainable elsewhere. I battled along its corridors and then searched the barrows on the crowded sidewalks without finding what I was looking for. I gave up trying and retreated bookless.

The following week I went to Oxford, to see a South African friend who was studying at Magdalene College. He suggested that I try Blackwoods in High Street, saying it was certainly one of the largest bookshops in England, and I should be able to get it there. It was huge, and it extended underground. I tried Blackwoods in High, wandering around its vast display of books before I asked where the secondhand section was. There, I told the salesman what I was looking for. He said "You are unlikely to find it here, it is mostly for Detective, Spy, and Gothic type paper-backs, why don't you go to our antiquarian department?"

The antiquarian section was outside, in a warehouse around the corner. When I got there, I diffidently asked for the "First Two Hundred Million Years." After referring to a manual of great length, he said they had a first edition signed by the author. It would cost two hundred pounds, or a first edition that would be one hundred pounds. Shocked, I told him that I merely wanted a standard copy at a reasonable price.

He appeared surprised, evidently most of their customers required first editions. Looking at me up and down, he decided that I obviously had not gone to either Eton or Harrow, and was probably merely only a Rhodes Scholar from America or the Colonies. Rather disdainfully, he produced a slightly worn copy and handed it to me for a nominal twenty-five pounds.

The wanted book had been found.

# 9

## *The Mantelpiece*

*A few years ago*, I was in Regent Street, London, waiting for a bus that would take me to Harrods in Knightsbridge. The first bus that arrived had "Harlesdon" written in large letters on its destination board.

Harlesdon was nowhere near Knightsbridge, but without a thought as to why or wherefore, I clambered on. From the recesses of my memory, I asked the conductor if the bus went past the Willesdon clock tower in Harlesdon High Street, a clock that I had not heard mentioned or thought of for well over sixty years.

"We don't actually pass it, but I can put you off at Gladstone Park nearby," he said.

Ah, Gladstone Park! Sitting on my own on the top deck of the bus, my mind wandered back in time to a host of childhood memories. One such was to a sunny day, walking with Daisy, my nurse, forming part of a caravan of baby carriages gathered around an oasis of a fountain. The whole area was alive with the shouts of children, the sound of gushing water and the chatter of nursemaids. The blue-jumpered sailors and the red-coated soldiers that soon gathered, added excitement and color with their laughing, teasing and chaffing, while getting quick-witted cockney backchat from Daisy and her friends.

Yet, all too soon, we left the park to walk along the dingy streets to a kitchen, set in the basement of a house, approached by white holystoned steps that led down from an iron fenced area at the side of the front door.

"I must visit my Ma, mustn't I?" Daisy would say. Her Mother was cook in a house nearby, and instead of getting exercise and fresh air, we crowded into a subterranean kitchen that always seemed to be full of Daisy's mother in a white and blue overall, entertaining her friends.

"All nice people mind you. My Ma is most particular," Daisy would stress.

The coal stove was always ablaze, and the temperature was probably unbearable, in those days before air-conditioning was thought of. But who cared! Certainly not me.

I had no complaints. If I looked restive, I was given another large slice of cake.

"I don't think the people in your 'ouse know 'ow to feed a child proper, ," said Daisy's mother.

"Just poppin' in to see how you girls are doin," was the type of opening remark of an endless procession of tradesmen, policemen and soldiers. Not one of them refused the tea and cake that always seemed to be forthcoming.

A background of talk and scandal went on continuously. Mostly it went over my head, but some items were within my scope and were wondrous, indeed. One such was The Green Man Epic, a serial that extended over several visits, and held me spellbound.

My host at the Green Man was a vast man whose remarks, usually spoken with great and kindly humor, were often quoted, as were those of several other local characters, who all became important stars in the private firmament of my own small world. This was a separate world from the one I lived in with my family, and certainly never mentioned.

At some stage, Mr. Ponsford suffered a boil. It was a boil that transcended all the other boils in my childhood experience. The cook from The Green Man used to report on it daily. It practically caused a complete breakdown in the Ponsford ménage. Daisy's mother, and others with experience, proffered advice as to its cure and eagerly awaited news as to the efficacy of the new treatment. Some of them wondered if his always fondling his favorite cat was the cause of it. Why it remained forever in my memory was apparently because the boil was on his behind!

"Gor Blimey," Mr. Ponsford had been heard to say, "Have I got to eat my bloody dinner on the mantelpiece for the rest of my life!"

Whenever I got home, I used to gaze up at our own mantelpiece with awe. In fact, ever since, I mentally visualize a vast ghostly Mr. Ponsford standing on the right-hand side of every mantelpiece I see, while he is eating off a dinner plate balanced precariously on its narrow shelf, a cat rubbing itself against his trouser leg.

When I got off the bus, I found my way to the High Street without much difficulty. To my great pleasure, it appeared that very little had changed. Everything looked just as I remembered it. I found the house where I was born, and although the ground floor was now a tailor shop, the upper two floors, as did the whole street, looked exactly as though time had stood still.

I continued up the road, looking for somewhere to eat, as it was well past my usual lunch time, and there, to my joy, was The Green Man. It was set back from High Street with a large inn signboard in front, depicting a man in a green coat holding a glass of ale. I went in and ordered a pint of lager and some bread and cheese. Although I had never been inside before, it was obvious not a bench or table had been changed over the years.

Everybody was very friendly and I was soon chatting freely with a group of regulars sitting at the bar counter, when the owner barman joined in the conversation. But the period just before the First World War was before their time, and no one had ever heard of Mr. Ponsford.

Suddenly, I felt an uncontrollable urge to attempt to see the famous mantelpiece. I told the owner barman that, as a boy, I had been to the upstairs parlor many times and would dearly love to see, it after all these years, to refresh my childhood memories.

"It is many years since anybody has lived there," He said. "I keep it locked up as it would cost too much to make it livable. But the parlor is open as we occasionally use it as a storeroom. By all means go up if you don't mind it being untidy."

On the landing of the second floor, the parlor door was closed, and as I pushed it open and peered into the darkened room I felt a cold shiver down my spine. When my eyes adjusted to the darkness I stood transfixed. There next to the fireplace, emanating out of ectoplasm that seemed to come from nowhere, a ghostly transparent figure of a man took shape. It faded as I looked at it but before it disappeared completely I felt, rather than heard, a faint hollow of an echo that sounded suspiciously like "Gor Blimey!

I found a light switch and just as the light came on a large cat that I swear was not there before, jumped down silently from the mantle and dragging one of its back legs as though in pain disappeared on to the landing behind me. Shaken, I went down to the bar and asked the barman if the cat had come down. He said he has never had a cat, as he is allergic to them. He implied I must have imagined seeing one.

I have no intention of ever going to The Green Man again—the experience is not one that I want to repeat. But if indeed the spirit of the late Ponsford still haunts the Inn, I will leave it to him to deal with the present owner, whose allergy to cats must be a problem.

# 10

## *People in Glass Houses . . .*

***On my first day*** to start work at Boss and Company, I had to pass a group of their factory workers who were standing in front of the office entrance, having their tea break. The youngest of them, obviously an apprentice, accosted me and very rudely put his face up to mine said, "If you are the new office boy I wouldn't give tuppence for your chances." An older man remonstrated with him, but the apprentice shook him off and spitefully continued saying, "I've worked here for only six months and I've seen five blooming office boys come and go."

Several of the other men apologized for his outburst, but I must admit I was shaken by it and wondered what I had let myself get into. Boss & Co was a glass beveling business that supplied mirrored glass to the furnishing trade. Mark Boss, the oldest brother, was a despot whose slightest wish was a command.

Phil, the second eldest, was a Beau Brummel of a fellow. He wore starched white shirtsleeve cuffs embellished with large gold cuff links exactly one inch below his jacket sleeves. He spent most of his time talking loudly on the telephone, mostly making sure that the dowager Mrs. Boss got the best seats at every new show that came on.

Ernie, the youngest, workmanlike in a khaki dustcoat, oversaw loading the vans, and constantly found me errands to run.

They were Boss by name and boss by nature. No sooner did one tell me to do something when another would tell me to do something else. I found it mind shaking, but managed to satisfy them somehow, and got involved in the firm's day-to-day affairs. One day Mark announced that they had obtained the job of supplying and glazing the new windows at Peter Robinson's, one of London's most prestigious stores. The most exciting aspect of it was that the main window had been built to hold the largest sheet of window glass ever made.

Pilkington, the famous glass manufacturer of St. Helens in Lancashire, were to supply it. We were to send vans there to fetch it. I was very keen to be a part of the undertaking and asked Ernie if I could go with him to fetch the glass, but he assured me that it was out of the question.

The Peter Robinson store stood on the north eastern corner of Regent Street and Oxford Street, one of the busiest corners in the west end of London. The glass would be packed in wooden crates that had to be unpacked at the site, which clearly could not be done during daytime. Two a.m. on Sunday morning was considered the most suitable time to do it. Without telling anybody, I decided to be there and see it done.

There was practically no traffic at that time of night and that Oxford Street corner was as quiet as it had ever been. Six men unloaded the huge wooden crate off the van and stood it upright on the road adjacent to the curb. As they reached down to get their tools to open the crate, to extract possibly the most valuable sheet of window glass ever made, an unexpected blast of a siren, a screeching of tires and a sweep of lights flashed the whole area as a fire engine swept around the corner of Regent Street North into New Oxford Street. The fire engine missed the crate by inches. The men had momentarily stepped away as the fire engine tore past, leaving the valuable crate standing unsteadily on its own, for a minute or two. If the wobbling crate had crashed it would have ruined the firm.

Unfortunately Ernie saw me there, and realized that if I mentioned the incident to Mark, the head of the firm, they would all be in trouble. So when I arrived at the office on Monday morning I was paid off immediately before Mark arrived.

Getting the sack at a moment's notice is always a terrible thing at any time, I am sure, but here it was for nothing other, than that I was in the wrong place at the wrong time and saw something I should not have seen.

Thinking back about it, I should have been prepared. That terrible apprentice had warned me that he had seen five blooming office boys come and go. He would now have the satisfaction of warning any new young expectant that he had seen six blooming office boys come and go.

# 11

## *Banbury Cross*

***Motoring from London*** on our way to Stratford on Avon we went out of our way to visit the town of Banbury. The name brought back to us the memory of the old nursery rhyme "Ride a Cock Horse to Banbury Cross, to see a fine lady on a White Horse."

There we found a ten-foot high cross in the center of the town square but not the fine lady, unfortunately. But we did find "The Original Cake Shop" that was still making and selling the Banbury cakes first made by Betty White in 1638. The lightness of the pastry stuffed with a currant mixture is legendary. Her husband 'Old Jarvis White' once said that a sparrow once entered the shop and flew off with one.

I had recently eaten an 'Eccles Cake that I was told resembles the Banbury in flavor and composition but is oval instead of round. I can personally vouch for the lightness of its pastry and the delicacy of its flavor. I think old man Jarvis's story of the sparrow may have more than a grain of truth in it.

Our curiosity was now awakened to find out more about such traditional treats. There seemed to be no literature on the subject but we found an old brochure headed 'Treasury of Folk Lore' published in the Isle of Man. The only thing I knew about the Isle of Man was that its unique Manx cat had no tail, so I was delighted to find that this peculiarity did not apply to the information given in the brochure. It was more full of tales than actual fact, and none the worse for that.

'Gingerbread Fairings' were said to have been sold in the Isle of Man for centuries. Their origin was that a worthy knight returning in his cups, accidentally knocked pots of treacle and ginger into the dough his lady was kneading. The dark color of these gingerbread men was not considered genteel and gilt paper was wrapped around them when served, hence the saying "Take the gilt off the gingerbread."

Muffins were first mentioned in 1706 when a Mrs. Glasse in her "The Art of Cookery" gave the recipe for a baked cake called a moeffin. The 'Crumpet' a cake with crumples, was referred to as a crisp or cramped bread in an old text of Exodus.

In the nineteenth century the muffin man with a tray on his head and a bell in his hand, was a feature of the London streets. At one time there were at least five hundred muffin and crumpet men in London. They certainly still plied their wares when I was a boy, until the mid-twenties, at least on Sundays when the teashops were closed.

Among a list of traditional cakes, was a Warwickshire Godcake still eaten in Coventry on New Year's Day. While in the Lancashire town of Bury, Simnel cakes are eaten on Bragat Sunday. The cakes contain dried fruits, spices and sugar, and Bragat is a drink of ale, spices and whipped eggs.

Funerals cakes abound; Yorkshire, Lincolnshire and Berkshire all have their own. Fourses cakes from Norfolk and Kitchell's from Suffolk also ease the mourners' sorrows.

Both Bath and Chelsea claim they were the originators of the bun. But although both are still eaten worldwide, the one-time melodious cry of the street sellers of the Chelsea bun is no longer heard. Bath is a spa town and a Doctor Oliver, who was a physician at the Bath Mineral Water Hospital, invented a medicated biscuit to improve the health of his patients. It was called a Bath Oliver.

Simnel cakes on Bragat Sunday; Simnels contain dried fruit, spices and sugar, and Bragat is a drink of ale, spices and whipped egg. Thousands flock to the town of Bury in Lancashire on mid-Lent Sunday to go "a mothering," that is to visit their parents and friends. The trip is accompanied by the consumption of large quantities of the cake and bragat. They probably need more mothering after their visit.

Shrewsbury Cake is peculiar to the town of Shrewsbury and is of indescribable flavor and crispness.

Maids of Honor, is a cheesecake beyond compare. As children we were always given them as a treat whenever we were taken to Hampton Court in Richmond. The story goes, that while being eaten by Anne Boleyn, then a Maid of Honor, she offered bluff King Hal a taste. She told him that she did not know what it was called. He said, "Let them be called Maids of Honor." One must hope that it was no fault of these cakes that she later lost her head.

Melton Mowbray Pie, the Cambridge Sausage, The Bath Chap, Cheddar Cheese and the Cornish Pasty are well known to this day, and indicate their places of origin. The recipes for most of them have remained constant over the years.

One cannot say the same for the Cornish Pasty; almost anything edible was likely to become an ingredient. In days gone by, it was said that the Devil himself would not enter the Duchy of Cornwall lest he should be made into a pie. These days, however, they are generally composed of either meat or fish, with potato and onion, so if you go to Land's End or Penzance, order a pasty with confidence. You won't be sorry.

Do not think that these traditional eats are all that there are. But I suggest if you go out of your way to visit the places mentioned here, and then endeavor to locate others, your next visit to Britain will be a filling as well as fulfilling experience.

# 12

## *My Battle of Trafalgar*

***On a recent visit*** to London I had asked my travel agent to book me into the Royal Trafalgar Hotel. Its central position near Trafalgar Square and Charring Cross Road was within walking distance of the theater district, which should save me the aggravation of the usually hopeless task of trying to get a taxi after a show.

I knew its location well because my wife and I had stayed there twenty years earlier. At that time we left it after only a two-day stay because we found that it adjoined the British Home Office, a government department. The news that Lord and Lady Mountbatten had just been blown to smithereens by I.R.A. terrorists while on their yacht so shocked us that we decided to move to a hotel that we hoped might be a less obvious future target.

On my arrival at the hotel, the receptionist told me that I had been given an upgrade to a larger room on the third floor. I was very pleased to hear that, but not so pleased when informed that as the two lower floors were being remodeled, the elevator to the third floor was not in use. She explained that I would have to go up to the fourth floor and walk down one flight. I did not like the idea but as I had written to ten different people to say that I would be at the Trafalgar Hotel, I had no alternative but to stay. At first it did not seem too onerous, but I was soon found it a chore, to have to walk up a flight of stairs every time I wanted to go down to the ground floor.

Any doubts I had about accepting the room fell way directly the porter unlocked the door. Recently rebuilt and redecorated, the bathroom was very modern, the bedroom well furnished, and as the room faced away from the street it promised to be quiet. A drawer contained china cups and saucers with a plug in water heater and an assortment tea and coffee bags, which were going to be very useful. A distinct plus was that the wardrobe contained a small safe with instructions on how to program one's private four letter code into it and so enable it to be locked and opened at will. My passport, airways ticket and spare money would certainly go in there.

I went down for lunch, having traversed a long narrow passage and walked up to the fourth floor to take the elevator down. The dining room was more like a brasserie, no tablecloths with a few eating utensils wrapped in a napkin on the table. The menu was less than ordinary. I could see that I would be eating out most of the time.

Before I went out of the hotel to explore my surroundings, I went up to my room. This entailed going up to the fourth floor, finding the stairwell and walking down to the third floor along the passage to my room. To go out, of course I had to go back to the stairwell, walk up the stairs to the fourth floor and await the elevator to go down.

That evening I decided to eat at Sheeky's, a nearby fish restaurant, but first I had to go up to the room before going out. Once again I took the elevator up to the fourth floor then walked down the stairs to my third floor room. After a wash and brush up, I again went up the stairs to the elevator, to go down.

By now, having gone through this performance a few times, I think I was getting used to it. Once, by mistake, I walked down the stairs when I should have walked up. But as it caused me to have to go back up two flights instead of one, I resolved not to do it again.

To get to Sheeky's, which was just off Charring Cross Road, I had to walk through Leicester Square, which seemed to be the nighttime center for all the young people in London. Vast crowds of them were all in different versions of undress so casual that, if I had been wearing a jacket, I would have stood out like an alien from another planet. Thank goodness, the weather was very warm all the time I was there and, wearing only slacks and an open shirt, I passed through the young well-behaved crowd without incident.

That night, my first night in London, having gone up to the fourth floor to go downstairs to my room once more, I was so worn out that quickly fell into a heavy sleep. The telephone ringing insistently woke me up. Who could be ringing me at this unearthly hour? I looked at my watch. It was half past one "Hallo" I growled. A frantic sounding voice answered. Please evacuate your room immediately Blearily, I pulled a pair of trousers over my pajamas put on a dressing gown and, half asleep staggered along the passage until I found the stairwell.

Down I went. The stairs were just bare concrete, no carpeting, below my floor, evidently. I tried the doors on each landing as I passed. They were all locked. Would I find the landing door locked when I reached the bottom? What would I do if it were? The concrete stairs and bare walls were like a prison but at least they were not flammable wood and plaster, which was some comfort.

At last, I got to a landing where the door opened and I fell through it into a side alley. Around the corner, I found the other residents, some in just their bedclothes standing outside the hotel. A fire engine blocked the road and the lobby was full of helmeted firemen standing around. We stood there for three quarters of an hour before it was decided to be a false alarm.

This time it took me a while to get back to sleep, but soon after I did so the phone rang and again I was told to evacuate the room once more. I made the time to put my trousers on again, after all my money and my wallet were in them.

After I arrived downstairs, I joined the now rather mutinous other residents to stand next to the same fire engine and watch the same firemen in the lobby, while the building was searched fruitlessly. This time they assured us that they found the loose wire in the fire alarm that was causing the trouble and we should not be bothered again.

Breakfast was a scramble. Evidently the hotel fills up with people who stay overnight and all go in for breakfast at the same time. It was a first come first served buffet, small boxes of different cereals that have to be pried open only to find that the contents were in thick plastic bags impossible to open. Toast and scrambled eggs in supposedly heated containers were all cold by the time I got to them. The assortments of jams in their little containers were plentiful but the butters were so frozen that they could not be spread. Often I did not bother with breakfast and ate something wherever I happened to be.

What was most annoying, however, was that the elevator that went up to the fourth floor kept going out of action. This happened so frequently that I spent more time at the National Gallery and the book shops in Charring Cross Road than I would normally have done, rather than haying to walk unnecessarily up and down the three flight of stairs to my room. In fact I often found myself walking here, there and everywhere, when I could have jumped on a bus or hailed a passing taxi.

By now, I felt I could not keep overlooking, without a protest, all the disconcerting things that were happening. Unlike Admiral Nelson, I did not have a telescope, nor even a blind eye, to pretend that I could not see the notice proclaiming that the elevator was out of action once more. But I could at least fire a shot over the enemy's bow. Speaking to the staff at the counter had been useless. I must complain to the manager himself.

A Miss Hardy, his secretary, told me that the manager unfortunately was out of town but asked if she could help. I listed all the many hardships I had put up with during my stay and thought I should get an apology and receive a considerable reduction in my bill. She agreed the remodeling the lower two floors had caused complications but it could not be helped, and no one else had complained. As for a reduction she could not do anything about it as I had paid in dollars to the hotel's American booking agent in New York.

Discouraged, the only thing I felt like doing, was saying 'Kiss me Hardy' as a throwaway line and walk away. I know that the circumstances were slightly different when Admiral Nelson spoke those immortal words, but I felt that it would emphasize my dissatisfaction with the hotel's handling of my complaints. At the last minute however, I stopped myself saying it to her, thinking it might be construed as sexual harassment.

Although I had complained about all the hardships that I had suffered, I was not really as serious about it as I had made out. I had never felt better; the exercise had done me the world of good. Walking up and down the stairs was something I should do more often. Not having a car I did much more walking than usual. Perhaps it was all a blessing in disguise. I probably had won my battle of Trafalgar after all.

# 13

## *Off With His Head*

***The Tower of London*** has a long history of providing an excellent venue for decapitations. "Off with her head" was quite a favorite saying of Henry VIII. Lewis Carroll had the Queen of Hearts say it on every occasion when she was displeased, which was often. It was Alice who answered her back in the royal rose garden. The King, who timidly pointed out that Alice was only a child, saved her from that dire fate. The Cheshire Cat was lucky in that its head appeared to have no body to separate it from.

Modern critics of children's literature have criticized Carroll's Queen of Hearts' ungovernable fury and constant orders for beheading. They feel that children's stories should be free of violence. Carroll is quoted as saying the horrors and decapitation in the Grimm's and Andersen stories are ones most children find amusing and are not damaged by them in the least. He suggests that perhaps Alice's adventures in Wonderland should not be allowed to circulate indiscriminately among adults.

On the occasion of Princess Di's funeral, her brother spoke feelingly about the way his sister had been ill-treated. A spokeswoman for the court said on television that Westminster Abbey was not the place, or the funeral the occasion to voice his anger. I do not know what time and place she thought it might be voiced. Probably never.

The Earl's words, magnificently delivered in the upper class accent of the English aristocracy, were a searing comment on her treatment by the press and general unfeeling behavior of the royals, and judging by its reception it seemed to echo throughout the land.

But his words were not in a children's story, but spoken in public, so it is surprising that his head remains on his shoulders, at least for now. He would be well advised to stay well away from the Tower of London. There must be many headless ghosts of people who, after criticizing past monarchs, still haunt its battlements.

# 14

# *The Curious Case Concerning a Cruel Canard*

**In retrospect** the case of the five C's was one of his most successful ones. It bought him not only a high degree of international recognition, but also the honor of earning the heartfelt thanks and lifetime friendship of one of the most intelligent and beautiful women in Europe. Her name remains unmentioned to this day.

On a typically overcast London winter day, a tall bearded man alighted from a Hansom cab. He looked furtively around, before instructing the cab driver to wait for him. Striding to the front door he checked its number, before peremptorily striking the brass doorknocker. Without a by your leave, he marched straight into the apartment as the door opened.

"Wait" said the occupant putting aside his violin and taking out a briar pipe from his jacket pocket. "I am honored by this visit albeit unexpected as it is. You are the Duke of Hentzau disguised as an English Country gentleman."

"How on earth do you know?"

"Your boots are crafted from mountain goatskin, your cravat is knotted in the Balkan style and the Norfolk jacket you are wearing is not a pattern worn in this country."

"That could apply to many people."

"May be, but you forgot to remove your signet ring bearing the Ruritanian Coat of arms."

"Touché! I can see that your reputation is richly deserved. I have come here hoping that you can help me find the perpetrator of a cruel canard. One that I fear, if allowed to circulate, will cause a throne to topple, heads to roll, and even worse, besmirch the spotless character of a beautiful woman. Read this slanderous document."

After reading it, the roll-top of the escritoire was raised, a quill pen dipped into the inkwell, and several paragraphs rapidly penned onto a sheet of linen notepaper. With a swirl of the wrist it was handed to the Duke with a flourish.

"Mon Dieu!" said the Duke, a ghastly pallor spreading over his face as he read the contents. "I would never have believed it. I must hasten to stop them doing any further damage. But how did you know?"

"That is something that I cannot divulge, but you must be on your way. Time is the essence. The 11:40 from Paddington will get you to Dover in time to catch the cross-channel packet that get to Calais this very evening."

The Duke rushed away saying, "You will be well rewarded and we will be forever in your debt."

A third man who had remained silent and unseen throughout, got up from the depths of the armchair in which he had been seated. He said, "My dear man, you have excelled yourself this time. How did you do it and who is the lady?"

"Too much is at stake to mention her name now. You heard that a throne could topple and some heads roll, but until I am assured the Lady's honor has been preserved, my lips must remain sealed. The solution, however was elementary, my dear Watson."

# 15

## *A Walk on the Wilde Side*

***While in Trafalgar Square*** in London some years ago, we were handed a pamphlet announcing that a youth orchestra would be playing Vivaldi's Four Seasons that evening in the St. Martins in the Field church.

Our hotel was just around the corner and as we had not yet arranged to do anything, we decided to go. It was still very early that afternoon and we were on our way to the National Portrait Gallery. To get there, we had to walk through a pedestrian paved walkway behind the church. In its center was a large memorial to Oscar Wilde. Although admirers of his plays, in these days of gay parades and talk of same sex marriages we had forgotten about him.

The memorial was a vast black marble coffin about ten feet long and four feet high, entitled, "A Conversation with Oscar Wilde." The sculptor was Maggi Hamblin and it was dated 1998. At one end, mounted on copper was the embossed head and shoulders of Wilde smoking a cigarette. Inscribed on a low raised portion at the other end, were the words, "We are all in the Gutter, but some of us are looking at the Stars," obviously written while in Reading Jail, at the end of his life.

Although, it may be a fact that "Old writers never die, they only fade away leaving their tales behind them," Maggi Hamblin, must have decided that Oscar Wilde's memory should be preserved in stone as well.

Carrying on to the art gallery we saw a large portrait of John Mortimer that had been painted by Maggi, herself. In it he looks more like his fictional character of "Rumpole of Old Bailey" than Mortimer himself. Looking at it, one could almost imagine him drinking another glass of his "Chateau Fleet Street" at Pommeroy's wine bar opposite the Old Bailey, rather than going home to "She Who Must Be Obeyed."

# PART II

# African Anecdotes

# 16

## *Efficiency*
## *From the Ridiculous to the Sublime*

*I was just sixteen*, and had just arrived from England when I got a job in a clothing factory in Johannesburg, It was owned by my grandfather's brother Henry Henochsberg. The year was 1926 and the business had been in existence about forty years.

It was probably the oldest clothing factory in the country and our methods and machinery had hardly changed over the years. A smart American super-salesman that year sold the guv'nor, as everybody called Mr. Henochsberg, fifty-two efficiency promoting colored posters. A different one had to be put on the factory wall each week. In bold colors a Bill Jones exhorted the workers to be on time, not talk so much, take pride in their work and so on. It had no noticeable effect on production.

In 1930 the Great Depression, which affected the whole country, meant there was no money for any sort of capital expenditure. Any modernization was out of the question. But in 1933, when I was on vacation in England, I visited some of the larger uniform manufacturing clothing factories. I took note of all their specialized machinery, some of which I had not even heard of. A lot of these machines were not readily available in South Africa in those days, but we managed to obtain most of them by the time war broke out in 1939. This was fortunate, as during the whole period of the war, new machinery was not available from overseas.

It was 1949 before I was able to get back to England and I found that generally most of the clothing factories were as antiquated as ours. The country had been under constant attack, and producing planes, arms and ammunition had taken precedence. Consequently the manufacture of new clothing machinery had been given very low priority.

At a conference of the British Clothing Institute I was told that several firms, with the aid of production engineers now freed from war work, were achieving an unheard of degree of production efficiency. The nearest such firm to London was the Westgate Overall Company in Egham Surrey. The director of the Institute telephoned Westgate and made an appointment for me to visit their factory the following week.

When I arrived at the factory, I was told that they had only agreed to my visiting them because I was an overseas manufacturer and not one of their competitors. I spent an hour chatting with the general manager and the production director, before being shown rounds the plant.

Three years before they had called in a team of efficiency engineers to investigate every aspect of their company's business. The plan they accepted was revolutionary. It completely reorganized their sales, accounting, storekeeping and work in progress, beside a completely new production method, that altered the method of paying factory workers from the previously hourly rate hourly rate to one based on output (piece work). Apart from the time it had taken to devise the plan, the Production Engineers had already spent two years putting it into force and were still fine tuning it while I was there.

The firm's business had traditionally been the manufacture and supply of seventy-eight styles of cotton work garments in a large variety of materials and colors. It had meant a lot of short production runs, and big stocks of raw materials. The finished garments were delivered to distributors throughout the United Kingdom in their own vans.

The new system now in effect cut the number of styles they manufactured to only four; a three quarter length coat, a coverall, a bib and brace overall and a jacket, all to be made from seven-ounce sanforised cotton material in any of four colors, either white, khaki, navy blue or brown. These standard items had always represented about eighty per cent of their sales and they had never been able to meet the demand.

Their scheduled output required twelve thousand yards of material a day. So a three days supply was kept in permanent stock as a reserve. Textile mills were contracted to deliver the twelve thousand yards, in the quantities of each color that were required from time to time. Thus the value of stock on hand was minimal. Goods were manufactured for orders taken well in advance and each day's output was delivered next day. Work in progress was, theoretically, not much more than one day's output. Instead of supplying the whole country they now confined their sales to the Four Home Counties thus cutting their delivery costs considerably.

On being taken through the factory I was impressed by the very up to date machinery and the overhead transport system. a system that automatically delivered garment sections to each machinist who, on completion of her prescribed stitching operation, hung it back on a passing hook to go to the next worker to sew on pockets, make button-holes or whatever. One machinist that I spoke to had to take off her earphones to hear me. After answering my question, rather rudely pointed out that in talking to me she was losing money.

Although impressed, I went away thinking it was unsatisfactorily impersonal.

Several years later I inquired how Westgate were doing and was told that they had gone bankrupt and closed down. It appeared that Hugh Dalton, the Minister of Trade and Industry, had the year before made a very negative speech on economic affairs that had caused a slump in the business world. Capital fled out of the country and sales plummeted. By narrowing their sales field they had lost their old customer base. And with the sudden huge drop in their sales volume, they were faced with fifteen thousand yards of cloth being delivered every day that they now could not use nor pay for.

Thinking back to the Guv'nor who, by placing posters on the factory wall, thought it would increase efficiency, was ridiculously naive. Westgate's bold experiment should have been sublime, but the fact it left no margin for conditions, however unforeseeable, to change, proves the old adage still applies, "Don't put all your eggs in one basket."

# 17

## *On Our Way*

*In 1924, my mother* accepted an offer to manage the dress shop in Johannesburg owned by two of her sisters. She took my sister, Vera, then aged ten, with her. We were to follow later if it proved successful. In 1926 my mother wrote to say she had settled in, and we could now all join her. My father was refused entry because of his tuberculosis but he encouraged us by saying what a wonderful future had opened up for us.

Preparing to go to South Africa was a major undertaking. My brother Jack and I were inundated with advice as to what we would need. If we had listened to half of what had been suggested, we would have had enough clothes and equipment for a major expedition to darkest Africa to find Dr. Livingston or whoever was lost there now. Thank goodness we did not have the money to consider buying other than what was considered essential.

September 6, 1926, was the first day of Rosh Hashanah. We asked the Reverend Bronkhorst, our Hebrew teacher and my friend's father, whether it was in order to travel on that day, and he said "What better day to leave for a new life than on the first day of the Jewish New Year."

The boat train left from Fenchurch Street station, to take us to Tilbury docks, near the mouth of the Thames, where we were to embark. My father and my maternal grandfather, Maurice Henochsberg, came to the boat to see us off. We all boarded the boat, and went down two levels below deck to locate our third class cabin. We returned up the stairs and followed my grandfather into the first class dining saloon for lunch. His reasoning was, he told us, if we were going to get a free lunch, why have other than the best.

He was an art dealer and using his monocle to read the menu, he ordered for all of us with the authority of a Rothschild. He may have looked like a first-class passenger, but I doubt that the rest of us did. He knew Johannesburg well, and his last words of advice to us was, to keep away from Turffontein Race course and not try to win back the money he had lost there. So with a rabbinical blessing and advice to keep away from horse racing, we were well equipped to face the future.

Our 8,000 ton ship rolled its way down the English Channel to the Atlantic, but when it hit heavy seas in the Bay of Biscay, its pitching had us feeling very queasy. Consequently, we were more than pleased to go ashore at Las Palmas, one of the Canary Isles, a surprisingly high mountain rising unexpectedly out of the ocean. Although it was only four or five days away from England, its sunshine, plentiful fruit, colorful flowers, and picturesque Spanish inhabitants made this, the first time we had ever been abroad, very exciting.

We had docked early in the morning and as the ship was to take on fruit and fresh vegetables for the voyage, it was not due to leave until four p.m. So Jack and I decided to explore the island. We wrote down the name of the street we were on, so as not to lose our way; it was Paragem. After wandering up, down, and around all day, we thought that we had better get back to the boat.

As the name of the street that we were now on was our old friend Paragem, we were quite sure that as we were going downhill, we would reach the dock. It soon became obvious that we were horribly lost, although we had assiduously followed the street sign Paragem. Fortunately, we found an English-speaking local who gave us clear instructions on how to get to the ship, which was in the opposite direction to the way we were going.

We arrived back with only a few minutes to spare, and on relating our experience to one of the crew, we were told that Paragem meant bus stop.

With sixteen days ahead of us before were due to reach Capetown, the sports committee, which had been elected on the first evening of the voyage, swept into operation. Everybody was press-ganged into participating into any and every event. Deck games of every description, violent or otherwise, were played all morning. Physical exercise classes even included three-legged racing. Apart from a break for morning tea, it was no rest cure. A daily event was the lottery on the ship's mileage the previous day.

As we approached the tropics, the heat became unbearable. There was no such thing as air conditioning in those days, and the four of us slept on deck most nights, awakening only when the crew swabbed the decks early each day. I remember suffering somewhat from prickly heat, getting rashes below my chin. At nighttime on our port side, flash lightning seemed to be continuous. The day we crossed the equator, we took part in the traditional "Crossing the Line" ceremony of being roughly shaved and dunked in the swimming bath by a relentless, hairy Neptune. We were given a certificate to prove it.

The last two or three days the tempo had slowed somewhat, and everybody could hardly wait for the trip to be over. We were up and packed at dawn on the last day, and stood on deck to see our first sight of Table Mountain. As it came into view, both Jack and I threw our bowler hats overboard as a gesture of freedom for the conventions of the old world. We were arriving in Africa.

We were met by an official of the Argus Company; publishers of The Star, the newspaper for whom my uncle worked and who was to employ me as a learner linotype operator when I arrived in Johannesburg. With his influence, we were rushed through the immigration and customs without delay. He then took us to the station to book in our luggage, and buy our tickets for the thirty-six hour journey to Johannesburg. The train was to leave at nine o'clock that evening.

He left us after suggesting how we should best spend our day, and we stood looking with awe towards the massive three thousand foot wall of grey rock that was Table Mountain which rose up sheer from behind the city. It was a dramatic backdrop to the city, and Table Bay itself. While we watched, a narrow strip of white cloud rolled up from behind it and came to rest on top. We must have looked to be strangers because a passer-by stopped, and told us that it was it tablecloth and always appears when the wind is from a certain direction.

We were in Adderly Street, the main street, in the brightest of bright sunshine. Here were Capetown's famed flower sellers. Brightly dressed women of mixed race, selling flowers in a variety and profusion that was beyond anything we had ever seen. We saw proteas for the first time and were shown velvet-like narrow silver leaves that we were told only grew on Table Mountain.

We walked towards the mountain and came to The Gardens, an unexpected quiet haven of cool shade. We strolled along its winding paths surrounded by sub-tropical shrubs and flowerbeds, with large brown squirrels scampering around us, and them we rested on benches under vast ancient oaks. This was in the heart of the city itself.

We had been advised to take food with us for the long train journey to avoid having to have all our meals in the dining saloon, which would be expensive. The train was waiting when we arrived, and we got into our pre-booked second-class compartment. Third class, we had been told, was only for black people. Six of us introduced ourselves and one of them showed us how two padded bunks opened up above the seat, on each side. These bunks would be let down at night-time and a bedding attendant would come round and supply sheets, blankets and a pillow at three shillings and sixpence for the two nights.

An hour or so later we arrived at Worcester, It was evidently a town in the heart of a fruit growing area and sellers of every kind of fruit pestered us to buy. We walked up and down the platform until the train was ready to leave, and with our beds now made, Jack and I being the youngest, climbed up to the top bunks. Early in the morning, a very strong cup of over-sweet coffee was brought round by a steward, and we drank the first of many cups of this South African Railway brew that we were to suffer in our fifty years stay in the country.

The next day was traveling mostly through the Karoo, a vast desert area bounded by low featureless hills with small scrub bush scattered over it that seemed to give succor to sheep that occasionally were to be seen. Apart from ranger's cottages, next to the track here and there, no life seemed to exist. Eventually we arrived at Kimberly and the train passed near enough to the famous big hole that had yielded vast amounts of diamonds in the past, for us to have a good look at it.

Another night, the steady click of the wheels rocked us to sleep and in the morning, we were given another cup of the railway brew, which shook us awake with a jolt. Now, mine shafts and huge, high, red soil mine dumps dominated the landscape in all directions. The dumps were the soil taken from the mines after the gold had been extracted. We had arrived on the Witwatersrand, the sixty-mile stretch of land that was supposed to harbor more gold than Midas ever dreamed of, and we would be in Johannesburg within the hour. Hallelujah!

Park Station, Johannesburg. There were Mother and Vera, our sister waving wildly. Hugs and kisses, tears of joy, we were here. Also on the platform was my Uncle Joe Emanuel, who had arranged the linotype job for me. He broke the news that there was no job after all. A printer's strike had just been concluded and the company had agreed not to take on any apprentices for two years. It did not break my heart. I did not know what a linotype operator was anyway.

It was imperative that we try to get jobs a soon as possible. So mother took us to her uncle Henry Henochsberg, who had a clothing factory that manufactured uniforms. He arranged for both of us to go to see Claude Leon, the owner of a wholesale soft goods business, who agreed to employ Jack at five pounds a month. I was disappointed and returned to Henry Henochsberg, who said, "You can work in my packing room until you find a job." I started work immediately at this temporary job, but was given time off to go to the department of labor. They sent me to The Castle Wine and Brandy Company who agreed to employ me.

When I told Mr. Henochsberg that I would be leaving at the end of themonth, he asked me what the job I had been offered, entailed.

"Taking inventories at all the firm's liquor stores," I told him.

"Nonsense, ," he said, "You will become a drunkard. You had better stay here." As it turned out I stayed there at Henochsbergs for the next fifty-five years. It was the start of a career that gave me a lifetime of absorbing fulfillment.

# 18

## *How Embarrassed Can One Get?*

**In Johannesburg** I was often invited to parties where both lawyers and doctors were present in large numbers. Invariably, they each gravitated to their own group to talk their own kind of shop. Knowing some of the lawyers and doctors personally, I went from one group to the other to chat, but often found I was interrupting a private conversation and moved on.

One such mixed social gathering will forever remain in my memory as the one I want to forget. In fact, it was enough for me to refuse accepting invitations to such affairs for a considerable time.

I was a clothing manufacturer, and the services of competent sewing machine mechanics were essential for the smooth running of the plant. The basic machines were not the problem. They were easy to repair. But, with the advent of many of the new electronically controlled, specialized machines, mechanics capable of dealing with them were in short supply. Van Heerden, my head mechanic, had been trained in America. There was no machine that he could not get promptly back into operation. We relied on him to a great extent. I was horrified when I heard that, while driving to his parent's farm at night with his elbow resting on the window-ledge, a speeding vehicle passed so close to his car that it hit his arm crushing the elbow.

He was rushed to Pretoria hospital where his arm was set. Weeks later when the cast came off, he was not able to raise his arm above waist level. This did not allow him to continue working. I telephoned

Doctor David Polonski, a friend, an orthopedic surgeon of national repute, and asked if anything could be done.

Send him along to me he said in his gruff off-hand manner. It won't be the first time I have corrected other people's mistakes.

The operation on the arm was so successful that after it, Van Heerden was able to bring his arm to shoulder height. Miraculously, this enabled him to continue doing his job. David refused to accept any payment.

A year later, my young woman secretary, was in a car accident and injured her arm badly. She was taken to the nearest hospital, but after her arm was set she found that she unable to type. She was broken-hearted when she came in to tell me about it. She thought her working life was finished.

I hesitated to phone David because he had not charged me last time. I did not want him to think I was taking advantage of his good nature. However, seeing that she was unable to continue working as a typist, I decided it would be foolish not to at least, discuss it with him.

I telephoned his office and was told Dr. David Polonski was overseas, but was asked if I would I like to speak to his partner Dr. Bernard Polonski, his brother. I did not know he had a brother, let alone a partner, but agreed to be put through. I told Bernard what the trouble was, and mentioned how David had been so successful in treating Van Heerden. Bernard was most receptive and said, 'By all means, send her along. I can't promise anything can be done, but I will certainly look into it.'

The long and the short of it was, that he decided to do an operation that should definitely give her more freedom of movement. She came back to work having regained almost full use of her arm. Like his brother he refused to charge, and I made a mental note that if ever I were to meet him, I would tell him how grateful we were.

Soon afterwards, I was again at one of those legal and medical social occasions. As usual, the doctors and the lawyers congregated into their separate groups. I was congratulating a legal friend of mine who had just been appointed to the Bench, when I overheard a group of doctors talking nearby.

One of them said, "I am a visitor from Capetown, Dr. Polonski, and I have been wanting to meet you for some time."

I looked around to see who he was talking to, and never having had the opportunity of meeting Bernard Polonski, I was determined to thank him there and then.

I turned round to him. Rather rudely, interrupted their conversation, saying Dr. Polonski, I am Leslie Herman, I must thank you for fixing my girl up.

Silence reigned, I did not believe that silence ever could reign, but it did. All conversation in the room stopped. Polonski looked at me blankly, appearing confused.

Someone, possibly my friend, the newly appointed judge, pulled me aside and said in a stage whisper that could have been heard a mile away, "That was the gynecologist, Jack Polonski you were talking to. He is David's youngest brother. You must have mistaken him for Bernard, David's partner."

# 19

## *Pagel's Circus*

***As a young man*** I was employed as a salesman in a uniform clothing factory in Johannesburg South Africa. I was asked to get to the factory very early one morning to open the front door to allow a few workers to do some urgent work. It was pouring with rain and I kept the door locked and did not expect to be disturbed.

After a loud persistent knocking on the door, I opened it to find a short, dumpy, untidily dressed woman demanding to come in. I said we were not open but as I hesitated, she pushed past me followed by a giant of man who stood passively by her side. Directly she told me that she was Mrs. Pagel, I remembered she was the owner of Pagel's Circus. She was a hard bitten character who was known to swear like a trooper.

In the small towns where they played just one or two-night stands, everybody would turn out to see the circus arrive at the railway station. The children especially, followed the procession led by the elephants to the circus site. She swore and chivied the workers until the Big Top was up, and the animal cages in position.

Her vocabulary was so luridly specific that mothers were known to threaten their children that they would be sent to Mrs. Pagel if they did not behave. However, this did not stop her being affectionately known throughout the land as Ma Pagel.

Both soaking wet, a very bedraggled Mrs. Pagel almost in tears gasped, "The elephants have run amok and the skips containing all the worker's clothing has been ripped to shreds, and I must have fifty sets of overalls for our opening here in Johannesburg, by the day after tomorrow. I calmed her down by showing her our stock of khaki overalls and said we can put red braid around the collars down the side of the legs by tomorrow afternoon. We would also embroider Pagel's in large letters on the back of the garments.

Relieved, she told me what had transpired. At dawn as they were unloading the circus in the railway goods yard, a tiger escaped and had been sighted roaming among some goods trucks. Her husband, the animal trainer had called everybody to help him capture her. In the excitement the elephants had been left unchained for a short while without their keeper. Alarmed by sudden bursts of steam and shrill whistles of nearby engines the elephants ran headlong onto the track. It was an hour or more before calm was restored. After things had settled down, she had caught a cab to our factory.

Next day we delivered everything to her. With customers like circuses who are always on the move it was impractical to give credit. Ma Pagel regretted that with the expenses they had incurred by yesterday's debacle she was unable to pay us there and then. She offered me two ringside seats for the night's performance so that when the show was over I could collect the cash from her in the ticket office. I was not happy to be given so much cash in notes and coins late at night that could not be banked until next day, but had no alternative but to agree.

It was years since I had been to a circus so I asked a friend to join me, and we both looked forward to going. We had been given cushioned wicker chairs next to the ring. It was frightening to be so near some of the animal turns when Mr. Pagel, whip in hand, was being snarled at by tigers and lions.

The clowns also performed some of their tomfoolery, right near us, and once included my friend and me in their act, which was fun. I was now finding my chair uncomfortable and was wriggling from side to side. My friend was also fidgeting in his seat. He diagnosed the trouble before I did. We were both covered with fleas.

We rushed to the box office to get the money and had to wait uncomfortably while Ma Pagel totaled the takings. She gave it to me in a heavy canvas bag apologizing that a lot of it was in coins. I did not mention the fleas. That was purely her problem, and did not want to ruin any future business by commenting on them.

# 20

## *Import Trouble*

***For many years*** after World War II ended South Africa was still short of foreign currency. Stringent import control regulations were enforced. Most cloth used by the clothing industry for garment manufacture had to be imported. Permits granted for such materials were often insufficient for the clothing industry's needs.

The year that I was President of the National Clothing Federation it was decided to invite the Minister of Economic Affairs to our annual banquet, to bring our problems to his personal attention. In my speech I was to stress how necessary it was to get government to allow us greater access to imported materials.

Hors-d'oeuvres, a good wine, and an excellent main course had put everybody in a good humor. Over dessert and coffee followed by a liqueur I rose to thank the Minister for his attendance. In making a plea for the issue of more permits, I told the following harrowing story.

Cohen, a clothing manufacturer met an old friend on the street who was surprised how ill he looked. He asked him what was the matter.

"I haven't slept a wink for weeks" Cohen said "And because of it I am not able to cope with the continual shortage of materials to keep the factory running."

The friend suggested that he count sheep when he lay his head down on his pillow. "After a few good nights sleep you will feel a different man and you'll find all your problems will fall away."

A few weeks later they met again. Cohen by this time had lost weight and looked much worse.

"Didn't you try counting sheep like I suggested?" said the friend.

"That's the trouble," Cohen said, "I did, but after counting hundreds of sheep, I was still awake. So I sheared them, washed the wool, combed and carded it, then spun it into thread. Though worn out from my efforts I was still very much awake. Not giving up, I weaved the thread into worsted suiting, but after that I was more awake than ever. Not giving up, I cut the material into jackets and trousers ready for stitching.

By now I thought my troubles were over, and I would be able to deliver back orders of suits to my customers. I was now ready to fall into a deep and restful slumber. But only then did I discover that I had no material for the linings because I had not received the necessary permit. So now you can see why I don't sleep."

The Minister rose and after saying what a pleasure it was to be with us, announced that the Government would eliminate all red tape and adopt a more positive attitude to the industry's many problems in the future. Jokingly, he said that he would hate to see clothing manufacturers not sleeping being short of material and lose weight on account of not receiving sufficient permits, but after the dinner we had all eaten tonight he thought weight loss was unlikely. At least in the near future.

# 21

## *Buy South African First*

*For many years* after the war ended, economic conditions were such that the importation of materials for the manufacture of clothing was restricted. Clothing manufacturers were to an extent forced to use inferior materials made in South Africa. The public naturally preferred to buy the imported article wherever possible.

The year that I was chairman of the National Clothing Federation, I felt it was my duty to buy South African whenever possible. Clare, my wife, was quite prepared to go along with it, until she found out how difficult it was. Shopkeepers looked at her with amazement when she asked for children's clothing or some underwear for herself made in South Africa.

She loyally persisted whenever she could, but had to forego a considerable difference in quality or comfort with the local article. For instance elastic was in short supply and she had to buy some items with tabs fastened with buttons, or tapes threaded through tunnels that needed tying like a shoelace to close.

It was our tenth anniversary and for a second honeymoon we decided to spend a week in Durban. We especially looked forward to going by the fabulous Blue Train that was about to make its trial trip to Durban. This world famous train attracts tourists from all over the world, but up to then had traveled only between Pretoria and Capetown.

We got to Park Station well before its nine o'clock P.M departure time. We put on our best clothes for the occasion and were shepherded in to our luxurious compartment, by the Station Master himself. A steward brought us champagne as we arrived. We arranged to go into the dining saloon for dinner at nine forty five.

The dining saloon was all that we had expected. In keeping with name of the train, blue was the color motif. A steward in a blue lapelled white jacket escorted us to our table. The immaculate white linen table cloth, topped by a handsome cut glass vase containing several exotic blue flowers, surrounded by some artistically folded blue linen napkins. This, together with the gleaming silverware that graced the table, heightened our expectation of enjoying the meal to come.

A dry sherry was served with the soup. The four courses following were excellent, each accompanied by a superb wine. It was certainly a gastronomic dream and ended with a liqueur brandy. Our second honeymoon had started in fine style. We may have staggered slightly as we rose to return to our compartment, but not so much that anybody would notice.

Walking down the blue-carpeted aisle between the tables we stopped to congratulate the chief steward. Then tragedy struck. The tape in the hem that had safely held up Clare's panties, through lack of clastic, somehow had come loose and they fell to her ankles.

She found it difficult to extricate something around her ankles with high heeled-shoes on, and did not manage it as gracefully as she would have liked. But I hastily bent down, picked them up and put them in my pocket. Walking on, trying to pretend that nothing had happened, Clare, still red in the face, looked rather wistfully at me, so I calmed her by saying, "It was lucky they were blue."

# 22

## *Capitulate*

***In 1949*** with the war ended, the head of the cap section of our factory gave me one month's notice of his intention to leave the firm. It came as a complete surprise because he had headed the department for twenty years. An excellent tradesman, he had learned his trade in Russia. There, he had made caps for the Cossacks. They were known to require only perfect workmanship in the manufacture of their uniforms.

After making enquiries we established that no suitable replacement was available in South Africa. We would have to find someone overseas. I immediately wrote to our shippers in London asking them to advertise for a cap maker in the newspapers there. On getting replies, they were to select the ones they considered suitable, and arrange for me to interview them when I arrived in London in six weeks time.

In those days it took mail and travel three weeks to get from Johannesburg to London by ship. Clare, my wife who was coming with me was prepared to go by plane. It would be a 36-hour flight on a D C 6, an unpressurized four-engine propeller plane that normally flew at five thousand feet. Flying up the length of Africa at this altitude, though bumpy, was compensated by the fact that often the pilot came down to two thousand feet to allow us to see game. We circled Kilimanjaro, and came down at Nairobi and Khartoum to refuel.

The City of London where my shipping office was situated, had been heavily bombed. Spaces that had contained offices and warehouses were now just empty craters. Thank goodness St. Paul's Cathedral managed to escape with very little damage.

The managing director of our shippers greeted me with the alarming news, that although advertisements for a cap maker had appeared in the usual newspapers for weeks, there had been no answers. I was shaken, had I come for nothing? I asked him whether there were any Trade Directories I could look through and found the names of several sewing machine companies nearby. Wandering around, without success, by chance I came across a small sewing machine mechanic's shop. The owner showed me a copy of a monthly sewing mechanics publication, and put me in touch with the editor. Who told me that this month's edition had just come out. It would be another month before the next one would be printed.

This meant that even if I got an answer it would be at least a further week or two before I could hope for a reply. What was I to do? I would have to remain in England for seven or eight weeks. Thinking it over, I realized that I had no alternative but to put the ad in, and hope. I worded it "A highly qualified cap maker was required for South Africa."

When I went back to the office, they agreed that I had done the right thing, and suggested that we find other things to do for six weeks or so. I phoned them every day to see if there were any messages. After visiting several uniform clothing factories, and seeing some of our textile suppliers. We motored on to Scotland where Clare had friends. To my surprise one day we were told, that they had several replies. Of course we rushed back.

They had interviewed the most likely ones, and highly recommended one man in particular. I saw him immediately, a charming fellow; he was the head cap maker at Gieves of Bond Street. Gieves were known to be the finest supplier of officer's uniforms in England. I was very impressed with the quality of the cap he showed me, and went with him to South Africa House to interview the immigration department. Unfortunately we were informed that because he had tuberculosis he would not be allowed in the country. I was heartbroken, and so was he.

The next one a Morris Kaye, they said he seemed to be capable, but a bit of a rough diamond. I arranged to go to his workshop in the northeastern suburb of Tottenham. He had his wife working with him making school caps for a department store. I showed him some of the detailed army and railway cap specifications and he assured me that they would be no trouble at all.

There and then he got hold of a sheet of cardboard cut a strip two and a half inches wide and about twenty-four inches in length. He cut another bit of the board into the shape of a cap peak. Then producing some calico from under the counter he cut out a circle about twelve inches in diameter, and then four quarters. Quickly stitching them together he added a leather sweatband and handed me a cap. I must admit I was impressed not only by his ability but at the speed with which he had done it.

He was prepared to come to Johannesburg, even eager; yes he could manage a large staff. The salary I offered was more than satisfactory, but there was a big catch. I would have to pay the cost of bringing his wife Ann, and their three children to Johannesburg.

The cap department ran smoothly and the quality of our caps was excellent. After a year, he told me that he was going to bring his aged mother over for a three-month holiday. The next thing I heard was that her visa had been refused. Her name was Mrs. Kayorskovich and she had been born in a village that was now in Communist Russia.

If there was one thing that the Afrikaans nationalist government were suspicious of, it was communism. Doctor Malan, the prime minister, was a narrow minded Dutch Reform Church Predicate, who openly denounced anybody who opposed apartheid, as a communist. Naturally the immigration department at South Africa House in Trafalgar Square refused her application.

One of Kaye's brothers lived in a district of London that Winston Churchill represented in parliament. To his surprise Churchill agreed to see him, after being informed that he was one of his constituents. On hearing the story Churchill straight away picked up the phone and got right through to Dr. Malan. "Malan old fellow, I don't think you know about it, but the elderly mother of one of my constituents a Mrs. Kayorskovitch has been refused a visa to see her grandchildren in Johannesburg, just see that she gets it. Thanks."

Caps off, and three cheers! If a man could beat Hitler he could surely get Malan to get his immigration people to capitulate.

# 23

## *The Strike*

***I had received*** an urgent called from the factory, to say that the workers are refusing to go into the factory. Naturally, I rushed there to find a group of angry workers restlessly milling around the surrounding streets. A large force of police had just arrived, a disaster as far as I was concerned because I knew the majority of Africans mistrust them, and it could easily lead to trouble. I also saw that a representative of the department of labor has just come. This is trouble too, as I know that it is this particular representative of the government who refuses to recognize black workers unions.

Here I am at odds with both the police and the labor department, because I recognize and am prepared to negotiate with any trade union, black or white. This is the first time my factory had been faced with a strike and obviously I have to do something about it.

Hesitantly, after speaking to the factory foreman and the trade union officials, I climbed on to a table to address the situation. The police officer in charge told me that they were here to protect surrounding property. The Sharpeville Incident, where a lot of protesting African workers had been killed recently, was in the forefront of my mind. Could I prevent a similar situation occurring here? In as loud a voice as I could manage I started to talk.

"My fellow workers, you are refusing to enter the factory to start work I see the police are here. I did not ask them to come, and have instructed them not to interfere with you in any way, or take sides on any issue between you and me.

"Standing here on a table in the yard it is impossible for me to hear your reason for striking. Please go into the factory and sit at your machines. Only then can we talk through the factory loudspeaker system. Knowing that you probably left your homes in Soweto at five o'clock this morning, I have instructed the canteen staff to serve you tea, bread and jam, at your machines."

The strikers agreed to go into the factory to continue discussions. I continued, "Thank you for going back in the factory. Through the speaker system your strike leader has explained your grievances and I have noted them with understanding and will appoint a grievance committee to meet with me next week to discuss and hope to solve some of them.

"Your main demand is that you want more money now. It is June and the new increased wage laid down in the Clothing Industrial Agreement does not come into force until July 1st. Many dress factories I am told, are paying this new rate already, but as I have explained to the secretaries of your unions, the average dress factory has only thirty workers and can increase the price of their dresses to the shops immediately. Whereas we have two thousand workers, making government uniforms, we can't increase our prices to the government until the first of the month.

"In an effort to ease matters, bearing in mind that as the oldest clothing factory in South Africa who have employed many of your mothers and even grandmothers over the years, I have arranged to pay the new increased wage rate in two weeks from now. One week earlier than the agreement lays down. Your union officials consider my offer reasonable. and I sincerely hope you will ratify it."

My offer was eventually accepted after considerable argument, thank goodness. I had never been more worried in my life. When I saw the police at the factory, my first thought was that we might be faced with another Sharpeville.

This was my first and I hope my last strike. In baseball, a batter is out after three strikes, but luckily I managed to get a home run off my first pitch.

## 24

## *Doctor Livingston I Presume*

***With the war over***, we decided, after suffering four years of gas coupons, to throw caution to the wind and motor to the Victoria Falls from Johannesburg. The Falls, known to be one of the wonders of the world, was like Naples something that has to be seen before one dies. Originally known as "The Smoke That Thunders," Doctor Livingston renamed it the Victoria Falls.

After eighteen months of waiting for the first cars to arrive from overseas, we, with a brand new car, were anxious to get going. The journey would entail a drive of fifteen hundred miles on a road full of potholes and corrugations.

At the end of the first one hundred miles on a paved surface we reached Warmbaths, a popular hot spring Spa, surrounded by orange groves. The road had been as smooth as glass up till now and we thought that the journey might be a cinch after all, but the buck stopped there. The rest of the trip was all on badly kept sand roads. With loose sandbox surfaces that caused us to skid as we rounded corners.

Just before reaching Pietersburg one hundred miles further on, we came across a signboard stating that we were entering the Tropic of Capricorn. Although now in the tropics, it would be another two or three hundred miles before there was any noticeable change in the climate or flora. Carrying on through the town of Louis Trichardt, we stayed overnight at a pleasant roadside Inn before facing the crossing the Soutpansberg Mountain range.

Narrow roads with blind rises twisted blindly around the bends. After passing through the mountain area we found the surrounding veldt dotted with Baobab trees. They give the impression of growing upside down with their roots reaching up into the air. What with these weird trees and the enormous eight feet high anthills, the scene was a surrealistic moonscape.

We crossed the Limpopo River, into what was then known as Southern Rhodesia, but now called Zimbabwe. After another three or four hundred miles we reached Bulawawayo, the industrial center of the country.

It was the beginning of October and we along with everyone else had to deal with the intense heat dominating the city at that time of the year. The people that we met were edgy and short tempered, they told us that they were impatiently awaiting for the rains to come.

Six months of winter in a cloudless sky without rain made for pleasant days and cool nights. But, brooding dark rain clouds gather early in October causing the atmosphere to be unbearably hot and humid from which there is no escape day or night. "Why did you come this month? It is called the suicide month," we were told.

Taking the advice of friends, we took the overnight train to Victoria Falls. They had said it can be seen at its very best before the rains arrive. The mist that envelops you, as while gaze at it from across the river, looks like smoke that can be seen from miles away, while the fury of its rushing water roars thunderously.

We stayed for two weeks, not wanting to get back until the heat diminished. On our way back to Bulawayo the rains arrived. It came down in a deluge; beyond anything I had ever seen, swamping everything in its path. Dried up riverbeds became raging torrents and the gutters in the city were clogged with the accumulated debris of six months without rain. Cars and people were stranded in the flooded streets.

Now that the temperature had dropped we decided after all to go on to Umtali in the Eastern Highlands, a welcoming portion of the country that even in the winter months was a holiday venue. But now that the rains had come, its hills and valleys had turned into a green wonderland. The setting of its many hotels and Inns, surrounded by trees and shrubs, had trails ideal for walking or riding, ranging in all directions.

Driving east across the country, cattle on vast ranches were nibbling on the green shoots that had sprouted miraculously from the previous dry soil. Tobacco farmers were on the land ploughing and planting seeds that would form a great part of the country's exports. An air of optimism now prevailed over the sullen despondence that had greeted us when we first arrived.

Returning home, we crossed the Limpopo River at Beit Bridge on the border post. Reviewing the trip, we agreed that the Victoria Falls must definitely be one of the wonders of the world, and the green oasis of its Eastern Highlands was wondrous beyond belief. It is obviously a country whose cycle of nature can turn 180 degrees overnight. But, we were lucky to be present when the country was at its lowest and see it reach its high point when the rains arrive.

The Falls no doubt is still referred to as "The Smoke that Thunders" by the indigenous people. But when Doctor Livingston named it after Queen Victoria, it was a fitting tribute to her as the beloved Queen of the then British Empire. Rudyard Kipling, whose "Land of Hope and Glory" epitomizes the times, I am sure would have done the same.

## 25

## *Lion Trouble*

***Eddie and Sonia Levin***, close friends of ours, lived in Krugersdorp, mining town just thirty miles from Johannesburg. Sonia invited us to a braaivleis (Barbecue) next evening. "Get here in the morning, and come with us to our local Game Reserve, I don't suppose you have ever been there."

"We'll come with pleasure," we replied. "Will about eleven o'clock suit you?"

We had never bothered to go there ourselves because we had thought it more of a game park than a reserve. One hundred acres or so, just a few miles out of town, seven or eight hundred acres, stocked with animals, would be rather like a zoo.

We were spoiled having been to so many proper Game Reserves all over Africa most of them encompassing hundreds of square miles. Wild animals roaming and hunting in their natural habitat must be considerably more exciting than in a park where the animals are fed. But, we were to find out otherwise.

Next day sitting in the back of their car and were pleasantly surprised at the variety and number of animals we saw. At a high fenced area, that according to the map given us at the ticket office was the lion area. Here we drove through a tall gate that closed behind us and continued through another gate, which closed automatically behind our car. We were now in a secure area supposedly containing only lions, although no lions could be seen.

The road led us up a very steep slope to a fair sized plateau. At the top we were forced to come to a dead stop. Any thoughts that we might have had that it was too like a zoo were quickly set aside.

We found ourselves hemmed in by a large number of seemingly angry lions. They prowled restlessly all around the car preventing us from going on. Not only were we surrounded but to make matters worse, one of the largest and angriest of them jumped on to our hood. He put his huge paws against the window as though to break the glass, and glared at us ferociously.

Sonia who was sitting in the passenger seat shouted out in horror, "My god! Look at the size of his paws." Each paw was almost the size of half the driver's window. If the window collapsed, the lion would be on top of her. She seemed hypnotized, and all she could say repeatedly was, "Look at the size of his paws." Terrified she tried to clamber over to the back seats, but before she could do so the lion jumped off the hood.

Eddie, although shaken, waited until he saw a lion free gap in the road before driving off. We reported the incident at the ticket office. Sonia still badly shaken was still muttering about size of his paws.

There, the only member of the staff we had seen all day seemed uninterested. He casually mentioned that they had put a newly arrived lion in there that morning, and supposed the other lions would take a little while to get used to it.

We told him that it was irresponsible to allow visitors in there until the pride had fully accepted a new lion. He seemed unworried, but at our insistence he promised to warn future visitors not to go into the lion section for the next day or two.

We had a bite of lunch in the area before returning back to their house to prepare for the barbeque that evening. Eddie took over the whole affair. This was evidently his thing. By the time the guests arrived in the evening Eddie had started the fire in the grill by lighting coal which he then layered with coke until the whole heating surface was red hot. Assorted haute cuisine sauces and condiments were on a side table as he put on his chef's apron with the lettering Master Chef on it. Meanwhile Sonia, still very shaken, entertained the guests with her horrifying tale of the lion on the car.

There was plenty of beer and other hard drinks available, but, knowing that we had a long drive home, I kept to drinking a soda. Saying goodbye to our hosts that evening, Eddie asked me if he could give me one for the road. Unthinkingly the advertising phrase came to mind and I said thanks I'll just have a "Pause that Refreshes."

"Oh my God," said Sonia as she handed me a coke, "Never say that phrase again in my presence. I'll not sleep thinking of that lion's huge paws on the windshield."

# 26

# *Namibian Venture*

**South West Africa**, now Namibia, was the only part of Southern Africa to which we had never been. So, Clare and I decided to take a two-week trip there.

Windhoek, the capital and largest city, was a one-hour flight from Johannesburg. The plane was to leave at noon and was expected to arrive at one PM, in time for lunch. A technical hitch delayed the plane for one hour, so we only arrived at two o'clock. No food was served on the plane, because normally it was such a short journey. Famished, we thought a short run into town, to get something to eat would solve the problem.

We had arranged for a rented a Volkswagen Combi (SUV) to meet us at Windhoek airport and expected no trouble. Unfortunately, when we went to pick up the car, only a battered old Volkswagen Beetle was there. The Hertz agent told us that the Combi that we had ordered would not be available until tomorrow.

Not happy about driving such a small car I had no alternative but to pack our luggage on to the back seat and get going. We had expected the terrain to be flat with the airport adjacent to the town. But to our surprise, we found the airport was in a mountain area, twenty-six miles from Windhoek.

It was a narrow twisting down hill drive, and to make matters worse, the steering on this horrible little vehicle was inclined to veer right. Only by firmly forcing the steering wheel to the left was I able to keep the car on a comparatively straight course. It was a nightmare of a journey and it was nearly four o'clock when we got our hotel. To our dismay they told us that the kitchen was closed and would only open at seven o'clock. They could only offer us a ham sandwich, which Clare decided not to eat.

It had been arranged that we phone the parents of a friend of our sons, a young man who was serving in the Air Force with them in Pretoria. They had been told we were coming, and asked us over after dinner. They owned the largest camping and equipment store in the town, and suggested they lend us various camping items that we might need.

They were an interesting couple and knew the country well. Having lived there for many years. We spent the next day with them and had dinner at their house for the next night or two. She was an American and he was Russian. He told us he was sometimes called upon to act as an interpreter when an occasional Russian ship limped into Walvis Bay needing assistance.

We complained to the Hertz people about the bad steering on the car given us at the airport, and picked up a Combi that thank goodness appeared to be in perfect condition. The country had been German South West Africa until it was taken over by South Africa during the First World War. The German influence was still very obvious, though Afrikaans was mostly spoken now. The indigenous people were Hereros and Ovambos.

The Herero women in their very Victorian, voluminous multi-colored dresses spread over layers of petticoats, reaching down to their ankles, were a picturesque feature of the town. Their upright bearing and natural dignity is no doubt the result of having carried buckets of water on their heads, and babies wrapped in blankets on the backs, since childhood. Despite their dignified appearance and seeming aloofness we found them friendly and helpful. The Ovambo men on the other hand were less than friendly almost hostile, quite different from the Bantu men in South Africa.

We were to discover, while driving around that in even the smallest village there was a first class bakery. Of course it had been German territory for many years and many Germans still lived there, and carried on their traditional trades.

There were signs on the roads warning us to be aware of buck crossing the road. It was just as well that we had been warned, because it enabled me to avoid an accident, when a huge Sable buck dashed across the road ahead of our car. It continued on, and jumped a ten-foot fence with inches to spare, before disappearing into the bush.

We changed over to another hotel that was nearer to the business center, and did not have made do with a ham sandwich because the kitchen was closed.

We stayed two or three nights in Windhoek and its surroundings, before going to Swakopmund, on the coast, two or three hundred miles away. The population of Swakopmund was mostly German and it has maintained its Bavarian atmosphere. It borders the Nabib Desert south of the infamous Skeleton Coast, the vast coastline bordered by the impassable Nabib Desert, where very few have survived when shipwrecked.

Here, standing in a lake of fresh water were thousands of flamingo. They were a wonderful sight to behold when they rose into the air as one, darkening the sky, only to return to the lake after a wide circular swoop. Arriving back, they stood stock still, like soldiers at attention. It was as though they had never moved. We were advised not to go on to Brandberg to see the famous Bushman rock painting "The White Lady" which was our original intention, as our car was did not have a four wheel drive.

So we carried on to Walvis Bay, the major port. There we found a large pool adjacent to the sea, with the largest collection of sea birds that we had ever seen. Clare ran out of film photographing them all. Adjoining the town was a huge salt mine, the main industry here. We were told that the atmosphere is so salty, that automobiles are badly rusted after twelve months here.

We intended to go to the Nabib Naukluft Park, renowned for a particular species of buck not found elsewhere. We found we needed a permit. Unfortunately it could be only obtained from the police station, which was closed for lunch. It was just one o'clock and it would not re-open until two. I spotted a barbershop across the road and decided to get a haircut. Clare was satisfied to go and do some shopping, in the meanwhile.

On entering the barbershop, I found several people already there. I sat down and looked around. There were two small boys and a man in front of me. The barber said. "I won't be long, please wait," so I took a chair and picked up a magazine. One of the boys was in the barber's chair and to my surprise the barber took a clipper and shaved off all of his hair. The second boy then got on to the chair and the barber did the same to him. Does everybody in Walvis Bay have their heads shaved? Making ready to get out in a hurry, I waited for the man to mount the chair to see how his hair got cut. To my horror the barber did the same thing to him.

Excusing myself, I went to the door, saying that I had an appointment to keep. The barber stopped me leaving by saying, "The boys go to a boarding school in the desert, and the gentleman is a teacher there." He went on to say, "Everybody there have their heads shaved for health reasons."

With some misgivings I went back. I explained how I wanted it cut, and he did the best he could. I really could not complain, but I must admit that I was pleased that I had got out safely, with a full head of hair.

Clare was waiting for me, and we rushed to get to the police station as it opened. We were issued a permit and they provided us with an African guide to show us around. It proved to be well worth the trouble we had taken to go there.

Next day, after booking out of the hotel, and loading the Combi, we drove back to Windhoek. While at the wheel, I remembered I had forgotten to ask Clare what she had bought. She showed me postcards and several T-shirts with Walvis Bay on them for the children. As the narrow dirt road was full of traffic, I was kept busy concentrating on driving, when she asked me how I had got on at the barbers?

It was certainly not the time to relate all the frightening details, so I said that it had been "A Hair Raising Experience."

# 27

## *The Greeks Had a Word for It*

*March is a wonderful month* to visit Capetown—the intense heat of December and January has passed, holiday makers have gone home and all the Cape's many attractions are at their best.

That March I had to attend some meetings of the South African Chamber of Industry there. Clare came with me saying that it would be an opportunity to go to Kirstenbosh, the National Horticultural Gardens at that time of the year. She even said that she might go to some of the entertainments laid on for the delegates' wives, if any were of interest to her.

We had arrived on Friday evening for the next week's meetings, and next day we went to Maskew Millar's bookshop. We asked them if Professor Skaife's new book on entomology was out yet.

They said, "No, not yet," but why don't you phone and ask him yourself, he'd love that! "They gave us his number and we phoned.

He said it was nearly finished, and we were very surprised when he asked us if we liked to go there, to talk about it that very afternoon. His home stood on the mountainside overlooking Hout Bay. Mrs. Skaife insisted on our having tea and some of her homemade cake while the Professor talked about his book.

Skaife said the book was practically ready for publication, except for the photographic illustrations he was still working on. He showed us a lot of miniaturized photographs of his grandchildren and some enlarged pictures of various insects and grasses. When he put them together, they would give the impression of children walking through a jungle inhabited by huge insects much larger than themselves. The story, he hoped, would bring the insect world into a greater perspective of its importance in nature, especially to children.

He then took us up to his laboratory, in a separate cottage, a good distance above the house. He showed us some of the various experiments that he was working on. For instance, in one such glass tube the complete life cycle of an insect could be observed. We also were much intrigued by him showing ants remove their eggs to an area that is exactly 60 degrees when the temperature changes.

Clare, as founder of the South African Spider Society, was particularly interested in the work he was doing with arachnids. He was very interested to hear that she was founding member of the South African Spider society and promised to let her have a signed copy of the book directly it was in print.

My meetings during the week were well-attended, but one afternoon the subject being discussed was of little interest to us in the clothing business. A competitor of mine, Everard Savage from Durban, asked me if I would accompany him to town to look for a book that he had been told he must read. He had been to several shops but had not been able to find it. We went to one two more bookshops and asked for "The Achilles Heel," but they had not heard of it. Eventually, I suggested that we try Maskew Miller, the bookshop that had put me onto Dr. Skaife. There they asked him the name of the author, but he had no idea who it was. He then suggested that perhaps it might be called "Hercules Elbow." They had not heard of that either. After looking through their list of recently published books, they said, "Could it possibly be the Five Fingers of Cicero."

"That's it!" said Everard. "I knew it was something to do with an ancient Greek."

# 28

## *Overnight Stay*

**The four hundred miles** to Durban from Johannesburg was by no means an easy drive in the days before they built the freeway. We usually stopped at Nottingham Road for the night. This would leave us just about one hundred and twenty miles to deal with, the long downwards drop into Pietermaritzburg, on through the Valley of a Thousand Hills in Zululand, over the heights of Botha's Hill to arrive fresh in Durban about eleven o'clock in the morning.

It was no hardship. It enabled us to spend the evening at Rawdon's Hotel, a large, thatched roofed manor house standing in many acres of land, with its own lake well-stocked with trout. Famous for gracious living and good food, Mrs. Rawdon herself personally welcomed you. Together with her two bachelor sons, they went out of their way to make you feel at home.

There was always a roaring fire in the huge fireplace in the lounge, around which were a large number of cretonne-covered armchairs. On our first stay there, there seemed to be no hurry to have dinner and we did not go into the dining room until about eight forty-five. The tables, lit only by candles, gave the atmosphere a special charm and a hint of good things to come. After an excellent soup and choice of hors d'oeuvres the waitresses brought in large dinner plates each with a large heated coconut standing upright in a mound of rock salt. The top of the coconuts had been sliced and tied back on with raffia.

After the raffia was cut and the top removed we found that the milk had been emptied and replaced with a superb, aromatic spiced heated concoction, its flavour enhanced by the white flesh of the coconut itself. The taste was beyond belief, so much so that we asked if it was possible to have any more. To our surprise a second one was immediately forthcoming, as though it had been expected that we would want more than one.

After dinner Mrs. Rawdon told us that together with her late husband Dr. Rawdon and her two boys, she had lived in Siam for many years and dined at the palace in Bangkok many times. This dish was a favorite of the king and often served there. The recipe was a state secret but she had managed to wheedle it out of the head chef. This was the first time she had served the dish at the hotel, and was pleasantly surprised to find how well it had been received.

Two weeks later, on our way back home we decided to stay overnight at the Rawdon Hotel again, looking forward to repeating the wonderful meal. We arrived expectantly into the candlelit dining room again only to be disappointed when no coconuts arrived.

Sitting in the comfortable armchairs around the huge fireplace after dinner we told Mrs. Rawdon how disappointed we that her Siamese delicacy had not been served again. Laughingly she said, "I am afraid you will never have it again. I have had to give up the idea altogether."

"Why," we asked, "can't you get enough coconuts?"

"Getting coconuts is not the trouble," she said. "But you try cutting the tops off one hundred of them, and you will see my difficulty."

# 29

## *There Came a Big Spider*

*After she had read* an interesting book on spiders by Bristowe, my wife, Clare, decided she wanted to know more about them. When we attended the monthly meeting of the Photographic section of the Johannesburg Nature Study Society, we found that although some very good studies of spiders' webs had been made, very little had been done about spiders themselves.

Clare asked the Editor of the Nature Study Notes to put an article in the next issue asking that anybody interested in the formation of a Spider Club get in touch with her. To our surprise an enthusiastic young woman, Astri Leroy, telephoned her. In no time Astri and her husband John met with Clare and myself and the South African Spider Club was born.

Within a few months with eight members, officers were elected. Clare was President, John Leroy the chairman, and Astri, the secretary. Professional entomologists from the Department of Agriculture and the Transvaal Museum were invited to our first Field Meet, and they told us what equipment we would require.

Sweep nets were a necessity with which to beat tall grasses and bushes, and we would need small glass collecting tubes to put any captured spiders in. These spiders should then be then taken to an assembly point to be sorted, identified and counted.

We were told that the purpose of a spider count is not just how many spiders are collected in the area searched, but in what type of flora they were found.

I, the least involved member of this original committee, did not take it as seriously as the others. I went off on my own in an entirely different direction to them. Swishing my catching net idly through the tall grasses that were growing in clumps here and there, I also swept odd groups of bushes, while day dreaming and enjoying the sunny warmth of this late summer day. I lost all count of time and indeed also the purpose of my journey. It was quite a while before I bothered to look to see if I had collected anything at all.

To my surprise the net was full of an assortment of weird and wonderful creatures; grasshoppers, beetles, bugs of all kinds, and of course, spiders. The most outstanding item in this mass of insects was a large ungainly spider, the like of which I could never have conceived. I certainly had no glass tube with me large enough to put it in. So I shouted out for help and ran back to the assembly table. It had eight legs identifying it as an arachnid but none of the members could imagine what it was.

Eventually, Hansi Dippenaar, the expert from the Department of Agriculture, proclaimed it to be a Pycnacanthus (a hedgehog spider) so named because of its prickly shape. It was so rare that as far as she knew, none had been seen in the last ten years, and never before in the Transvaal.

"Where did you collect it?"

"I have no idea. I walked here and there, and then I think I went in that direction, and then I may have gone through some of those bushes or those, but I can't be sure."

Frantically everybody present was asked to beat everywhere in the area I may have been. But it was to no avail.

Photographs were taken of my spider and they argued who should take it home to study. But I, the intrepid collector of the spider, was forgotten. Nobody bothered to photograph me.

Its capture made a paragraph in the daily press and a column in Nature Notes (Overseas Arachnid Societies please note").

The newly started South African Spider Club thus became internationally known by the surprising capture of a Pycnacanthus, an extremely rate spider, by an anonymous naturalist.

In retrospect, I don't think that I received the amount of recognition that I really deserved, although I walked and walked, around and about, in the hot sun for an hour or so before I found the spider in my net. My name was never mentioned in connection with its capture.

Whereas, little Miss Muffet's name is world-famous by her merely sitting idly on a tuffet, eating curds and whey when her Big Spider arrived.

# 30

## *A Ring in the Dark*

*A strident ring* shook me out of a deep sleep. I fumbled for the telephone. Not properly awake. I looked at the clock before I put the phone to my ear. Three o-clock in the morning, it could only be bad news. It was. It was Jack, my brother, to tell me that Madge, his wife, had died on the train on the way back from Kalk Bay in the Cape.

Madge had been very ill for a long time. Her cancer after lying dormant for some years had returned, and the doctors had warned Jack that it was terminal. There was nothing they could do. Jack took her to Kalk Bay, a holiday resort thirty miles from Capetown, hoping that the sea air would improve matters.

He was phoning from De Aar, a sheep farming town and railway junction in the middle of The Great Karroo. De Aar, in the center of this vast desert, was a place as difficult to get to from Johannesburg, as any place could possibly be. I said that I would get down there as soon as I could, not knowing how, when or where.

Although it was the middle of the night I rang Bill Jolly, my firm's cost accountant, at his home. Bill had been with me since the war ended. He had battled glaucoma for many years but was now completely blind. Notwithstanding this, I relied upon him more than ever. His quick thinking, his keen mind and unfailing memory were invaluable. I told him my problem. He said he would deal with it and phone me back.

When he phoned about six o'clock, he told me that he had booked me on the first plane to Kimberly leaving at 7:30 a.m. Rental offices were not open yet but he would arrange for a car to meet me. He said it was about two hundred miles from Kimberly to De Aar, and I should be able to arrive there about eleven thirty or twelve.

On arrival at the exit g–ate at Kimberley airport I saw somebody holding up a placard with my name on it. He was an employee of Jaff & Co., the maker of Delswa dresses. Ever resourceful, Jolly had remembered that Jaff & Co., the manufacturer of Delswa Dresses in Johannesburg, had an auxiliary factory in Kimberley, and decided to phone them.

He was put through to the manager who without hesitation said they would have a car and a driver at the airport to meet me, adding that the driver would drive me to De Aar and would be at my disposal all day.

I telephoned Jack from the airport to get the address of where he was staying. We started on our way. Sitting in the front with the driver, I was pleased to see that he was wearing a Henochsberg uniform made by my own factory. Perhaps I should suggest to my wife that she should buy some Delswa dresses.

Arriving at De Aar, I found Jack writing down his thoughts and memories of Madge, saying in effect that he would turn his house into something like a shrine. He made me read a page or two. It stunned me, as it was so personally sentimental. Without comment I asked him what had happened.

Madge had died on the train before it reached De Aar. The conductor got in touch with the stationmaster there, notifying him of the death. The stationmaster had a policeman with him as well as an ambulance when the train arrived. After questioning Jack to make sure that it was not a homicide, the body was taken to the mortuary.

Where was Jack to go? Establishing that Jack was Jewish, the stationmaster explained, that although at one time they had had a sizable Jewish population, now Mr. and Mrs. Isaacstein, who owned the town's shoe store, were the only Jewish family there.

Late as it was, he insisted on ringing Mr. Isaacstein who immediately offered to put Jack up for the night. It was from there that Jack had phoned me. The Isaacsteins were both most sympathetic. They gave him a room and a bath, and served him breakfast in the morning. Mrs. Isaacstein told him to use their lounge, with its desk, and stationary and have full use of the telephone, while they went to the shop.

Jack, who was an accountant and a very organized person, must have got down to making telephone calls as soon as he could. First, to Rabbi Bernard of the Oxford Shul, who recommended he phone the Chevra Kadisha right away. The Chevra Kadisha is the Benevolent and Burial Society that every Jewish person belongs to, at least in Johannesburg. We all pay in and those in need or want, turn to it, and never get refused; burials are arranged free of charge.

They arranged to send a van to De Aar next day, to bring the body back to Johannesburg. They would arrange for the burial to take place as soon as possible after that.

Jack was told that a small plane arrived at De Aar at four regularly every afternoon. He had already booked for the two of us to fly to Kimberley, and then take the regular 5:30 p.m., plane on to Johannesburg. I told him that I had a car and a driver outside to take us back to Kimberley. He would hear none of it, and insisted on going by plane. I had no alternative but go and explain what had happened to the driver. I tipped him handsomely for his trouble.

Twenty-five years after the De Aar/Kimberley episode a friend here in La Jolla introduced me to Phillip Jaff, a South African, who was here on a visit. He told me that he managed the Delswa factory in Kimberley. It was he who lent me his car to take me to De Aar,

He was very interested in learning all that had happened when I got to De Aar, and I was very pleased to be able to thank him personally. However, it reminded me of the terrifying "Ring in the Dark" that started it all.

# 31

## *The Tin Temple*

***This corrugated iron*** structure was originally erected in the nineteen twenties. It was to be used as classrooms, while The School of Mines was being built nearby. The School of Mines was eventually renamed The University of Witwatersrand, and moved to Parktown, a northern suburb of Johannesburg. Adult education courses continued to be held in this now old, almost derelict shanty for many years. It was not demolished because it served a much-needed purpose and had become known affectionately to many people as The Tin Temple.

Before arriving in South Africa at the age of sixteen, I had already passed some of the primary accounting examinations of both the London Chamber of Commerce and the Royal Society of Arts. Now, in Johannesburg, I enlisted to continue my studies in the classes held by the Transvaal Education Department.

I attended lectures there from 5:30 to 7:30 every weeknight, but as I could not leave my job until 5:30 p.m. I usually arrived about ten minutes late. A front row seat was saved for me, but as my job was physically tiring, I usually dozed off soon after we arrived. The lecturers mostly put up with it for ten minutes or so, but eventually tapped me on the head with a ruler and asked what I thought of a point the lecturer had just made. Still half asleep, I wearily struggled to come up with a feasible answer when the point was repeated.

The roof leaked when it rained, forcing the students to huddle in any dry corner. The lecturers, obviously prepared for it happening, put up umbrellas and continued on. The country was in the throes of a depression and we all knew that no money was available for the luxury of getting the roof mended. The lecturers were mostly young professional lawyers or accountants just starting their careers who badly needed the extra money, so they, like the students, put up with it as a matter of course.

Over the years, having taken most of the senior and diploma levels of the accounting and company law courses that were offered, I decided to stop studying and live a more social life. But, to my surprise Mr. Gunn, the principal of the Tin Temple, called me to his office. I hardly knew the man, but it appeared he had been told I was leaving.

"You have been wasting your time taking all the subjects without any real purpose," he said. "I consider you are amply qualified to take the examinations of the Chartered Institute of Secretaries."

"I have never thought about it," I said. I knew it as a professional body governed by a British Royal Charter, known for the high standards it required of its members. It was rumored that never more than ten percent of people writing its final examination were accepted. In fact we had several people in the class who had written the final examination several times, and failed every time. "In any case I have never matriculated."

"Don't worry about that," he said. "I am on the acceptance board of the Institute and will arrange for you to have an oral test for a matriculation exemption."

It was the last thing I wanted to do, to go on studying for three or four years more, even if it would enable me to put the magic letters ACIS (Associate of the Charted Institute of Secretaries) after my name. But, having looked over some of the examination papers of the last few years and had been assured that I could have the oral matrix exam next month, I said I would give it a try.

The old Chartered Institute Exam papers he gave me did not seem to cover much that I had not already studied. The exams were to take place in June, nine months from now. I paid the necessary fee and entered to write the intermediate exam. When I received the confirmation stating the date and time, I noticed that one week after the intermediate exam was scheduled, the final was to take place. The fee to write the final was not large, so I entered for it also, to give me an idea what I would have to deal with, the following year.

I snuggled with both exams and was not satisfied that I had done that well. Several months later two foolscap envelopes arrived by registered post. My hands were shaking as I slit them open, and found so my amazement that I had passed both exams.

The Final Certificate was a work of art bearing an impressive seal, one that befitted a Royal Chane. The only catch was not really a catch: I was not allowed to use the lens ACIS until I was twenty-one.

Hallelujah! It was as though an alchemist had waved a magic wand and changed my alma mater, that temple of learning, from tin so gold.

# 32

## *Black Tie and Candles*

*I was sixteen*, when I arrived in Johannesburg from London. My grandfather's brother, Henry Henochsberg agreed to employ me.

His clothing factory specialized in the manufacture of uniforms for the government. I started work in his packing room at five pounds (10 dollars) per month.

I enjoyed working there, and gradually became involved in every aspect of the business. Five years later in 1931, unfortunately, Mr. Henochsberg died unexpectedly. Of necessity although I was only 21, I now had to take a more senior position in the firm.

I had very little time for dating because I was busy all day and studying every weeknight for an accounting degree. With only Saturday evenings at my disposal, girls I took out were mostly casual acquaintances. I had no time or desire for anything more serious.

Of all the clothing firms that manufactured high quality garments in South Africa, it was generally accepted that the one firm that stood out from the rest was Monatic Alba Ltd, which had its main factory in Capetown. The company's suits and trousers were advertised extensively with slogans, such as "Be Emphatic Buy Monatic." And their shirts "His Tern" and "Her Tern" bearing the emblem of the small sea bird were much sought after.

One day the receptionist phoned to tell me that a Mr. Nathan Jacobs was asking to see me. He was the sales director of Monatic and lived in Johannesburg. Introducing himself, he recalled the occasion where we had met once before.

After I had acknowledged that I now remembered it, he invited me to dinner at his home next evening. "Black tie and candles" was the phrase he used. I never had heard the phrase before, and it took me awhile to realize what it meant.

Next night was a Friday night when the Sabbath is welcomed in by lighting candles and saying a prayer before dinner. Dutifully, I put on a dinner jacket and a black bow tie, and arrived at the hour he had stipulated. I soon realized that the purpose of the whole exercise was to introduce me to his niece Paula, the daughter of a brother who lived in Liverpool.

She was a tall, good-looking girl, but I had difficulty coping with her accent. Liverpudlian, she called it when I commented on it. We were seated together at the dinner table, which I found rather obvious and embarrassing. Paula told me she had been given the family's season tickets to the orchestral concert at the city hall that evening. "Of course I'd love to," I said when she asked me if I would care to take her.

I parked in the underground garage in the city square to find that it was pouring when we came up. We got drenched, crossing the road to the hall's entrance. Sitting in wet clothes did not improve matters. Paula could not hide her annoyance although she tried hard enough. When I battled through the crowd to get drinks at the interval, someone knocked my arm and caused me to spill the drink over her dress. My effusive apology was not well received.

I found that we had very little in common. Her background and interests were very different from mine. I might have been partly at fault when I did not defer over several minor points.

It was still raining when we got out. I fetched the car and picked her up at the entrance. Unfortunately, we could not avoid getting soaked again, as we walked from the car to the front door of her house. Altogether, it was not a successful evening.

After saying goodbye, I am sorry to say I merely pecked her cheek and rushed away.

Mr. Jacobs, her uncle, invited me to lunch with him, soon afterward. Hinting that if I ever became a member of the family I would certainly be offered a seat on the board and be the owner of the necessary number of shares in Monatic that a director was required to have. I told him politely, but in no uncertain terms, that I was not interested.

Paula married a doctor soon afterward. I don't know if it was 'His Tern' or 'Her Tern' to be 'Emphatic' about accepting a few shares in Monatic but I didn't care.

# 33

## *Late for Dinner*

**My wife Clare** and I were to take the long drive from Capetown to Durban and make a first night stay at George. As we were not able to start until noon, we would be unable to stop en route if we were to arrive there in time for dinner. The drive would be a strenuous one, entailing many hours along winding roads and mountain passes. However, the thought of reaching this pleasant country town situated on the tree-lined slopes of the Outeniqua Mountains made it worth the effort.

The town of George is where the famed scenic Garden Route begins. It was named for George Rex, a reputed illegitimate son of Queen Victoria who lived there in the nineteenth century. The point of making a stop there was that the following day's travel through the Lake District to Knysna and its forests, before arriving at Plettenberg Bay, would be sheer joy.

We arrived at six o'clock in the evening and, by a stroke of luck, came across the Hawthorndene Hotel set back in its many acres of formal gardens. It proved to be the overnight stop of our dreams. We were warmly welcomed and the atmosphere of informality, combined with unassuming luxury, was exactly what we needed after our tiring journey.

Clare said, "You change first and go and have a drink, that will give me a chance to bathe and change without having to rush, and we can meet in the lounge at seven o'clock before going in to dinner."

It was a comfortable, dimly lit bar with large leather padded stools, a wide mahogany bar counter, and elaborate fittings that had displayed an impressive display of liquors on its mirrored shelves. Mine Host, the manager, presided, pouring out the drinks while adding his local knowledge to the general talk. Feeling at home immediately in this friendly atmosphere, I found myself sitting next to a genial gray-haired gentleman who introduced himself as Mr. Trotter, the managing director of the much advertised Trotter's Jelly company, who was staying overnight on his way to Capetown.

He had obviously been imbibing for some considerable time and was now the mainspring of the conversation in the room. He seemed to have an unending flow of absorbing stories and every now and then insisted on paying for a round of drinks, and civilly never refusing when one of us did the same. I had a very enjoyable half hour I thought, until I looked at my watch and found to my surprise that two hours had passed.

Clare was waiting in the lounge, by no means too patiently. She told me later that I staggered into the lounge, and over dinner I pointed out my friend from the bar as being Mishter Shtrotter of Shtrrotter Jellish, who was a great teller of tall tales.

A year later, doing my annual business round trip, we flew the first leg down to Capetown and continued up the coast by car again to Durban. Clare came with me again, as it gave us the opportunity of visiting our son at Stellenbosch University. We made our first stop at George once again, and I pulled happily into the Hawthorndene Hotel. I changed quickly and went downstairs to have a drink.

"I hope you don't meet that terrible Mr. Trotter again," said Clare jokingly, as I departed.

Entering the bar from the brightly lit reception area, I groped my way to the counter and settled myself comfortably on to a bar stool and ordered a scotch and soda.

"Hullo, haven't we met before?" came a voice from the dark area on my left. I turned, my eyes now adjusting to the half-light, and there was, yes, it really was, Mr. Trotter himself. Round, jovial, several glasses ahead of me, he looked as though he had never left the spot where I had first seen him He assured me that he had only got in that afternoon and was leaving next morning. We both agreed that it was an extraordinary coincidence.

This led him to tell me what the bishop said to the cardinal in a similar circumstance, and after a few more drinks and many stories later, I found it was eight-thirty. In self-defense, I insisted this time that he accompany me and join Clare and myself for dinner. I suppose both of us would have failed an alcohol test for driving, but our condition was nothing that a good dinner could not nullify. A bottle of wine chosen by Trotter, combined with his genial manner and fund of good stories carried the day.

After dinner we moved into the lounge and settled into the deep cretonne-covered armchairs, and over coffee, with the help of a liqueur or two, we carried on a convivial conversation until well after eleven o'clock. Then, insisting that it was time for bed, we got up to go. Trotter, after saying goodbye, turned back, obviously loathe to let two good listeners escape, and said hesitantly, "Did I tell you the story about my meeting George Bernard Shaw when he was living in Knysna?"

Catching one another's eye, we both said, "Yes, you did," almost in unison as we rushed up the stairs. We had had a long day and if we had admitted we had not heard it, we may have been there all night.

It is improbable that I will ever meet Mr. Trotter again, but if I should, I will certainly ask him to tell me what happened when he met Shaw, even at the risk that under the mellowing influence of yet another round, I again finish up late for dinner.

# 34

## *Decisions*

**Matilda, known as Matt**, and her husband were the owners of Emmanuel Reynardt, a wholesale warehouse catering to the toiletry trade. Their two sons, Stanley and Ernest were employed as salesmen in the business. There was no doubt that it was Matt's tightly strung energy was the reason for the firm being the leader in its field. A born manager, she made all the major decisions, and insisted that they were carried out promptly to her satisfaction.

Her decisive way in dealing with everyday affairs was difficult for those most closely involved with her. Her husband, an easygoing man, was quite prepared to leave most decisions to her. However, Stanley, the eldest son, strained at the curbs reigning him in. He took a job elsewhere where it allowed him to use his considerable talents freely.

Ernest, the younger, accepted life to be a giant chess game in which he was a Pawn with blinkers on unable to move left or right. The game had a King, who could only move one square at a time, and was dominated by a Queen, who was willing and able to move any distance in all directions.

Matt's main hobby was playing bridge. An enthusiast, she loved teaching young people her quicksilver approach to the game. She had taught her sons to play her way, but was looking for someone else to teach,

I had just arrived from England and her cousin, my uncle Joe Emmanuel, introduced me to her. Her eyes gleamed with anticipation; here was one possible bridge student. She only needed to find three more to make the four players that were necessary to get her lessons started. I found one fellow who was willing to try, and she talked two others into joining us.

After the four of us sat down at her bridge table, she told us of her philosophy of playing the game. "When you call or play never hesitate, you will be giving your opponents a clue as to what cards are in your hand."

Two packs of cards then were put on the table and a card had to be cut to decide who would be the dealer. That decided, her next pronouncement was, "Always say blue. This will save you hesitating whether to take the red or the blue."

The dealer then dealt out the cards. After we had sorted them, she said, "Call the suit you would like to be trumps. Don't mess around, don't let your opponents think that you have another suit that could have been called as well."

After some months of making such quick decisions applied to every aspect of the game, we played with other teams. Although our card playing was by no means good, we found that most of our opponents dithered around before deciding what to call or play, to the extent that it became boring.

Ernest, with exuberant encouragement from his mother, married Natalie Harmel. She like his mother had a strong personality. Her eldest brother was a wealthy accounting wizard who managed the vast complicated financial affairs of John Schlesinger, a playboy who had been left millions by his father.

Norma moved in her brother's social circles, where high finance and fur coats were a main subject of conversation. Norma never understood why Ernest took so very little interest in this life style. He still worked in Emmanuel Reynardt, where his mother made all the decisions. While at home Norma insisted that they attend continual social occasions and every charity ball, without ever consulting him.

His daughter, a lovely young girl of sixteen, came to see my wife one Sunday. She told her that her father had recently walked out of the house without saying a word, and never came back. They had since discovered that he was living with another woman in London. The girl was broken hearted about it and could not understand why he had done so. "I loved him," she said. "My dad and mother never had a quarrel in their whole life."

Could this have been the one decision in his whole life that Ernest had made on his own?

# 35

## *Pat Farley*

**Mrs. Schmidt's boarding house** in Hillbrow Johannesburg in the late 1920's housed and fed an ever-changing population of young people. None of us had any money and were probably better off without it. There was a definite feeling of camaraderie among us and newcomers were readily welcomed into the fold.

In those days, everybody worked a five and a half day week. On Saturdays we all helped with watering, rolling and marking the lines on the brown sand tennis court directly we got in from work so that we could start playing immediately after lunch.

It surprised us that Pat Farley, newly arrived from Ireland did not play tennis. He came from Belfast, the center of the Irish linen trade, to work for Nunnery's, a wholesale firm that specialized in linens. He did not know anybody in Johannesburg, and so we went out of our way to be friendly with him. He had a ready charm and responded warmly to our efforts to include him in our midst.

One Sunday, I took him for a long walk in the then undeveloped north-eastern suburbs of the town. The walk was a favorite of mine leading as it did to the heavily treed green fairways of the Royal Johannesburg Golf Club. From there it was a comparatively easy distance to Orange Grove, where we could catch a tram back to town.

While at the golf club, we followed some players for a few holes who I thought were playing extremely well. But, without his making any comments, I got the feeling that he was not impressed. It was only on the way home that he mentioned casually that he had been junior champion of Ireland, and would join a golf club here as soon as he could afford it.

In 1930 I moved to another boarding house but saw Pat from time to time both in business and socially. In June 1933 we traveled from Capetown to Southampton together on the Edinburgh Castle. He was on his way to see his folk in Ireland, and I to see my father and grandmother in London.

I do not remember seeing him during the war. The weeks were spent trying to keep up with the army's demands and all my weekends in camp at Booysens were spent with my regiment of the National Volunteer Brigade. I was much too busy to know what anybody else was doing. But I do remember meeting and lunching with him just after the war. Both of us enjoyed recalling old times.

You can imagine my surprise, however, when one day I saw him walking towards me on Eloff Street, Johannesburg's Broadway, seemingly purposely crossing over to the other side of the street. Perhaps he had not seen me I told myself, it could not have been intentional. A month or two later, it happened again. This time there was no mistake he was definitely avoiding me. I tried to put it out of my mind, but wondered how on earth I could have slighted him somehow without realizing it.

It was Christmas 1947 when I met him face to face in the bank and he was obviously uncomfortable but did not try to evade me. I asked him straight out why he had avoided me. He pulled me over to an empty space near the window, and said he must apologize but at that time he had been too upset with the world and me as a Jew in particular. His only brother while serving with the British Forces in Palestine had been killed in August 1946 when the King David Hotel in Jerusalem was blown up.

# 36

## *Graham Daniels*

***Graham, an only child,*** was a first cousin of my wife. He was an affable chap, but spoiled to the extent that if everything did not go his way, he could turn disagreeable, and let you know it.

His mother, Mabel Daniels, the younger sister of my wife Clare's mother, lived in fairly modest circumstances. Her husband Gerald was a bookkeeper in a small way. When the South African Chartered Accountant Society was first established in the country, he, in common with every other firm operating as bookkeepers, was allowed to add CA (CPA) after his name. This in no way had any effect on him, he still rode around on his motorbike, dressed in a white dustcoat looking more like a meter reader than an accountant.

Graham his son on the other hand, dressed immaculately. If one could criticize him at all it would be to say he was too gentlemanly. It was a facade. He was about my age and I had occasionally played bridge with him. When the game did not go his way, if his partner played a wrong card or an opponent queried his play, he would lose his temper in a flash, go red in the face and be positively unpleasant. On the other hand, when the game was over he would apologize profusely for his bad behavior.

He was quite a simple fellow and that was probably why he was such an excellent salesman. He had complete confidence in whatever he was selling irrespective of its merits. He married Lydia, an attractive woman, soon after his parents died from heart trouble, inheriting the sum of forty thousand pounds, a considerable sum in those days. He convinced Lydia that Johannesburg's six thousand feet altitude put too much strain on the heart so they moved to Capetown, because he believed that at sea level he would live longer than his parents had.

With his inheritance they bought a house in Sea Point and with plenty of cash in the bank they were prepared to live happily ever after. They had two lovely daughters and often when I was in Capetown on business, I would look them up.

He was a top furniture and appliance salesman. When he changed jobs, it did not change his successful selling technique. He sold whatever refrigerator or what-have-you his new firm offered with the same enthusiasm he had previously given to an opposition product. He was naive and believed implicitly in the merits of whatever he was told about the article he was now selling.

What, I did not know at the time was that soon after they arrived in Capetown, they went to Milnerton racecourse and became involved in horse racing. At first they won considerably, and it was probably the worst thing that could have happened. They became inveterate gamblers. Over the years they must have lost heavily, but were always convinced that next week their luck would change.

I suppose I did occasionally I hear them arguing, and sometimes he seemed bad tempered, but I never gave much thought to it. I may have mentioned it to Clare once or twice, but had no idea there was any real trouble.

One evening, Lydia phoned Clare and sobbingly told her that Graham had shot himself that day. She was at her wits end and did not know who to turn to for help. I flew down immediately and found the position was worse than I had hoped. She had no money in her bank, but knew that they had a Life Insurance Policy on his life, and understood that an amount of two thousand pounds was guaranteed in the policy for her. Would I look into it?

I went to see the Insurance Company and found that Graham had gone in there the day before, cancelled the life policy and had withdrawn the two thousand pounds. The money was never found, I gave her fifty pounds to go on with, and promised to see Graham's mother's eldest sister's husband, who was a multimillionaire.

He expressed shock and sorrow when I told him what had happened. He said he would instruct his lawyer to see if that two thousand pound meant for her, had been illegally withdrawn, and claim on the insurance company if possible. Other than that he was prepared to pay her fifteen pound per month for twelve months, if I would do the same. I should have known. Twice before I had gone to him when members of his wife's family needed help. He had said both times, Leslie, "I will give whatever you do."

# 37

## *Leo Jacobs*

***Soon after my arrival*** in Johannesburg in 1926 I was introduced to Leo Jacobs, a fellow about my own age, and found we had mutual interests. We became close friends, so much so, that over week-ends we often walked from Clarendon Circle along Houghton Drive and turned down Kloof Road. About two hundred feet down we climbed up to a flat rock that overlooked the sloping roadway. Kloof Road was a gap in the hills that wound its way to the as yet undeveloped area that eventually became the select suburb of Lower Houghton.

From our elevated position there was merely open veldt between us and Sogot's Corner on the corner of Tyrrwitt Avenue and Oxford Road Rose bank, a mile or two away. Here we talked and talked for hours about ourselves and the world in general. We may not have solved anything, but were completely happy doing so. Such was our friendship.

One of the many things we did not try and solve was the fact that the two heroes of the Boer War, General Smuts and General Hertzog, were at loggerheads. Hertzog wanted South Africa to have a new flag, and Smuts wanted to keep the Union Jack. Of course the essential difference was that one wanted to break away from being a the British Empire and General Smuts wanted to remain.

Among the many issues of the time that was given much media attention was that the first Jewish Judge. Justice Greenberg was trying the case of a Jewish farmer in the Bethal area being charged with murder. He was accused of having a farm worker flogged to death. Would he be more lenient because the farmer was Jewish? I personally have no idea what the final judgment was, but it caused a lot of discussion at the time. Leo and I certainly kept away from the subject.

It was now 1927. Leo and most of my friends were in their last year of High School. The school year finished as it had for many years with the Inter High sports competition in all the High schools. Both the Afrikaans and the English schools competed. With the Afrikaans element encouraged by General Hertzog to change the flag and demanding that Afrikaans be the official language, animosity between the English and Afrikaner high schools became too much to cope with. Future Inter-High competitions between both English and Afrikaner schools were cancelled and never resumed.

Leo's mother had died soon after I arrived. I hardly knew her. But I had met his father, generally known Coffee Jacobs. Whether it was because he was an importer of coffee beans or for the dark color of his skin, I do not know. Unfortunately his business had recently failed and Leo, instead of going to college, was forced to take a job that would pay an immediate living wage.

He applied and was accepted to be a learner miner in the Robinson Deep Gold Mine. It paid a very much higher wage than any other entry occupation. The learning period took many months and included spending some considerable time at working sites underground, after which he obtained a blasting certificate. Only a qualified miner could insert and ignite the dynamite that was necessary to crumble a new section of reef into a vast amount of dust-filled, broken rock and soil. African miners would load it on to trucks that ran on rails to the shaft to be hoisted to the surface, where the gold would be extracted. The residue was added to the huge reddish brown mine dumps that were such a feature of the Witwatersrand landscape.

The animosity between the races that had caused the inter-racial Inter High to be cancelled, had become general. Most of the white miners objected to Leo speaking English. Besides, he probably was the only Jewish miner on the reef. Which didn't make Leo's life any easier.

He took his job seriously and made a study of the cooling and ventilation systems that made working at these tremendous depths possible. Management recognized his interest in the technicalities of deep level mining, and he was sent to other mines in the same group to suggest possible improvements. All this did not increase his popularity with his fellow workers.

His brother had a concession store on Nourse Mine and had married the daughter of Leonard Jenks. Jenks, after his first wife died, married my mother's youngest sister, Florrie. Through this family tie, I got to know his family well.

I was not surprised, therefore, when one day his sister-in-law phoned me at my office, but was horrified to hear that it was to tell me that Leo had been killed in a mine accident that day. I got into my car and rushed to Benoni where they lived. When I arrived I found that the information they had received about his death was incredible. They had been merely bluntly informed that he had fallen down the mine shaft. No more information than that.

They, like me, were skeptical. A preventive barrier is kept in front of a shaft until the elevator comes up to the surface, and there is only a narrow gap to step over to get on to it. It was so out of character for Leo to take any chances of any kind that we were faced, and still are, with the question that will never be answered; "Did he fall or was he pushed?"

## 38

# *A Train of Evidence*

**Ernest Samuel,** a pipe smoking, affable man, was popular with farmers throughout the country. For more than twenty-five years he had been a traveling salesman for Greatorex, manufacturers of top quality leather goods. In the 1930s there were no paved roads outside of towns, so going by train was the only way to get from place to place. Farmers were notified well in advance of Samuels's itinerary, the dates that he would be in their nearest town, and the location of the sample rooms.

The saddles, bridles and multifarious items with their brass fittings, had to be man-handled on and off the train at Johannesburg station, and repeated as each scheduled town was reached. The samples had to be rearranged for display to the local farmers, most of whom were old friends. He had not considered any of it a chore when he was younger, but now he felt his age. He was looking forward to retirement; these last six weeks of travel had become too much for him.

Thankful that he had at last arrived back at Johannesburg station, he put on his jacket and picked up the two briefcases that contained the record of his sales. He walked down the corridor and reached the exit as the train came to a stop. With a case in each hand he stepped out of the carriage door. Before his foot reached the platform, the train, without warning, lurched forward. Thrown off balance, Samuels fell heavily on to the platform.

Not able to get up himself, a man and his wife lifted him up onto a four-wheel luggage cart and called an ambulance. They told him they had nearly fallen themselves when the train jerked forward. Unfortunately they did not leave their name. At the hospital, he was found to have a broken hip. His firm engaged an attorney who advised Samuels to sue the Railways as they were clearly responsible. The amount claimed was considerable, and was to be heard in the High Court.

As the South African Railways was a government department headed by a cabinet minister, the government denied the claim in its entirety, and engaged a leading barrister Millin KC. (Kings Council) to represent them. Millin with his white wig and flowing black silk gown was an imposing figure. Two attorneys in their plain black worsted gowns sat with him at is table, which was spread with legal tomes. Each of the books had pages pre-marked showing the decisions in cases that were similar to the one now before the court.

Samuels's attorney put a clear-cut case before the court, of how his client in the course of his employment had been thrown rudely to the ground when the train jerked forward as he was alighting. He mentioned Samuels's long service with the company, but because of the injury he had now sustained, was no longer able to work.

The Right Honorable Millin KC (Kings Counsel) rose impressively from his chair adjusted his gown, and centered his wig. Acknowledging the judge, with due respect, he sad how sorry he was to hear of Samuels accident. He was a well known figure himself, but his wife, Sarah Gertrude

Millin the famous author, was even more well known. Her book "God's Step-Children" was acknowledge to be an important part of South Africa's literary heritage. Consequently the case attracted tremendous media attention. Millin assured the court that Samuel's accident unfortunately had nothing to do with the railway. Alighting from the train and stepping down to the platform, with both his hands full, was a foolish thing to do, and falling was clearly his own fault. After the train stopped, it did not move again. To save wasting the courts time, to show that the railway was not liable, he was going to produce several credible witnesses to show that the train did not move again after it had stopped.

Samuels's attorney with an incredulous look on his face, said he was surprised to hear that trains never move after they come to a stop. With a railway time table in his hand, he challenged the court to adjourn to the station to watch a train arrive. The judge thought it would be interesting but the opposing counsel Millin KC. dismissed it as ridiculous.

The court adjourned until next day. Millin produced several witnesses who assured the court that trains never move after they have come to a stop. The witnesses included the Johannesburg stationmaster, several guards and the senior man operating the signal system.

Samuels attorney was unable to locate the man and his wife who had nearly fallen themselves when the train jerked forward. He had hoped that with all the publicity in the press that they would come forward. Nevertheless, confident that he could show the court that trains very often move after coming to a halt, he asked if the court would repair to the main platform when the train from Capetown arrived next morning.

Notwithstanding a protest from the railway's counsel, the judge agreed that the court would assemble at the railway station at eleven o'clock next day. Wearing robes and wigs, the judge, and both counsel lined up on the platform, together with reporters and photographers who were present to see the unusual sight of the court in full legal regalia, assembled on the station platform. The train from Capetown pulled in, and came to a stop. But, this time it did not move. The railway officials who had given evidence at the trial, must have been pressured to say that the train had not moved.

The Judge adjourned the proceeding, until two o'clock that afternoon. When the court re-assembled, the Right Honorable Millin KC asked the Judge to deny the claim. It was granted and the case was dismissed.

Unfortunately the couple whose evidence would have been essential to Samuel's claim had been temporally out of town and apologized for not coming forward before. The lawyers recommended that they should appeal. Especially as the couple who had been on the platform were prepared to testify. But Samuels said it would be too expensive to consider it, and he had no intention of going to court again. With his wry sense of humor he said, "I'll file it away in my own mind as a railway miscarriage of justice."

# 39

# *A War Time Story Never Told*

*I met Morley* at a reunion of the 2nd battalion of the National Volunteer Brigade a year or two after the war. At one time he had lived two houses away from mine, in Johannesburg. I had not seen him since he had volunteered to go on a supposedly secret mission in 1943. Volunteered was a polite word for it—dragooned would have described it better

\*     \*     \*

South Africa declared war on Germany in September 1939. Soon afterwards I joined the Civic Guard, whose main duty was to police the neighborhood while so many men were away in the army. After the Japanese attacked Pearl Harbor, in 1941 however, I decided to join the National Volunteer Brigade instead.

The NVB was a military unit comprising men who were essential to the war effort. It entailed training every weekend at Booysens military camp, in addition to mounting guard duty one night a week at an oil refinery, or some similar essential facility. However, it was the compulsory one-month camp we had to attend that was the most onerous.

Cullinan Diamond Mine, near Pretoria had been transformed into a military camp. When we arrived there, were shown into several large bungalows. A military sergeant of the permanent force was there to impress upon us the importance of making up our beds in the squared up uniformity that a morning inspection demanded.

After some initial drilling on the parade ground under the shouted commands of a gravely voiced permanent-force sergeant-major, we were told that after dinner in the mess, we would be marched into the main hall where the whole battalion would receive a lecture on compliments and saluting. This sounded like a pleasant entertaining evening about an aspect of army life to which none of us had given much thought.

Twelve hundred of us settled comfortably into our seats in the hall. An army captain introduced himself, and pleasantly enough said that he would be giving the talk. Suddenly, unexpectedly, he raised the level of his voice and demanded that we sit up straight and pay full attention. We immediately shuffled ourselves into a more upright position, endeavoring to look like real soldiers eager to listen to what he was about to say.

After explaining the basic principles of saluting, but just before proceeding as to who, when and where, he stopped abruptly. Pointing to a man in the front row, he asked him to repeat what he the lecturer, had just said. The man, who probably had dozed off after the rigors of the day, admitted he had no idea. In a voice that reverberated around the hall like thunder, the captain demanded that the company sergeant-major take his name and ensure that the man does pack drill for the whole period of the camp. Twenty times every day he was to march around the parade ground shouldering his rifle and carrying his full pack. It was surprising how closely we concentrated on listening to every word for the rest of the lecture.

After a week of drilling and more drilling, we were introduced to some of the army's intensely concentrated methods for weapon training. Every platoon in turn had to train with rifles, machine guns, mortars and antitank guns. Each weapon had to be stripped and reassembled in the correct order in the shortest possible time. A complicated series of mnemonics were relentlessly drummed into us on the pain of death to achieve the seemingly impossible results the instructors required. At the point when the individual consonants and vowels in the correct order had been seared into every crevice of our brains, a new and even more worrisome situation occurred.

The officer commanding was to deliver an important message and ordered the whole regiment to assemble on the parade ground. He informed us that four hundred men were required to volunteer for an important mission, one that required them to be away from their homes and families for a period of at least six months.

No leave would be given and no incoming or outgoing telephone messages allowed, until four hundred men had volunteered. He said this was an order from high command and he himself had no idea what the mission entailed. But it was of the highest priority. There were no ifs or buts: we would be kept in the camp indefinitely until the quota was filled.

Not able to get in touch with our families or employers, it was seemingly an impossible request. My occupation was such that I could not be spared, but my immediate worry was that my wife was almost due to give birth to twins, and would not be able to get in touch with me.

Constant threats were now the order of each day. Every man had to face an individual inquisition to pressurize him into volunteering. The number of men, who had already agreed to go, was read out each day. Fifty, then one hundred, then two hundred, but when three hundred was reached, the number of men volunteering came to dead stop.

Threats and pressures were now increased. The Spanish Inquisition would have been child's play to what we were subjected. Getting the last hundred names was painful. It got to the point where the circumstances of being confined to camp became unbearable and, I am sure that the last man to give in did it out of sheer desperation.

When the target was finally reached, we all breathed a sigh of relief. I knew that my neighbor Frank Morley had volunteered early on. On a mission yet to be disclosed and without any fanfare, the gallant four hundred were marched to an unknown destination.

\* \* \*

At the re-union after the war, I asked Morley about the so-secret mission. He said that after the four hundred men were marched out of Cullinan camp they still did not know what the mission entailed, but they were given one week's leave to finalize domestic matters. They then entrained to Capetown, one thousand miles away. There, only after they were incarcerated into another camp, were they informed what the mission was. To ensure complete secrecy they were once more not allowed any communication with the outside world.

They were to act as guards on the White Star liner Queen Mary to ensure that ten thousand German soldiers taken prisoner at El Alamain reached New York. They were issued with the standard tropical kit as worn by the South African forces in the desert.

A cursory four weeks of training was meant to acquaint them with their duties, as well as with the complicated anatomy of the vast ship. Morley told me that the boat was one thousand foot long, and eight stories high. Its vast interior was a rabbit warren of passages. Most of the cabins had been converted into prison cells. This minimum amount training proved to be insufficient for them to cope with all the problems they would encounter.

The journey was a nightmare. Several armed ships escorted them, as the ship zigzagged at full speed to avoid attack by submarines,

Their arrival in New York was the epitome of irony. The arrangements to deal with the ten thousand German prisoners went off without a hitch. They were transported quickly and inconspicuously to a pre-arranged camp. But the citizens of New York were not prepared to let such an important occasion go unmarked. The city, famous for its ticker tape parades, did not let the first allied troops, who had arrived there since the war started, go unnoticed.

After all, the battle of El Alamain was the first major battle to turn the tide of German victories. New Yorkers came out in full force to welcome these desert heroes, as they marched down Broadway, shouldering rifles, and wearing their exotic looking desert uniforms, comprising pith helmets, khaki bush shirts and shorts with their canvas gaiters atop their army boots. The Mayor thanked them officially, and the gallant four hundred were entertained royally for the entire period of their extended stay in America.

The fact that they had never faced an enemy, or fired a shot in battle was never mentioned. But whether forced into it or not, they had volunteered for a mission without knowing what it was, had left their families with only one week's notice, besides zigzagging across a submarineinfested ocean. So what if New York gave them a big hand. Who is to say that they did not deserve it?

# 40

## *Shoulder Arms*

***In South Africa*** every man had to register with the department of defense when he reached the age of 16, and was attached to a peacetime regiment of his choice by the time he was 18 or 19. This Active Citizen Force training was not onerous, merely a parade at night once a week. By law, the purpose of this Active Citizen Force was to defend the country only within its borders.

When South Africa joined England in declaring war on Germany in September 1939, men and women in the army were pressured to agree to fight outside the country's borders. They were then issued with one-inch red-cloth tabs to put across the base of their epaulettes to indicate their willingness to do so. Soldiers or policemen not wearing such red tabs were looked on with suspicion.

I had been nominated a key man, one not allowed to join the army, as my job was essential to the war effort. I therefore joined the Civic Guard. an auxiliary police force whose main duty was to police one's neighborhood at night.

In January 1942, a month after Pearl Harbor, I resigned from the Civic Guard and enlisted in the National Volunteer Brigade, a military Home Guard regiment attached to the army, thinking that if the Japs arrived, I would have a rifle in my hand instead of a baton. After being issued with a uniform and a rifle, I joined a crowd of new recruits at the Union Ground.

After we were lined up into companies and platoons, a fearsome looking Sergeant Major barked. "Stand to attention,—Shoulder arms,—Quick march,—Left right—Left-right!" This on my first parade was not as easy as it sounds. My legs were going left—right while my arms were going in the opposite direction and my shoulder felt like hell.

The routine of guarding an oil refinery one night a week and spending every weekend at a military camp became part of my existence for the next few years. But my job was becoming more and more onerous as the army's demands on my firm became greater.

The already overloaded telephone system got worse. I often had to travel the thirty-six miles to Pretoria and back several times a day, as I was unable to reach it by phone.

Hoping it would make my life easier, I applied and got a U license that allowed me to drive army trucks. I found that being in the transport section had many benefits. Extra rationed gas coupons were not the least of them. Also, despite the fact that I was only a private, while driving an army vehicle I was completely in charge of its occupants. This knowledge I found useful on more than one occasion.

Although at times I had to drive heavy truck loads of sand and building material to new sections of the camp site, I was still attached to 'A' company and had to participate in the intensified drilling and weapon training that was now being imposed on us, as the war continued.

Hard-bitten permanent force instructors, some just returned from the battlefront, put us through our paces. Rifles, mortars, anti-tank and Vickers machine guns had to taken apart, oiled and re-assembled in record time. On the whole they were demanding but fair, and gave us credit when it was due.

The one exception was Captain Madison. Although he was the Captain of "A" Company and not an official permanent force instructor, he insisted on training the machine gun group himself. He was never satisfied with what we did or the time in which we did it. He was determined that his Vickers Machine Gun crew would break all records at any cost.

On that last Sunday on which the machine gun competition was held, he had us take the gun apart and re-assemble it ten or twelve times before he was satisfied. Although worn out, we eventually achieved the time he had in mind. We had broken the record and beaten every other company in the regiment.

Megalomaniac that he was, he insisted that we all come to the rifle range to watch him compete for the revolver shoot. He fancied himself as a sharpshooter and although tired out and bored, we had to stand around for an hour, watching him perform.

Now, late Sunday afternoon it was time to go home. The troop carriers were all lined up ready to take us. The weary men thankfully piled into them, took out their cigarettes and lit them up. My troop carrier was to lead the convoy, but before I could get to it, along came Captain bloody Madison who, seeing the men contentedly settling in, shouted "No smoking in troop carriers.

There was nothing they could do about it. Sergeants in every carrier had to ensure that his orders would be carried out.

I walked to the front of the line got into my carrier and to my surprise Captain Madison jumped in beside me. Once we got on our way, he took out a packet of cigarettes and offered me one. "No smoking in troop carriers, sir," I said, and he sheepishly put the packet away.

# 41

## *Invisible*

**The Quartermaster General** of the Union Defense Force in Pretoria told me confidentially that they intended to incorporate a regiment of Marines into the South African Navy. The officer commanding had been appointed and was leaving in two days time for training in England. Not a word about it must leak out because it had not yet received Cabinet approval.

I was soon to find out why he was burdening me with something so secret. He said the newly appointed marine commander insisted on seeing me before he went away.

I was then informed that I would be transported on an air force plane next morning to the military aerodrome in Durban. There was no time to get official permission to transport a civilian on an air force plane or vehicle, so my journey must remain a secret. I was told that I was to be an invisible man. Semi-jokingly he said if the aircraft crashed, they would deny I was ever on it.

After a bumpy ride on a DC3, I arrived at the air force station in Durban in time to join the pilots for breakfast. I did not have to be invisible there, but when a transport sergeant arrived in his drab green UDF vehicle to take me to the Bluff, he was told that I was an unofficial passenger, and in a light-heartedly manner they added, "If you are caught with him in the car you will be court-martialed."

The future Marine Headquarters were evidentially on the Bluff.

To get there we drove along the Esplanade around the Bay and weaved our way through the overcrowded streets of what was mainly an Indian residential and trading area. Mahatma Gandhi had practiced law there many years before.

The Colonel there had been told that I had copies of all the British navy and Marine dress regulations, and he wanted to see and discuss them with me.

He was a busy man and I wasted no time before I asked the sergeant to take me back. However, the streets through the Indian area that I thought had been so crowded earlier that day were now chaotic. Traffic jammed the streets. Religious ceremonies were taking place around all the Indian Temples. We had to travel slowly to avoid dogs and children darting haphazardly between the slow moving traffic. Even cows, possibly sacred, were ambling here and there. I could have been in Calcutta, only the Ganges was missing from the scene.

Frustrated, the sergeant accelerated into a gap only to knock over a dog that sped across his path. He intended to drive on knowing that if he stopped a hundred people would claim ownership and demand compensation. Out of nowhere an Indian municipal policeman arrived pencil and notebook in hand. Turning to me the driver shouted, "For goodness sake get out, you will have to find your own way back. I have to deal with this myself." Thrust unexpectedly into this Asiatic setting with everybody speaking in an incomprehensible tongue, I was not happy at all. I wished I was really invisible. I threaded my way through the crowded streets and telephoned from a general store for a taxi.

On getting back to the air force station, they chuckled at the plight of the transport sergeant. I was thanked for saving them from all the complications that would have resulted had I not rendered myself invisible so quickly. After a bite of lunch, they put me on a plane that was just leaving for Pretoria. They introduced me to the pilot, and with their straight-faced sense of air force humor told him that if he ran over a dog en route, he had better drop me over the side with a parachute.

When I got back to Pretoria I reported the details of my conversation with the Marine colonel to the Quartermaster General in Pretoria, who once again impressed me with the importance of secrecy. I got back home in time for dinner, after just another day at the office.

A month or two later, I was told that the whole scheme for a marine regiment had been shelved indefinitely, for some obscure political reason. I hope that I will never again have to accept the mantle of invisibility. I found it too much to take.

# PART III

# Trials and Travels

# 42

# *Hong Kong*

***I have very fond memories*** of the trip that we made to the Far East many years ago. Our first stop was Hong Kong, which proved to be an excellent introduction to the rest of the tour.

Our plane touched down at the airport at 8:30 in the morning after a fourteen-hour flight. Mike, who was to be our guide while there, met us. He took our worries about getting our luggage through the custom off our shoulders, and managed to appease us when we were told that we could not get into our hotel rooms until one o'clock.

Tired out after the flight, both Clare, my wife, and I certainly were not yet in the mood for serious shopping when we streamed out into the surrounding narrow streets. Tiny little shops, ground level, basement and upstairs, offering unheard of bargains, spread out in all directions. We literally staggered around taking it all in, but managed to resist buying hardly anything.

At last we got our room, had a bath, fell into bed and only surfaced after dark. With another couple, Mavis, who used to work in my office, and John, her architect husband, the four of us went out for our first oriental dinner. John, whose firm did business in Hong Kong and knew it well, took over the ordering of the meal. He ordered a variety of dishes: fish, chicken, walnut shredded beef and vegetables. This was all put together in the middle of the table and we were provided with bowls and chopsticks. The thing to do was to stretch over and dig out something of each dish and put it into your bowl. This was washed down with continually refilled cups of china tea. For dessert we had a slightly overripe, light colored mango that had a banana-like flavor.

Refreshed and well-fed, we went out into the exciting atmosphere of streets that sparkled with lights and swarmed with people and children. All the shops were open for business and conventional nightclubs vied with nude shows and sex joints for customers, with bigger and bigger flashing electric signs that blazed on and off. Clare and Mavis had the idea that John and I were being awkward and prudish when we did not want to take them to one of the shows. Under pressure, we gave in, but they could not get out quick enough once they were inside. This meant they got down to serious shopping and it was very late when we got back to the hotel.

Our hotel was in Kowloon and next morning we were taken by bus through a one and a quarter mile tunnel under the harbor to the Island of Hong Kong. We took the funicular to the Peak and from the height of some fifteen hundred feet we had a bird's eye view of the entire colony. From there we were taken to the Tiger Balm gardens that adjoin the home of the late Aw Boon Haw who made a fortune from his ointment. It is a mass of violently colored poured concrete statues that defaces the hillside with its sheer vulgarity. From there we moved on through Repulse Bay to Aberdeen. (I wonder whether these names have been retained now it no longer belongs to Britain.)

Aberdeen is a spacious bay where the River People live. Here they are born, marry, work and die, aboard their boathouses. We traveled in a sampan (water taxi) along channels between the boats that were all individually decorated. We ended up for lunch on the famous Jumbo Restaurant. It is an enormous floating boat with seven restaurants spread over its four floors all elaborately decorated in the garish Chinese manner.

We sat at tables of ten in a room filled with 400 people. We nobly struggled eating with chopsticks. The seven or eight courses were all served hot, starting with soup, baby prawns, lobster pieces served in onion chunks, chicken, fried fish, lettuce boiled with crab meat purée, shredded pork and noodles (which we gave a miss) followed by fresh orange quarters. One member of our party didn't fancy the set menu and asked for half a chicken instead. She nearly fainted when she got her half chicken, literally: half a beak, half a head, one eye, one leg, and half of everything else.

Bundled into a bus again, not used to traveling with a tour, we were not entirely happy being cramped in and taken hither and thither to see something, whether we wanted to or not. We arrived at the New Territories where we were able to overlook Red China, and were pleasantly surprised to see how well-farmed the land was there. On the way back we passed high-density buildings built to cope with the refugees that pour in, in vast numbers. Here we were told whole families live in one room without water toilets or cooking facilities. A lot of the houses and buildings have circular mirrors on them to counter a bad spell that a person living opposite may be casting. The idea is to reflect the evil spirit back from whence it came. In some cases the person or persons on the opposite side put up an even bigger mirror to re-reflect it back again. The exercise must keep the spirits very fit, I should think.

That evening, after dining at the Hotel Furama's revolving restaurant we went on to the Beggar's Market, a daytime parking lot. Clare had her fortune told by a man squatting on the ground with a birdcage full of sparrows. In front of him were about 25 envelopes and after she gave him a sufficient number of Hong Kong dollars, one of the birds was let out of the cage. It hopped up and down the envelopes until it picked out one. This, the man gravely handed it to her, as her fortune.

It was in Chinese and she had to sign the fortune, which was then placed back in the envelope and shuffled with all the others. A bird was taken out of the cage again and after much ado it picked an envelope, which was given her with much ceremony. On opening it, there was the fortune with her signature on it. She was so surprised that she forgot to ask what the fortune predicted.

Although tired out, we returned to the bus and were taken to a nightclub.

Here we saw traditional dances performed by enchanting Chinese girls. Their hand movements were fantastically graceful and expressive and were a delight to watch. However so many other tours had now poured in, that the hall became jam packed with people standing at the back as well as sitting in the aisles. The room became hot and uncomfortable and I looked around to see how we could get out in a hurry if we had to. Yes, there were two doors with a lighted sign shaped very much like a five-bar gate above them. This must be the exit sign I decided and made a mental note of it. This knowledge came in very handy when we got to Japan where very few people speak English. The music was unappealing and repetitive to our ears and having had a long day we were glad to leave.

Next day we had a late breakfast thank goodness, as it was a day of leisure. At last we could do what we liked. We would not have to be packed in the bus to do something because it was on the itinerary, which had to be ticked to make sure we got our money's worth. This time, joined by Mavis and John, we took a taxi, quite a relief, and went through the tunnel to the newly constructed Ocean Park. A whole mountain has been converted for the project. It contains an oceanarium, zoological garden and a botanical park plus a museum and restaurants. We took a cable car to the mountaintop and then a fifteen-minute ride over the vast complex of buildings housing the oceanarium and restaurants. The heat was intense and when we left at 4 p.m. tired out, we were thankful the taxi was air-conditioned. Our legs ached so, that after a hot bath we rubbed them in with Tiger Balm, which eased them greatly. So much so that we almost forgave the horrible brightly colored concrete statues in Boon Haw's garden.

The Information office in the City Hall suggested we should go to the "Cat Street" area. This is the real Hong Kong and certainly where tourists are not. The streets were on the steep slope at the foot of the mountain, and were so crowded that even crossing them was a major problem. Market shops open to the sidewalks offered meat, fish, vegetables and fruit, many kinds of which we had never seen before. Unfortunately both the meat and fish were covered with flies.

Turning a corner we found row after row of shops in which every sort of trade was being practiced. Front rooms, back rooms and mezzanines were full of people manufacturing or packing every conceivable thing Most of them on the mezzanine level had mainly children working there, the floor being so close to the ceiling that grownups would not have been able to stand. We saw umbrellas, caps, artificial flowers, straw mats and much more being made by family groups. At the back of the shops there were little shrines with a glowing red light. Some of them had little figurines on them, which we were told kept unnamed bogies at bay.

We got back to Kowloon by ferry for one Hong Kong dollar, about nine cents for each of us. In the afternoon we shopped in a quaint shopping area behind the hotel. Clare got annoyed with me because I suggested she should not bargain, as the prices they asked seemed too cheap. This did not stop her. She said, "Here we are in the most exciting shopping place in the world and if you can't bargain it is no fun. The shopkeepers expect it, and would be disappointed if you accepted the first price they asked."

Clare found a store that had a vast assortment of goods that Clare simply had to have, over which, she and the seller haggled at great length, to the obvious enjoyment of both of them. We had to buy another suitcase to put the purchases in, because most of our cases were already packed, as we were leaving for Taiwan next day.

# 43

## *My First Time in Italy*

***The Italian Department*** of Foreign Trade invited South Africa to send a representative to an exhibition of uniform clothing held in Milan in November of that year. The government offered it to me and I accepted.

I was given a return ticket on Al Italia, and told that the South African Consulate in Milan would book accommodation and handle all arrangements for my stay. The exhibition was to be for one week from Thursday to Wednesday. I booked a flight to leave on that first Wednesday. That week, North Italy was hit by the greatest flood of the century. Florence was flooded and Milan severely battered.

Consequently, I cancelled the trip. However, on Sunday the newspaper stated that weather in Italy had cleared, and still very keen to go I telephoned the Johannesburg airport and found that an Al Italia plane was leaving in an hour or two for Rome. They accepted my booking and I boarded the plane with very little time to spare.

We arrived in Rome at 9:30 p.m. A taxi took me to a hotel in Via del Tritone near the Trevi Fountain. Next morning on my plane for Milan, I found that on internal flights in Italy, seats are not allotted. In the cabin, I sat in the first vacant seat. Regular meals were not served, but a steward came around with a tray with sandwiches and buns.

I had not given a thought to the fact that the captain' 's announcements were only in Italian. So, when we arrived in the airport, it took me at least thirty minutes to find I was in Genoa and not Milan. It must have been announced in Italian on the plane that fog made it impossible to land in Milan, but I did not know. It was an hour or two before we were shepherded into a bus that was to take us to Milan.

I had left suddenly on Sunday and had been unable to notify the South African Consular office of my change of plan. Consequently on arriving in Milan, with visibility only about a yard or two, I told the taxi driver to take me to the nearest American Express Office. They booked me into the Hotel Continentale in Via Manzoni. When I arrived there, the fog was so thick that I could hardly see the brightly lit entrance, and certainly not the other side of the road.

The comfortable red carpeted and mahogany entrance foyer gave me a feeling of relief after my last few hours of trauma. But, when I showed the concierge the handful of large Italian lire notes the taxi driver had given me as change for my 100 dollar note he expressed dismay, saying that it was all worthless money that had been demonetized and withdrawn as acceptable currency two years before.

Next day, having been given instructions on how to get to the consular offices by the metro I was pleasantly surprised to be told the Italian Overseas Trade department had laid on all sorts of entertainment for myself and a guest during my stay there. A junior consular official named Giovanni Scribante, an Afrikaner of Italian decent, would be at my disposal for the whole period of the exhibition.

We went straight on to the exhibition hall and I found that Giovanni, although Afrikaans was his home language, could speak enough Italian to make it easier for me to follow up possible business opportunities.

Two seats in the center of the front row at the La Scala had been reserved for us. It was the opening night of La Traviata, seats that we could never have got for ourselves in a lifetime.

The next night, the entertainment provided was for a concert and a fashion show in the theater of the newly built Pirelli Building. Two charming hostesses accompanied us for this occasion. One was very much at ease speaking Italian with Giovanni, but I found my supposedly English-speaking girl more than difficult to deal with. Her English was only high school level, which was certainly not conversational, and her only experience at speaking English was her six months with a Scottish family in Glasgow. The Scottish influence on her Italian-accented schoolgirl English did not make her any easier to understand.

The concert consisted of operatic quality divas singing well-known arias from Italian operas, and the fashion show was a preview of Milan's first fashion show of the season. Neither entertainment needed much conversation and my struggle to understand Scotch-accented schoolgirl Italian English was forgotten. Actually, we all enjoyed it and had a first-rate dinner afterwards.

I spent two weeks following up business contacts that I had made at the exhibition, and was ready to go home. I then remembered that I had promised to try to look up a Jean Silverman, a daughter of friends of my wife. She had gone to Milan for singing instruction some time before. They were worried that they had not heard from her.

I had her phone number and address but could not get through. The concierge told me that the telephone operators had been on strike for two days. Strikes of some kind or another were a common thing in Italy at that time, and not reading the papers, visitors like me would be the last to know. So he sent a messenger boy with a note from me inviting her for dinner that night.

She came, and arrived with a sorry tale to tell. The singing lessons that she had come for were much more expensive than expected. She could only afford to pay for a one-hour lesson a week. Further, although there were opportunities for singing engagements that would provide an extra income, foreigners were not allowed to work for pay. A lot of South African hopefuls were in the same position. She made me promise that I would not let her parents know, as she was determined to battle it out on her own.

I was leaving next day, so I phoned the South African Consulate and got Giovanni to promise to introduce Jean to Mimi Coetzer who was a friend of his. Mimi was South Africa's most famous opera star, and she was then living in Milan.

As promised, I did not mention Jean's plight to her parents. But this, my first trip to Italy, was not only successful business-wise, but I hope that Jean's introduction to Mimi helped solve her problems.

# 44

## *Sanctions May Not Be Fire Resistant*

***Prototype fire-resistant*** sample garments, used by armies of several other countries, were given to my firm by the South African Defense, to copy and suggest improvements.

The Israeli Army's garment was said by them to have saved many lives when tanks caught fire in battle during the six-day war. Their experience had shown how important it was to mount the tank and yank the driver out through the turret as soon as possible. To achieve this the overall that we copied had a heavy one inch tape stitched up the inside leg seam, through the crutch, finishing up the back of the garment with a loop, to an opening at the nape of the neck. The design of such a tank suit for the South African army was approved, but the eventual material had not yet been finalized.

Dupont had a fire-resistant cloth was called Nomex. We had been successful using it in garments worn by racing drivers and firemen's tunics. Because of sanctions, American firms were not allowed to sell it to the South African Government if it was to be used for military or police purposes.

Nevertheless, the local Johannesburg agent phoned Dupont's European sales office in Geneva, for suggestions. As the quantity of Nomex yarn was considerable, they expressed their willingness to help. If I was too come Geneva, they would put me in touch with several firms who may be prepared to supply us.

Dupont had booked my wife, Clare, and me at the Hotel Du Rhone at their expense. It was internationally famous hotel on the bank of the Rhone River. It was a much higher-grade hotel than I would have thought to go myself, and being shown into an elaborate suite embarrassed us.

In the dining room that evening, the Maitre d' took our order with a flourish, after which several waiters danced attention on us.

Commies (learner waiters) brought the food from the kitchen as far as some adjacent tables, then our team of waiters took the dishes from there One served us hors d'oeuvres, another the entrée and yet another offered an elaborate assortment of vegetables from silver dishes kept warm on hot plates. A sommelier (wine steward) placed the wine, wrapped in a linen napkin, into an ice bucket. After drawing the cork he poured a mouthful into a wine glass for me to approve before filling our glasses. "I hope we are not paying for this," said Clare. I assured her that we were not, saying "If we were paying for this ourselves, we would have been out of here long ago, directly I found out the price that they were charging for the room.

Next day, I took a taxi to Dupont's office where I met not only the Geneva manager, but the managers of their British, French, and Spanish sales offices as well. It appeared my visit coincided with a European group meeting. I told them of my requirement for Nomex of a particular count of yarn and they looked up their records to see to whom they had previously supplied with a similar yarn before.

Their records showed that a manufacturer in Barcelona had satisfactorily used it in the manufacture of a material very similar in weight and thread count to the South African specification. They told me that the price was likely to be considerably lower than any other country's quotations.

That night the lot of us, including Clare, had a splendid dinner at a fancy restaurant. After the meal, while smoking cigars and drinking liqueurs, it was arranged that I be taken to Barcelona to meet the proposed supplier and discuss my requirement with them.

What did surprise me, however, was that all were coming. Of course the head of the Geneva office and the Spanish office I could understand, but why the British and French managers were joining us was beyond me. The Spanish manager spoke Spanish well enough for ordinary purposes, but he thought their official Spanish interpreter should come, too, thus avoiding any possible language misunderstanding. At the last minute they decided to include a textile technician as well. I did not know if some of them were using me as an excuse to go on a trip at Dupont's expense, because in a strange country, not knowing the language can be a big gamble. With several hundred thousand dollars involved, I welcomed all the help I could get.

On the plane we took up most of the first class cabin. It appeared they had such a good time when they last attended a conference in Barcelona that they wanted to repeat the experience. On our arrival we booked in at a hotel and were told our rooms were not yet available. We left our luggage with a porter. Then, like a troop of schoolboys, we marched joyfully down the Ramblas. This majestically broad avenue starts at the city center and goes in a straight line all the way down to the sea. One of the show streets of Europe, splendid shops, cafes, bars and theaters, line its sidewalks. But, it's very wide median is its most distinctive feature. Here, interspersed among lawns and trees, are fascinating stalls and entertainers. Definitely a place in which to ramble, I decided to come here again if time allowed.

After lunch, we went to a bullfight in the magnificent stadium filled with most enthusiastic fans. But I was pleased that we left the arena early, as they wanted to show me the city. That night we went to a Fado performance. Magnificently costumed dancers did their intricate steps to music that was hauntingly memorable. I was surprised it seemed so sad. I suppose I had expected an exuberant Flamenco. In the evening we went down to the docks to a rough and ready seafood restaurant famous for its paella. The un-scrubbed wooden tables, heavy pottery plates, and crude flatware were not inviting, and I am afraid I did not enjoy the paella as much as I should have. Everybody else declared it excellent so I must have been wrong.

Next day we went to the village in which the factory was situated, the one we hoped would manufacture the material I required. I was horrified that nobody in the whole organization understood a word of English. Now I appreciated the Spanish interpreter and the textile man. I would have gotten nowhere without them. I got them to explain that the Nomex fire resistant material would have to be inspected by the South African Bureau of Standards to ensure that it meets their specification in all respects, otherwise it would not be accepted.

They did not appear to be at all worried about that, and promised to send several three yard samples for approval before starting bulk manufacture. I was worried that they did not show me the factory, and began to suspect it may be a village industry where every house has several looms. Dupont's men told me that I had no need to worry; past experience in dealing with this firm had been satisfactory in all respects.

We then went to a charming restaurant in an old fashioned villa overlooking the sea, for lunch. Everybody was happy and although I could not make direct verbal contact with the principal of the firm we, through the good offices of our interpreter, came to understand one another. I left with every confidence that he was honest and responsible. I placed the order with him at a satisfactory price and arranged that Dupont would supply and invoice their yarn to him.

When we got back to Geneva, Clare had happily found an old school friend whose husband was attending a conference. The two of them had a wonderful time. The fact that Clare was able to spend enough time in Le Petit Palais, her favorite small art museum was a big plus, because on previous visits we had only been able to spare an odd hour or so there. This time they were able to do Geneva properly, something neither of them had previously done, because husbands on business always seem to have to be somewhere else in a hurry.

It was a month before we got back to South Africa. The army was delighted that I would be able to supply them with Nomex fire resistant tank overalls. The Quartermaster General said that they had applied through the South African Embassy in Washington and been refused. "How did you manage it?" He asked.

I said, "I merely went to Dupont's European office in Switzerland and told them what I wanted. They did not ask who I was going to supply it to, and I had no reason to tell them."

# 45

## *Alpine Wonderland*

***We had seen a home*** movie our brother and sister-in-law had made of their trip with their family in the Austrian Alps. It looked so much fun that we decided to go there ourselves, with our two 16 year-old sons, next December.

We lived in Johannesburg South Africa, and had never had the opportunity to ski; so going to Austria to ski would be a complete adventure. Our travel agent had booked us on a flight on South African Airways to London and, after a week there, we were to fly to Innsbruck. We had intended to rent our ski clothing from the well-known Moss Brothers, in London, but were told that it would be better to rent them in Innsbruck, and not have the bother of lugging them back to England to return them.

To our dismay, we were told that the airline on which we were to fly to Austria had gone bankrupt and no other airline would fly into Innsbruck in the winter. Surrounded as it was by mountains it was considered too hazardous to land there in the snow. However, they managed to get us on another airline, which would take us to Munich, and from there a bus would take us on to Innsbruck.

Arriving at Munich airport we were taken to the main railway station and told that our bus would arrive in about a half an hour. While waiting we went down a flight of stairs to the restrooms. On getting down, Clare went to the Women's on the right, and I to the Men's on the left. It wasn't long before there was a loud shouting "Mishter Herrmann, Mishter Hermann," from an irate ladies' room attendant, demanding money. An anxious Clare peaked around the door, saying "she insists on my giving her only German money before she will open a door."

Now, we had Austrian money with us, but evidently it was not acceptable in Germany. Looking around I spied a bowl full of coins on the counter. Evidently in Europe you are expected to tip the restroom attendants. Thinking quickly, I took out a handful of these coins and handed them to the women, who took the lot with a satisfied. grunt. I walked on, not bothering to look back in case the men's room attendant had seen me filching his tips. The bus was waiting for us, and shaken by our restroom experience, we flopped into our seats thankful that we were now on the last lap of what had been a much more stressful trip than we had anticipated.

Innsbruck stood in a bowl surrounded by tall snow-covered mountains. An imposing statue to a local hero stood in the center of the main street that was lined with excellent shops and cafes. There we had no trouble renting all the clothing and equipment we needed. At the railway station we took a twenty minute train journey to the village, in which we had pre-booked accommodations at its hostel. We arrive in time for dinner and were shown to a table that we were to share with an English couple, Mr. and Mrs. Morgan, and their daughter Ellen aged 11.

Next morning, we took a cable car up a nearby hill and followed the crowd into much larger cable cars each holding about 20 passengers. Here we were swooped up at a perilous angle, high above a tree-filled valley, to the top of the Mountain. We alighted at a plateau on which a restaurant, restrooms and sports shops awaited us. The boys, with the help of an instructor, had little difficulty in managing the skis and even did a few short runs, but Clare and I did not even attempt the learner's slope. We spent most of our time in the restaurant enjoying the crisp cool air and wonderful view.

The next morning, before starting off for the day, Clare looked on the dining room door to see what would be served that evening. Apart from soup, the only entree was breaded pork chops. Going into the kitchen she explained that we did not cat pork. "Don't worry, the manager said. "I will see you will be given something that you will be happy to eat. "That evening in the vast dining hall the waitresses brought trays of huge breaded pork chops and gave them to everyone including us. Clare rushed into the manager's office to complain, but he laughingly assured her that ours contained only veal. "They all breaded to look exactly like the others because we did not want you to feel awkward if your meal looked different from what everybody else was eating." After our experience with the restroom lady in Munich, this was definitely one up for the dining manager in our hostel.

The boys skied every day and we found plenty of other things to do. One day for instance we were driven in a bus up to a restaurant that provided us with sleds. We had much fun tobogganing down the slope all the way to our hostel. Joining others we walked along snow-filled roads to charming cafes but came across fallen snow blocking our path here and there. With heavy snow covering the mountains that towered above us, our guide warned us that the weather had not been as cold as usual, so we should keep our voices down because the risk of avalanches was always present.

On the day before Christmas we visited the cottage of a highly recommended sculptor and were delighted to get a charming wooden figurine. He suggested that we visit the graveyard that night. It was the custom for everybody to light a candle on a grave every Christmas Eve. We went, and were enthralled to see all the candles flickering in the breeze—what a wonderful idea. Whether it was the custom only in that village or a general thing in Austria I do not know.

A few days later, the Morgans' daughter broke her leg while skiing. The nearby hospital was well equipped to deal with this sort of thing but the doctor insisted that she must not fly for a week. This put the Morgans in a quandary. He was the mayor of Tunbridge Wells and had an urgent council meeting on the second of January, and she had just been appointed headmistress of a new school, and had to be there to interview her new teachers. After much talk we suggest this that we would bring her back to England with us. Thanking us heartily, they agreed and said that they would be at Heathrow airport to meet us.

To entertain the child we went to the Village bookshop, and were delighted to find they had a section just for English books. More especially, they had books for children of all age groups. We chose Alice in Wonderland; it was on the shelf marked as being suitable for a child of eleven. She enjoyed reading it but we had to find her other things to do occasionally. I only looked at the book just before we left and was horrified to find it was an annotated version. Its marginal comments implying sexual connotations. I am sure it meant nothing to Ellen, but I feel that her mother would not be too happy about it.

The Morgans were at Heathrow to meet us. Thanking us, they hoped Ellen had been no trouble. Clare assured them that she been very good indeed, but I could not resist saying jokingly, "Here is your child safe and sound, we would not do it again for a thousand pound."

# 46

## *"Parlez Vous Francais"*

***The only French words*** I can remember having learned at school were the words for "The pen of my aunt." Why anybody could possibly be interested in an aunt having a pen I can't imagine.

A lifetime later, after an extravagant business dinner and too much wine with a group of Dupont's European representatives, at the Hotel du Rhone in Geneva, I mentioned that my son Derek was about to leave college and I would like him to get clothing manufacturing training in Europe. Everybody was in a good mood while smoking cigars and drinking liqueurs after the meal, so the idea was given more thought than it might have done under normal circumstances. The French representative said he thought that Monsieur Brouchard, a manufacturer of uniform clothing in the North of France, might be prepared to do so, with the proviso that he would have to be French speaking as nobody there spoke English.

Derek knew no French whatsoever, but I knew a teacher at Kingsmead girls' school who took a party of girls to Paris every Christmas to polish up their French. I got her to write to Madame Simon, the head of the Rothschild chateau in Paris, now an orphanage, to ask if she was prepared to take a young man in some capacity for training. Madame Simon who held many medals for aiding the De Gaullist underground movement during the war, wrote back saying "For the sake of Anglo French accord she would take Derek into the Chateau as a soccer coach, for the time being.

Derek wrote us many amusing letters of his experiences while there, but unfortunately we never saved them. I do remember one however. When accompanying the butcher to buy meat one day, he chided the butcher for stopping for a drink at every saloon they passed. The answer with much hand wringing was always the same "Porquois?"

Whether he taught the orphans soccer or the rugby he played at school, we will never know, but after three months Du Pont's representative in Paris told us that his French was good enough to start at Brouchard's factory.

After working in the factory in San Quentin for six months his letters indicated he was lonely. Nobody there spoke English and had there was little entertainment of any kind in the town. To cheer him up we wrote that we were coming to visit Paris in May and would look him up. He answered enthusiastically and said that when he had told Monsieur Brouchard that we were coming, he had insisted that we dine at his home the day of our arrival. Derek warned us that nobody had spoken a word of English to him since he had been there, but he thought that Monsieur Brouchard might speak a little English because he had sent out for an English pamphlet listing English business terms. To get there from Paris he told us to go to the Gare du Nord and book tickets to San Quentin. He would borrow a car and meet us there.

It was not as easy as it sounded. We had to stand in a long line to buy a ticket. I was met with a completely blank look when I asked for tickets to San Quentin and could not get the ticket agent to understand where I wanted to go. The people behind me were getting annoyed with the hold up, and were protesting angrily. I was in danger of getting lynched when an Australian who had been at the back of the line came up and told me I wanted "San Kantong." I was given my tickets just in time to prevent a riot.

We booked into a hotel when we got to San Quentin and after changing we went with Derek to the Brouchards' for dinner. To our surprise he his wife and two daughters all spoke perfect English. It turned out that Brouchard had served with the American Air Force during the war. Derek had never had a hint that he spoke anything other than French.

We were made to feel more than welcome. Business matters were not mentioned apart from him inviting me to visit the factory next day. His wife was Brazilian and one girl was at the Sorbonne, and the other was just about to start at a cooking academy in Lyon. The family had traveled extensively and so we had much to talk about. Dinner was to be at eight,

Here we were to be faced with problems. The dining table was set most formally with immaculate white linen tablecloth with matching serviettes. There were more silver knives, forks and spoons arranged on each side of the large English china table plates than we had ever seen. How many courses were we to be served and what spoon, fork and knives were we to use for each? There were even knife rests, something we had heard about but had never used. We had hors d'oeuvre, soup, and much else followed. The only way to cope was to watch which item of cutlery our hosts picked up each time a course was served.

The next day at the factory I was amazed how even the most utilitarian uniform is transformed when designed with a French flair. I must admit that the uniforms made in my own factory were very staid in comparison. I now see that "the pen of my aunt" is much improved when it is "le plume de la Tante."

# 47

## *A Visit to Vancouver*

***Vancouver that July*** was a joy to behold. It lay beneath dark green covered mountains still topped with snow, I had arrived at Vancouver's new airport that had only been opened a week before. It was an airy symphony of glass and steel that could well be a setting for a modern ballet. A girders and glass "see-thru" airport and bright green carpeted passages with low railings allowed you to look over every level, both above and below. Well-displayed notices clearly indicated the way to the immigration, customs and baggage areas. I got through with the minimum of red tape and felt welcome.

Derek, my son, met me and we drove to his apartment on Beach Avenue. It overlooked English Bay, a wide expanse of sea, edged by land on three sides. In the distance ships lay, waiting to be allowed up the Frazer River to the harbor. As both he and Serena, his wife, work, it was obvious that I would have to get about and entertain myself on weekdays.

For my first jaunt, I turned left on the bayside path just thirty or forty yards across the road from their apartment, and shared it with walking couples, cyclists, joggers and in-line skaters. Within ten minutes I found that I had arrived at the False Creek Ferry. I did not have to wait long for the ferry to arrive that would take me to Granville Island. It would have held ten or twelve people but as I was the only passenger, I doubted that the one-dollar senior fare I paid would even pay for the amount of gas used to make the trip.

There, beneath towering road and rail bridges, is the Granville Island Market, where an unparalleled display of ethnic goods, fish, meat, vegetables, fruit and baked goods are for sale. Chinese and other Asian minorities who live in Vancouver in great numbers vie with one another to get you to partake of their offerings. The shop, stalls and restaurants, all teemed with people.

That weekend we drove to the fishing village of Steventon. At one time it was the largest fishing port in the world with twelve large canneries. All have since closed and the village's main claim to fame appears to be the excellent fried fish served in vast quantities at its many restaurants.

Monday was Canada Day, their main holiday. Bright sunshine greeted us as we drove to Jericho Bay and on to Spanish Camp. These busy beaches were full of family groups taking advantage of the first bright sunshine for days. Facing the Bay, to the right we could see the fully built-up area of West Vancouver, as well as the entrance to the mouth of the Fraser River, which is navigable for large boats for many miles upstream. On the left was the wide sweep of the North Shore Mountains. One behind the other, still with snow on the higher levels, they form a most dramatic backdrop to the city.

It was lucky that we had bright sunshine while I was there as Vancouver has the reputation for persistent rain. The locals are said to say, "When you can see the North Shore Mountains it is going to rain, and when you can't see them, it is raining."

I had no difficulty going to the city and back by bus. Going in, the direction board was marked Gasstown, the old area in city's center. The same bus now re-marked Beach returned me by a circular route back to the apartment. To get my bearings I took a tour bus that circled the town and drove through Vancouver's pride and joy, its justly famous Stanley Park. Huge trees cover its vast acreage that is hidden from first view. The park's lawns, lakes and all its many other areas provide facilities for every kind of activity.

Another day I took the False Creek Ferry to Vanier Park, in which were a planetarium and several museums. But it was the Maritime Museum that most intrigued me. Here an actual ship, the RCM St Roch, was on display in a vast hall, obviously built around it. The vessel's purpose had been to enable the Royal Canadian Mounties (who always get their man) to police the country's northern areas that were inaccessible any other way.

I entered the ship at floor level and followed a marked route through engine room and the crew's quarters until I arrived up on the main deck. Here I joined the crowd who were being shown a film of its voyage, narrated in the film by a Norwegian with a baritone voice, salted in the brine of the sea air, which would have carried resoundingly from the poop deck to the mizzen in a gale. He related the story in great detail with such dramatic effect, that I suffered with the crew, all its trouble and near disasters, as they were encountered. I was exhausted when he finished and surprised that I was not frostbitten.

I was intrigued that Canada Place the Convention Center was interestingly built on a spit of land jutting out into the ocean. It adjoins Gasstown, the old portion of the town presumably named for being originally lit by gas. Not only were the shops there fascinating but also so was the large variety of places to eat. The streets were crowded and the restaurants full. I had to wait for a considerable time to get a table.

On my last Sunday we motored up the coast and had lunch at Furry Creek, a golf course and country club situated on the side of a mountain overlooking Howe Sound. The Sound was spectacular beyond belief. Sunshine highlighted a vast circle of mountain peaks tinged with snow, their slopes dressed in dark green close-fitting suits of Douglas fir, redwoods, beech and maple. Creating a panorama that embraced The Sound and all its tree-covered islands. Too impressive to forget, it will remain forever in my mind.

I carried home to San Diego all the many pleasant memories of this trip to Vancouver. The Granville Island market, the North Shore mountains, Stanley Park, the Ship "St Roch" and certainly not least, the wonderful panorama of Howe Sound.

On the way back to the airport we were further rewarded by the seldom-seen uninterrupted view of all fourteen thousand feet of the snow covered Mount Washington, a view seldom seen by the people that live there, and as happy that we had seen it as our guide in Japan had been, when clouds covering Mount Fuji cleared away just in time for us to see it

# 48

## *Out of the Blue*

***Vancouver British Columbia*** is probably the last place that one would expect the unexpected to happen.

Without a care in the world I stood waiting for a tour bus to take me around the city. I was standing just outside the Conference Center, which stood on a spit of land surrounded by the sea on three of its sides. Behind me was a fountain consisting of a large, ornamented, slanting bronze wall over which cooling jets of water flowed down and splashed relentlessly into the fountain pool that was edged with a low parapet. The sound of the rushing water attracted the passing crowd to stop, throw in a coin and murmur a silent wish as it entered the water, while one or two shoppers were quietly resting on the low wall at the edge of the fountain, tired out.

Oblivious of them I stood waiting there by the tour bus stop. If I was thinking about anything at all it was certainly not of my past in another continent, a lifetime ago.

The bus came up from the Gaslight area on my left. I waited for a party of tourists to alight. The first to get off was an elderly man, dressed in a business suit wearing a tie, definitely a visitor, because his outfit was unusually formal for this part of the world. Obviously arthritic, he put his cane down to the road, before carefully stretching a leg over the gutter to reach the sidewalk. He nervously steadied himself, before looking up. Once he was settled, I asked him what the bus tour was like. Instead of answering me, he looked at me quizzically before saying "What part of London do you come from?"

I was taken aback, having lived in South Africa and America for so long, that any remnant of my speech indicating my London boyhood had long since been obliterated. Completely surprised by the question I jokingly said, "You must be Professor Higgins to even think of asking." But after collecting myself, I tardily admitted to "Stoke Newington."

"I thought your accent was familiar; I lived in Kyverdale Road. Do you know it?"

The rest of the party all similarly formally clothed had now got off and surrounded us. A woman probably his wife in a very British accent interrupted us saying "Sam you are always asking strangers silly questions people will get annoyed with you."

I took no notice of her interference and said, "I lived there from 1915 for some years."

"Don't tell me that you went to Northwold School."

"Of course I did."

One of the party very loudly said, "We will all be late for the ship's passengers meeting, lets go!"

The man taking no notice, continued to say "Then we must have been there, about the same time. Do you remember?"

The rest of them now crossed the road and called a taxi. His wife, grimacing, obviously impatient stood by Sam's side, violently grabbed his arm and rushed him away, against his will.

I nonplussed, angry and perturbed was left on my own with a host of questions forming in my mind, that will obviously remain forever unanswered. Kicking myself, that I had not even asked his name, I should have at least asked him that.

It was as though a flash of lightning had exposed the darkened landscape of my long forgotten boyhood only to vanish before I could take it in. A strange coincidence out of the blue, it was frustrating. Nevertheless, I am not sorry it happened. At least I now know there is somebody else still alive, who may have scored a run playing cricket on the meadow in Springfield Park, or scored a goal playing football on Hackney Downs or even rowed in one of the outboard skiffs, on the river Lea, the same time as I did.

# PART IV

# America Here We Come

# 49

## *The Policeman's Story*

***Soon after we arrived*** in La Jolla, we joined the contract bridge club at the Cove. One of the regular players was a senior official of the San Diego Police Department. He, knowing that we were South Africans, asked if we would consider helping the department out of an awkward situation.

It appeared that the Chicago Police Department had arranged for a South African police officer to spend several weeks in Chicago to take one of their special courses. The man had arrived there, but the men's union refused to let their members co-operate with a police officer from the country that upheld the Apartheid System.

The Chicago Department was very embarrassed about the situation, and knowing San Diego had a similar special training course asked if they would take him over. San Diego did not object, providing Chicago would pay the costs involved. Chicago accepted full responsibility for the whole matter and would send the man down to San Diego at their expense, accompanied by one of their senior captains.

The two men would not know anybody here and it was hoped that my wife and I, being South Africans, would do something about their entertainment. We did what we could and on their last evening we took them to a restaurant for dinner. They were both in good spirits and the captain especially had a fund of interesting experiences to relate.

One that capped them all was the story of the wealthy Irishman who after living in Chicago for forty years, went back to the Emerald Isle to retire. He arranged with a pet travel company to put his dog in a suitable container and ship it back to him in Ireland.

Unfortunately, the ship that it was to go on was delayed. The next ship was not to sail until two weeks later. A completely new staff of the travel company was on duty that week, and when they checked the animal container box before shipping, they found that no food or water had been put inside, and the dog had died.

The packing staff were horrified, and were so worried that they would be blamed and be sued for a considerable sum, they decided to replace the corpse, with an identical live one.

They purchased an Irish terrier from a Kennel that was as far as they could judge, about the same size, age and weight as the one that had died. The dog's collar with its nametag 'Paddy' still on it was put on the replacement Terrier and they were confident that nobody would know the difference.

The crew on the ship was given full instructions to see that sufficient food and water was supplied, and to make sure that it got constant exercise during the journey.

On its arrival in Ireland it was delivered to the owner in the quickest possible time. On opening it, he was amazed to find a live dog inside. "Begorra!" he cried, "It's a miracle. I swear by St. Patrick himself that it was dead when I left Chicago. I intended to bury it here on the family farm in Killarney."

# 50

## *Gone With the Wind*

***On the way*** to attend our son's wedding in New York, my wife and I intended to spend two or three days attending The Bobbin Show, in Atlanta.

In those days it was a thirteen-hour journey from Johannesburg to London. This was because South African Airways had to go considerably out of the way to refuel on the Isle de Sol. This tiny Portuguese island off the coast of West Africa was barely large enough to hold a landing strip and very little else. South Africans were politically unwelcome elsewhere on the continent. Here we had to alight and put up with the island's most unsanitary facilities. We walked around for an hour or so in the middle of the night, in intensely humid conditions.

From Heathrow we were taken by helicopter to Gatwick to catch a Delta Airline flight to Atlanta. On arrival, it was only a short walk to the bus that was to take us to town. This was a year or so before Atlanta's new airport opened, so we did not have the complication of the circular train ride from terminal to terminal, or have to walk the long distances that later trips to Atlanta entailed. The woman driver of the small bus kept up a continuous stream of talk to the twenty odd passengers, but the local dialect and the speed at which she spoke was such that neither Clare nor I could make head or tail of what she was saying. In fact, we wondered whether it was indeed English that she was speaking.

The exhibition was held in the Georgia World Congress Center adjoining the Omni Hotel that comprised a large shopping and theater complex. The Bobbin Show was an eye-opener. The clothing industry was just entering a revolutionary new electronic phase and the vast display of completely new ideas and machinery was overwhelming.

We stayed with Jack and Shirley Moore, who had visited us in Johannesburg the year before. The Moores recommended that in the one day we had to spare we would be well advised to spend it at the Fernbank Science Center, some distance out of town. The center comprised they told us, not only an excellent exhibit hall, but an observatory, a planetarium, and some forest walks.

Shirley dropped us in town at the seventy-story Peachtree Plaza. We took a taxi from there and asked the driver to take us to the Science Center. He did not move for some considerable time while he studied a map and turned over several pages of a direction book. It seemed obvious to us that he did not know the way, perhaps it was so far out of town that he had never before been called upon to go there.

Leaving the city behind us, we drove through a heavily forested area and I noticed, among some trees, a low building bearing a sign that said Science Center on it. We had already passed it, when I drew it to the driver's attention. He appeared surprised, turned back quickly and pulled up beside what was merely a small research lab.

Annoyed, he turned to us and said, "Ah like mah clients to have confidence in mah." We apologized profusely as he drove us the several more miles to the Center.

We spent a considerable time there as we found much of interest. A door at the back of the main hall led us on to a circular, gravel forest path. On the inside of the track, three-foot stakes supported a taut continuous rope. The rope was knotted wherever it passed close to a bush or a tree, where a plaque indicated the tree's name in English and Braille. The path had been donated to the museum by the Society for the Blind, and a notice stated that audios with earphones were available free of charge at the reception desk.

Having taken a special course in escorting blind groups through museums to let them experience the sculptures by touching them, Clare went back inside to ask for the audios. This caused some consternation as no one remembered ever being asked for them before. The curator thought that they were in a particular locked cupboard, and it was some time before they located its key. Eventually when they were produced, the batteries were dead, and they had no spares. Shamefaced, they promised they would get some next day, but of course that was no use to us.

A bus took us back to the Peachtree Plaza. We were amazed that its vast seven-story atrium included a restaurant, a lake, trees, a swimming pool and much else. The hotel was on Peachtree Street. We had noticed while on our travels in the town, Peachtree had a N.E. and a N.W., and probably a S.E. and a S.W. section as well. There was also a Peachtree Road with all the same directional variations. What with this Peachtree Plaza, the Peachtree Playhouse, the Peachtree Academy and all sorts of other things that we had seen, Peachtree was definitely the dominant theme of the town.

Inside the atrium lobby, we looked at the trees that were around the artificial lake, but a peach tree was not one of them. We had always associated the United States of America with the cherry tree that George Washington had cut down as a boy. But here in Atlanta, a non-evident peach tree takes pride of place. Had a later President cut it down? Or had it just "Gone with the Wind."

# 51

## *The Fifth Sunday*
## *A woman for all Sundays*

***In 1986 the members*** of Temple Beth Israel in San Diego, enthused by the excellent work being done by Father Joe Carroll, were eager to do their part in helping the community. With Joan Kutner, a member of the congregation, offering to organize and run it, the members of Temple Beth Israel accepted responsibility for the "Feed the Hungry Project" at the St. Vincent de Paul Center every Sunday.

In May 1987, my wife and I, knowing that a considerable number of helpers were needed every week and not having been called upon for some time, offered our services again, if ever they were short of volunteers. To our surprise, we were asked if we would be available to help out the very next Sunday. Naturally we said of course, we would be there.

"Thanks," the caller said, "Meet us at seven-thirty tomorrow morning in the parking lot on Third and Laurel to collect the food and equipment Come in your oldest clothes."

When we arrived, we were handed several large bags of cast-off clothing to put in our car while several station wagons were loading up with food and equipment. Joan Kutner was there as usual, having run the program since its inception. She called us together and said, "It is the fifth Sunday of the month and Social Security and Welfare checks will not be available until Monday or Tuesday so more people than usual will be without money to buy food this weekend."

Joan looked round and saw that there were several newcomers. "For the benefit of those of you who are helping for the first time, bear in mind that a lot of our guests are street people, dirty and even disreputable looking, who are generally ignored by society. They are the invisible portion of our community, mostly passed by without a second thought. Please make them feel that they are people. Look them in the eye, be pleasant and talk to them even if they do not reply. At the same time there will be respectable looking men and women, probably out of a job for the first time in their lives, who are terribly self-conscious because of it. Do not make them feel like charity cases. Chat, joke and be friendly."

Joan's humanity was infectious. Any subconscious feeling of self-righteousness we might have been harboring fell away. We were not in the vanguard of a mission to help our fellow men preserve their self-respect. Our cars now full of cast-off clothing, we proceeded to the Joan Kroc Center.

As cleanliness in preparing and issuing food at the Center was essential, plastic aprons and gloves were to be issued to us. We were also told that the tables and floors would have to be scrubbed and trays and equipment sterilized before use and again before we left. The unloading was accomplished quickly under capable direction. The efficient kitchen staff immediately started heating the previously prepared thick, vegetable soup, which was a meal in itself.

As soon as the tables were scrubbed, mounds of bread, peanut butter and jelly arrived on one table, and towers of bagels together with jars of cream cheese arrived on another table as if by magic. Everybody was allocated a job, whether it was opening cans, slicing bagels or making sandwiches, and good humor prevailed. You were one of a team. Our customers had been lining up outside since early morning, and the first group would be let in soon after nine-thirty, so there was no time to waste.

Joan, who was here, there and everywhere all the time, appeared to sense when anyone was idle. Were we ready for another job? Of course we said, "Yes." "No," was not in the vocabulary that fifth Sunday of the month on Sixteenth Street.

The other jobs were many and various. You name it, Joan had it! We wiped dry the food trays as they arrived hot and wet from the sterilizers, wrapped spoons and forks in paper napkins, opened crates of fruit, and we worked full out.

Nine-thirty arrived, and we were preparing to commence issuing the meal that we had been getting ready. With their trays loaded to the limit, recipients made their way to find seats in the dining hall. The behavior of everybody, young and old, well-dressed or ragged, was excellent. I was sorry to see so many young mothers with children arriving. As each group finished eating, they went out through a door on the other side of the room, many of them helping themselves to donated garments that had been laid out for them to take.

Apart from seeing to it that everything proceeded without a hitch, Joan, with a bell in one hand and a megaphone in the other, was also controlling the outer gate. She let fifty in at a time to sit on benches in the yard and await their turns to come into the hall. Five hundred or more had come and gone. Tired but undaunted, we scrubbed and put away the tables and swept and vacuumed the floor. Then, after reloading the vans, we left at one o'clock.

It is now 1994, seven years since I wrote the first part of this report and eight years since the program was started. Joan Kutner is still there as enthusiastic as ever. For four hundred and twenty consecutive Sundays the program has continued without a break.

A new, enlarged St. Vincent de Paul Center has been built, and the number of people requiring meals has doubled. I volunteered to help recently, and noted how efficient the whole operation had become over the years. A retired admiral was there seeing that everything flowed from the kitchen to the worktables with naval precision, and the regular workers saw that we casual volunteers performed the work allocated to us in their approved method.

After donning my plastic apron, gloves and paper hat, I applied cream cheese to many hundreds of previously slit bagels. Joan was doing several things at once. Even so, she noticed that I had finished and immediately asked me to assist placing items of food on the trays prior to distribution to the dining hall.

Seventy-five people were allowed into the hall at a time, with Joan standing at the entrance from the yard to control the flow. While she Heated everybody with consideration, I noticed that she saw that women and children got special attention.

I now stood in a line at a counter and put sandwiches on to the partitioned tray that came to me from my right, before pushing it along to my left. Nine hundred and forty trays passed relentlessly before me, until we were told to stop. There was a chart on the wall that showed that the number of people fed exceeds twelve hundred on some days. We scrubbed, sterilized and swept until everything was as we had found it. Joan even noticed that there were a couple of scraps of paper left on the floor after I had swept there. I picked them up.

This Sunday operation that goes off so smoothly is only the tip of an iceberg. A vast amount of preparation takes place during the whole of the previous week. Barbara, one of the hard core of key workers, later told me that Joan tries to take the day off on Wednesdays, if she can.

While it is true that Temple Beth Israel's concerned congregation provides the wherewithal and, generally, enough volunteers to help, it is the small group of regulars who carry on week after week without any desire for personal recognition that makes the whole effort possible.

But, Joan Kutner is always there keeping everybody activated, as firm in her commitment as Joan of Arc and as dedicated in her self-imposed duty as Florence Nightingale. She is truly a woman for all Sundays.

# 52

# *Life Class*

***Soon after my arrival*** in San Diego, and finding how close it was to the Mexican border, I decided to take one of the Spanish courses offered by the Community College.

When I opened the classroom door, I was surprised to see a group of a dozen or so people gathered around a low raised platform, some of them still unpacking drawing books and paint brushes. As I stood there, a young woman took center stage, threw off her light cotton gown, and without a stitch on, moved unconcernedly into a set pose.

I did not have to be Sherlock Holmes to know that this was not the Wednesday Beginners Spanish Class. I had made a mistake in the day. It was Thursday, not Wednesday. How foolish can one be? Seeing me hesitate, the instructor quickly introduced herself as Amanda and implored me to stay.

"You are heaven-sent. We are one student short of the minimum number the Community College requires us to have. Please! Please, don't go."

Put like that, who could have refused such a plea? So with some mental reservation, I diffidently agreed to stay.

Amanda showed me to a table that I would share with two others, and handed me some newsprint and a pencil. During this first period, Elise, the model, was to do very short poses only. After the coffee break, we would be given more time to do some complete studies.

Immediately, everybody got down to drawing boards and canvasses, but I found that every time I put pencil to paper, Elise had changed her pose. Frustrated, I decided to see how the others in the class were going about it. Walking around and chatting with this mostly denim clad group, I found that they included commercial artists, book illustrators, and even architects, all of them enthusiastic about having the opportunity of working with professional models.

Later, over coffee, we discussed marketing, Amanda stressed that from her experience, and it was essential to have an agent in New York if one hoped to break into the advertising or publishing world.

After the break, Elise posed for longer periods. The class, now using whatever media they preferred ranging from charcoal to oils, became thoroughly absorbed in their work. This did not stop Amanda from giving a monologue of her various "Adventures in the Wonderland of Madison Avenue" where she had gone hoping to get some illustrations accepted for Jane Fonda's aerobic exercise book. Struggling with the drawing of Elise's arms and legs, as seen from my very difficult angle, and awash with the even flow of Amanda's verbal battle against the art world of New York, the time passed all too quickly. I went home tired, but with every intention of carrying on with the course.

In the weeks that followed, we were fortunate that Amanda was able to engage a variety of widely diverse and interesting models. One night we had two male models who obviously enjoyed displaying their muscular bodies, striking martial poses in exciting adversary-like positions.

Another evening, two graceful Asian young women used exotic arm and hand movements to give variety to their poses. So the weeks flowed on uneventfully, with the class concentrating on their drawing and painting to the soothing ripple of Amanda's art world chatter in the background. That is, until the setback occurred, an impossible situation, at least as far as I was concerned. It happened one evening when the model did not arrive. At first we puttered around doing this and that for ten minutes or so, until a frowning Amanda came to a frightening decision, one that I was horrified that she could ever have thought feasible.

She announced in a voice, leaving no room for contradiction, that we would have to draw bare. I was thunderstruck. My whole conformist background was against it. I am a private sort of man who, even if in the shower and alone in the house, will put on a dressing gown to speak on the telephone.

I looked despairingly at the lank blonde haired girl on my left who was in the process of taking off her jacket, then on my right, my other neighbor, the bearded architectural draftsman bent down to what I supposed must be to slip off his shoes. The girl opposite was fingering the zip in her skirt. This was too much! There must be a limit beyond which one cannot be expected to go. I had had enough.

Grasping my belongings but still facing into the room, I began to edge backwards, hoping to slip out the door unnoticed. I was almost out when a heavily built woman holding a large carrying bag knocked me sideways. She rushed past me crying out, "I am sorry, Amanda, I was held up in a traffic jam." I slunk back, and had my drawing board ready, by the time the model had taken up her position on the dais.

When the lesson ended, Amanda asked if we would mind clearing up. as she had to leave right away. When she got to the door, she gave a shrill whistle and a large black Labrador retriever came bounding up to her, resting his huge front paws against her breast.

"Down, Bear, Down!!" she shouted, and then lovingly attaching his lead, she waved good-bye. I stood bemused as Amanda and "Bear" hurried off to the parking lot.

## 53

## *First Time in America*

***My wife and I*** flew British Airways to New York. It was a business trip and my agent had booked us accommodation in the Doral Hotel in Madison Avenue. Unfortunately the weather was extremely hot and the window air-conditioning machine was not coping, and my wife refused to stay there.

I returned to the office for them to get us other more acceptable accommodation but I was assured us that most of the hotels were fully booked. However, they did suggest that an office building on Thirty-Ninth, between Park and Lexington had allowed one of their clients to stay over a weekend. "Go and see them, to see if they will help you."

On going there, the two elderly owners told us, "The whole building is fully let to Merrill Lynch through out the year. They bring their staff from all over the country to stay and attend lectures."

However, when we told them we came from South Africa, their whole attitude changed. One of them very excitedly asked if we knew Rabbi Bender.

"Of course" we said. "We would never go to Capetown without visiting him. His congregation in Garden Synagogue is known throughout the country."

It appeared they had studied with him at the same Yeshiva in Jerusalem. Well, after that they could not do enough for us. Yes, we could have an apartment on the eleventh floor as long as we liked. The position was wonderful; Clare could investigate Macy's,

Bergdorf Goodman, and Lord and Taylor to her hearts content while I went to the office to do my business.

I was given an office to work from, and kept very busy getting in touch with suppliers and making new contacts. So much so, that I was surprised when the manager, Chuck Herberg, came in and asked if I had had lunch. I had forgotten the time. He and the office staff had lunched an hour or so ago. He sent out for a sandwich and stayed while I opened the package. He stood and watched me eat it, saying he wanted to see someone cat a pastrami sandwich for the first time.

I must admit it was very good, I now remembered Damon Runyan's Harry the Horse, eating a Reuben Sandwich at Lindys while awaiting the result of a horserace.

After several weeks, it was time to get back to London, and I thought we should confirm the booking at the British Airway's office on Fifth Avenue. We were to travel on Tuesday, the day after tomorrow. That morning I had my haircut at a barbershop around the corner on Lexington. While waiting for a chair I picked up a paper and saw on the sport's page that the British Soccer Cup Final was to be held at Wembley Stadium on Thursday the day after we get back. What a pity. If I had been there I would have attempted to get tickets.

On our way to British Airway's office on Fifth we passed a bank window on the corner of Park and Madison given over to a huge advertisement for British Airways. Standing as its centerpiece was a life-size cut out of the famous actor and humorist Christopher Morley with printed bold lettering coming out of his mouth, "There is nothing we won't do for you." Was this the answer to my prayer?

At the counter they confirmed that we were indeed booked on the plane to arrive on Wednesday. I asked the girl behind the counter if they could get me tickets to see the Cup Final to be played on Thursday. When she said they couldn't do that sort of thing, I pointed out that we have just seen a big advertisement with Christopher

Morley saying on British Airways behalf, "There is nothing we won't do for you." I insisted that she see the manager and find out what he will do about it. I must admit I was a bit more adamant than I usually would have been, because we were traveling first class.

She did not come back for over a half an hour, and I wondered what was happening. I insisted on waiting although Clare had been saying let's go, this is so much nonsense. Eventually my counter lady came back with a big smile on her face, saying that they had been in touch with London, who told them that the Cup Final had taken place last Thursday.

# 54

## *The Sound and the Fury*

***Michael Hochschild,*** a South African living in Connecticut, needed to relax after a busy day in Manhattan. He asked my grandson Dean and me to go fishing on Long Island Sound with him that evening. Land lubber that I am, I unhesitatingly said, "No."

Notwithstanding my diffidence, Dean said, "Come on Gramps, you'll like it." Thus encouraged, and not wanting to seem an old fogy, I agreed to go. It was a mistake I came to regret.

His boat was docked at the nearby town of Mamaroneck, just ten minutes away. When we got to the dock, we found the boat, sitting well below the level of the dock, and we had some difficulty climbing down to it.

Michael, who evidently had not used it for some time, found the two gas tanks to be completely empty. Taking one of them, he climbed up to get it filled. It was at least fifteen minutes before he returned.

We found several fishing rods under the back seat but no bait. Dean was sent off to buy some. He found the bait shack was closed, and had to borrow some from a reluctant yacht owner who said he was short of it himself. While we waited for the bait, Michael, tinkered with the motor and adjusted the rudder, he asked me if I would mind bailing out water that that had seeped through the floorboards. This dampened my spirits as well as well as my shoes, but I was assured me that the boat did not leak.

Remembering the Titanic, I looked I looked to see if there were life jackets aboard, but there were none. We were now ready to be cast upon the waters without any life support. No one was worried but me.

After much pulling and whirring, the engine still refused to start. It had a bad connection. Dean offered to go and get a spanner to tighten the terminal so that we would have no more trouble, but Michael said, "No, I'll do it when we come back."

All set to go now we found that two yachts were blocking our path, so we had to drag them out of our way and lower their anchors before leaving them. With the effort of dealing with the anchoring, Michael's glasses got broken, "No matter," he said "I can see fairly well without them." I hoped he could, because it looked, judging from what had happened already, that he might have a fair amount of tinkering to do before we got back.

When we were well away from shore we were treated to a magnificent view of Manhattan. From this unique viewpoint The Twin Towers and the Empire State buildings dominated the exciting skyline. It was the first and only time on the trip that I felt pleased I'd come.

The sun was setting over the shore, a wonderful sight that Michael tried to capture with a small camera that he had with him. Meanwhile Dean, who was steering, let go of the rudder while he struggled to catch a fish, letting the boat to drift firmly on to a sand bank.

As it was now overcast and getting dark, we decided to make our way back. This time the engine once again seemed determined not to cooperate, and it was some while before we got it to start. We eventually managed to push the boat off the sandbank with the one and only oar. With the engine now ticking over, we were ready to return, only to find that both the lights and the radio were out of action, and the only flashlight had no batteries.

We carried on blindly in the dark, until Michael with much fumbling located a loose connection and the lights came on. At least we would now be able to see where we were going. A storm warning was being announced as we turned on the radio. The boat now started to rock uneasily, and we began to ship some water, dampening my feet as well as my spirits, which were already low.

The rocking movement was too much for the loose battery terminal and the lights failed again. Without his glasses Michael was unable to reconnect it.

Lights on shore enabled us to steer toward the harbor. But it was so dark when we got to the dock itself, that we were unable to avoid banging into the side of several anchored yachts before we found our mooring spot. We climbed ashore, but without a flashlight we had difficulty treading our way along the wooden platform to the boat shed.

I refrained from commenting on the casual irresponsible manner with which the trip was handled. But am furious that I allowed myself to be talked into going.

# 55

## *I Don't Understand Art, But I Know What I Like*

***While in Manhattan recently,*** I decided to see the extension to the Guggenheim Museum. This addition to the famous circular building, designed by Frank Lloyd Wright, was built only after a storm of protest. The fact, that like so many of Wright's buildings, it was by no means suitable for the purpose for which it was intended, did not matter. It was considered to be a monument to the architect himself.

Guggenheim never saw the building finished and I doubt that he even approved the building's final design. But he probably would have agreed with me that the art on display did not deserve such expensive housing.

After entering you travel by elevator to the sixth floor and then wind your way down the curving steep slope to see the pictures on your left. It certainly makes for lopsided viewing. Fortunately, the art that is displayed does not delay you. After exiting the elevator and rounding the first downward curve or two, I was reminded of the Hans Christian Andersen fairy tale of the Emperor's New Clothes, by what was termed 'Minimalist Art.' The first item that took up a lot of space was the outline of an eight-foot square and only some small print reading, "Everything is purged from this painting but art. No ideas have entered this work".

If this was not enough, the others were no better. For instance, a completely otherwise blank wall had "Flare... The residue of a flare ignited upon a boundary," in small letters on it.

Continuing downward, the offerings did not improve. Any idea that the next section called "Non-Objective Art" would be worth looking at proved wrong. The only difference here was that if there were any objects pictured on the canvasses at all, they were certainly not recognizable

As I had arrived by taxi and gone directly into the original building, I had forgotten to look at the new addition that had caused such controversy. So, I went out, walked across to the other side of Fifth Avenue and looked back. I liked what I saw. The tall square addition fits neatly on to its circular counterpart, enhancing rather than spoiling it. I re-entered the museum and went up the elevator again. On exiting I turned right this time, and right again, into the new extension and found the floor was level and walls that were hung with paintings that commanded attention.

I was fortunate that the Thannhauser Collection was on view. I had never heard of this particular collection but I can assure you that old man Thannhauser, whoever he was, would not be ashamed to pit this collection against those of all the other millionaires who were collecting art in those halcyon days before income tax became a burden.

For the next hour or two, I was wafted into a world in which the

Impressionists and other European artists of the period held sway. Van Goghs, plenty of them, Picassos from the period 1900 to 1906, Renoirs to spare. Excellent Marc Chagalls, Kandinskys, a large group of Franz Marcs and a gallery of Paul Cézannes and more.

What luck. As for the furor over this tall graceful addition to Frank Lloyd Wright's circular masterpiece, I say, mind you, they will take no notice of me, but I still say, "Knock down the original building, keep the addition, and by all means hang on to The Thannhauser Collection, if you can."

# 56

## *A Day in Tacoma*

***Situated as it is*** at the southern end of Puget Sound, Tacoma is an easy drive from Seattle. My wife Clare and I, together with our Seattle hosts Charles and Frances Nathan, set off at about 9:30 to revisit the Port Defiance Zoo and Aquarium. When we were in the area the year before, we had not given ourselves enough time to see it properly.

After we turned off the freeway at the Tacoma exit, we stopped at the Tacoma and Pierce County Visitor and Convention Center, as we were not sure which was the best way to get Point Defiance Park. Two friendly elderly men, presumably volunteers, manned the office. They were big chaps and, judging by their checked shirts and the ten-gallon straw hats lying on the counter, were probably ex-lumber men.

Obviously bored with their own company, and now having some visitors requiring information, they were not going to let us get away too quickly.

"Hi," said one of them putting out his hand, "I see you are members of the club."

"What club?" I queried.

"The Volvo Club," he said, turning towards his mate and pointing. "Both Fred and I have Volvos. What year is yours?"

"82," I said.

"So is mine," he said, slapping me on the back.

I agreed that it was a remarkable coincidence, but not wanting to get too involved with car talk, I said, "How do we get to Point Defiance Park from here?"

"That's easy. Fred will give you a map of the area. But, where are you from?"

Admitting we came from South Africa, both of them recalled knowing somebody who had been there and liked it. What a small world, we agreed. Fred had now poured our four cups of coffee, while Dick, the first one, was saying, "If you went to the Zoo last time, why not spend some time at Fort Nisqually; that's something you should not miss, isn't it so, Fred?"

Our coffee break was interrupted by a new arrival going up to the counter and speaking to Fred. Although not specifically listening, we heard the word "spider". Intrigued we went and joined them. It appeared his son, a science teacher, had visited what he termed a spider farm somewhere in Washington State, and had told his father he must not miss it. Unfortunately, he had forgotten both the name of the farm and the town where it was located.

Clare, having rather decried the oddness of the Volvo coincidence, had not agreed that both Fred and Dick knowing somebody that had visited Africa meant that it was a small world. Now, as past president of the South African Spider Society, she was prepared to admit that finding somebody else interested in spiders on a cool day in the Far North West was unusual.

Neither of our Volunteer Information Experts knew of such a place, but that did not mean that they were not willing to try and find out. Ten telephone calls later a pet shop thought that he might be referring to Bob's Tarantula Ranch in Redmond. However, the name might not be Bob's and it might not be Redmond but the name of the town definitely began with an "R".

More coffee, and as more visitors came in with other odd requests, we entered into the spirit of the thing by making suggestions when Fred and Dick did not readily have the answer. Nothing could stop them, however, from seeing coincidences in almost every situation.

Before leaving, we were given various colored round-headed pins to insert on a large map on the wall. To help give the international character of the Kiosk, we pinned ours to Johannesburg, London, and San Diego and our friends pinned theirs to Swaziland and Seattle.

Fort Nisqually, we found, had been the first outpost of the Hudson Bay Company on Puget Sound. Built to develop the fur trade, it was more like a small village in an almost impregnable high-walled enclosure. Inside we found knowledgeable volunteers who, dressed in early nineteenth century costumes, made the recounting the Fort's early history so interesting that we did not have time to go to the Zoo and Aquarium again as we had intended. We did, however, drive down to see The Narrows suspension bridge that replaced the infamous Galloping Gertie Bridge that swayed so violently in the wind that it finally collapsed only four months after it was completed in 1940.

On our way back to Seattle, we did not go back to the Visitor and Convention Bureau to say goodbye, although it was still open. There had been nowhere to have lunch in the fort, and we feared that another series of surprising coincidences might well make us late for dinner.

# 57

## *The Puget Sound*

***It was October*** and we were in Seattle for the first time. Luckily, the warmth of our welcome overcame the chill in the air. Our hosts met us at the airport and drove us to their home. The town, we found, was on long narrow strip of land lying between the Puget Sound and Lake Washington and is intersected by the ship canal and various lakes and bays.

Our hosts were newcomers to the town and when they were driving, we often found ourselves going in the wrong direction. The day we went to the Chittenden Locks we went south instead of north and ended up at Queen Anne Hill where most of the roads come to a dead end. We had to go back and turn several times before finding a bridge that returned us to the northern side of the Locks.

We munched our sandwiches while looking down on the assorted craft that lay below us. The crews were performing odd nautical tasks while waiting for the water level to rise sufficiently to continue on their way. We then walked along the Lock wall across the canal to a building that housed the Salmon Fish Ladder. Here we saw through lighted windows salmon battling their way upstream to spawn.

We discovered The Museum of History and Industry by chance, having lost our way to somewhere else. We decide to go in for a few minutes, and stayed two hours.

We were thrilled to see a reprint of the Seattle Post-Intelligencer dated June 1889. Here was a report of a fire that destroyed twenty-five city blocks in a matter of hours. "No more wooden buildings," was the heading, and the following paragraph captured the drama of the moment.

At an assembly called at short notice in the Armory, Mayor Moran called the meeting to order. In response to loud cries, Judge Hannaford mounted a chair saying this is opportunity to turn disaster into a benefit. Let us widen the waterfront and rebuild the wharves and business buildings out of brick and stone." Seconded by the ex-Governor, the motion was carried. The ban on wooden buildings remains to this day.

Next day we went to the University Arboretum in Washington Park. We found our way to The Azalea Way, a wide, grassy, mile long stretch of meadow, graced by an exciting collection of trees and shrubs. They were a joy to behold. Although officially out of season, we were entranced by the varying colors and textures of the bark as well as the leaves.

As though this was not enough, our enjoyment was heightened by sounds that floated eerily over the pond toward us with bewitching clarity. Could it be the great god Pan down in the reeds by the water? We rounded a bush and found two young Taiwanese men, sitting cross-legged, playing homemade flutes. We stepped back, not wanting to interrupt the music that blended so naturally into the surroundings. But they had seen us. Smiling self-consciously, they stopped playing.

"Where did you learn to play like that?" we asked.

"All Taiwanese boys play such pipes."

They started to play again when we were out of sight. We made our way back to the car with the sounds of their music hovering wistfully around us.

Another day we went to Space Needle, an observation tower with two revolving restaurants about five or six hundred feet up. Built in 1962 for the World Fair it is to Seattle what the Eiffel Tower is to Paris. The Needle is situated in the grounds of The Pacific Science Center, its science museum we found so interesting that went on more than one occasion.

We spent a full day at St. Helens fairly soon after its tremendous eruption. On the way up its winding sand roads we passed a moonscape of stunted trees and scorched earth covering a very large area. Driving up as far as we were allowed to go, we were pleased to see plenty of side roads marked as escape routes.

The days had passed all too quickly and the picnic basket that had served us so well on our trips until now, needed a complete refill for our full day's jaunt to Deception Pass State Park at the North end of Whidby Island.

The coastal road was devious and the villages quaint. Stopping to ask the way, I was surprised to be told to turn left a mile after passing the "slew" (slough). I had always considered a marshy inlet to be a "slough" as in "bough" of a tree, and accepted "cough" being pronounced "coff" and "enough" as in "cuff", but "slew" was new to me.

Deception Pass Bridge turned out to be in effect, two bridges. The first part reaches an inlet, and the second continues on to Whidby Island at an angle of forty-five degrees. We stopped at the bridge, to walk across and look down to the torrent of water that was compressed into the narrow strait far below. However, the wind, now roaring through the pass, was too strong for safety, and we retreated back to the car, and drove across.

We followed the winding road to the Ranger's office and he directed us to the camping site. There we found picnic tables and benches. The camp itself was closed until next summer, but the picnic area seemed well protected from the wind by the forest. Before settling down to eat our lunch, we opened the brochure given us by the ranger, and read, "Here in the depths of nature is the voice of yesterday and the sound of tomorrow. Can you hear it?"

Unfortunately we only heard the sound of today-the unexpected heavy muffled roar of a jet plane. As it passed out of range, we relaxed and prepared to eat the lunch that we had given so much thought to that morning. However, the jet noise returned, and although the sky was overcast and nothing could be seen, it was obvious that many planes were now circling above us. Although the trees provided protection from the wind, they seemed to magnify the noise. There was no escape, and we were forced to eat our lunch in the car, with the windows up.

We drove the twenty-five miles down the Island towards Nisquilly Ferry, without escaping the sound of the planes for more than a few minutes at a time. Then, as we passed through a more built-up residential area, we came across an imposing entrance gate over which was a sign bearing the name of the Naval Air Station, followed by the words, "Pardon our noise. It is the sound of freedom."

We returned to California with the glorious vision of the Olympic

Mountains and of snow capped Mount Rainier still in our minds. But badly shaken and still questioning, which was the right Puget Sound?

"Here in the depth of nature is the sound of yesterday and the sound of tomorrow. Can you hear it?"

Or, "Pardon our noise. It is the sound of freedom."

# 58

## *The Race at Nisqually*

***Dick and Fred,*** the two elderly men manning the Tacoma Visitor and Convention Center, were amazed to learn that on our on our previous visits to the southern end of Puget Sound, we hadn't visited Fort Nisqually in Point Defiance Park. Dick said, "Go there and ask for Hank. He knows more about its history than any man alive."

Hank met us when we arrived. He was dressed in the costume of the period and obviously had steeped himself in the fort's history. He told us that the fort was built early in the nineteen century as a trading post to develop the fur trade in the Puget Sound area.

Hank's involvement and enthusiasm for its history was such that in no time we became involved ourselves in re-living incidents of one hundred and fifty years ago. We were shown a faded manuscript that recorded the arrival of furs traded with the Indians in Oregon and brought to Fort Nisqually by a Brigade of the Hudson Bay Company. It was signed by Edmunds Huggins.

That year, 1855, the company headquarters had instructed that the furs be sent to Nisqually because the Fort was overstocked with goods for trading. Ahead of time the people at the Fort had packed the trading goods into compact eighty pound bales. Two of such bales made a load for the pack horses, taking into consideration the rough trails and mountain passes they would encounter on their return journey.

On the 2nd of July Macdonald, the leader of the brigade, confidently cantered in on his own and was warmly welcomed.

Evidently, he was a well-known and liked figure in the territory. Hank's telling of his arrival was so dramatic that we almost welcomed him ourselves.

Within a day or two, the first detachment of the Brigade came trotting into the Fort, followed by others, until more than two hundred pack animals were in the yard together with some 25 men.

Although it was happening in another century, it was as though we were there in the packing room with Edward Huggins and his helpers when they unpacked and totaled the skins. Thirteen hundred bear's skins, two hundred badgers, two thousand beavers and many others were finally listed.

Over drinks in the evenings the men of the Brigade boasted that one of their men, was a champion runner and promised he could outrun anybody the locals could put up. The fort people resented their continuous boasting and begged one of their men who were known to be a good runner to accept the challenge.

He was a young man who doubted that he could beat such a powerful looking fellow but, under pressure, eventually agreed to run a 100-yard race against him.

Macdonald laughed at the idea of anybody thinking that they could compete against their champion, but agreed to act as starter. The race was to be run in the evening after the day's work was done. A large crowd assembled at the water gate, the starting point was to be down the road. 100 yards was measured off, terminating at the gate. All were now ready for the race. The Brigade's man was cool and confident of success, as were his fellows. To the last one, they were willing to bet their shirts and every inch of their tobacco on the outcome.

At an agreed upon signal from Macdonald, a fair start was made. To our surprise, the young Nisqually man led at the halfway mark, after which the brigades champion speeded up and approaching the finish line they were neck and neck. To the intense disgust of Macdonald and his company, the young Nisqually with a last minute surge, won by a yard

Hank showed us some newspapers of the time recording that the young man's fame quickly spread over the entire Indian country from Scovil right up to the base of the Rockies. He was hailed as a great runner who had defeated the hitherto unbeatable Rocky Mountain Champion.

Nowhere in the manuscript is the name of the young man given, but Edward Huggins himself fits every descriptive detail of the winner. In fact, I know for sure it was he. Although it took place more than a hundred and fifty years ago, I had got so involved in the story as related by Hank; I was at the water gate myself, shouting encouragement with the rest of them.

# PART V

# Family Fun

# 59

## *Dining Out*

*It was sometime* early in the 1950's that we took the family on vacation to Lourenco Marques, in Mozambique, now called by the much less exciting name Maputo. There we met an interesting Italian man on the beach, Francisco Garibald, who had come to South Africa when the immigration laws were eased for the opening of the Empire Exhibition of 1936.

He had been trained in the hotel business in Italy, but was employed temporally as a wine steward at the Grand National Hotel in Johannesburg. He introduced us to his wife and daughter when they joined him on the beach. We were all staying at the same hotel. Our two seventeen-yearold girls became friendly with his daughter so we saw a lot of them.

Lourenco Marques, the capital, was a favorite seaside holiday resort for people living in Johannesburg, not only because of its continental atmosphere, but being only four hundred miles away it could be easily reached in one day. It was a Catholic country and perhaps it must have been a particular time of the year because there were several very colorful religious processions during the period that we were there.

No Portuguese women were to be seen out in the streets on their own. Out-door cafes abounded, and were always full, but only occupied by men. On Sunday Clare and I went to a soccer match, but the person at the ticket counter had a problem. He had never seen a woman there before and did not know what the entrance fee should be for her. After much thought he decided to let her in free.

That evening we went to a movie. It was "Some Like It Hot" with Portuguese sub-titles. Every girl there had a presumably specially selected boyfriend with her and all were closely chaperoned by the girl's parents who followed and sat behind them in the theater.

I can only imagine that it was because of our girls that every day our hotel was serenaded by men on motorcycles or fancy cars that followed us everywhere we went. It was obvious that because Portuguese maidens were kept out of sight, under lock and key, the men were starved of female companionship. They became a damn nuisance, but there was nothing we could do about it.

A year or two later, I met Francisco in the street and he told me he had gone into partnership with Sobardi, a man who was generally accepted as the best Italian restaurateur in the business. Their restaurant was in the Rissik Hotel, which was very popular at the time. We had an anniversary coming along and decided to celebrate it there.

When we arrived at the restaurant, Francisco, now the Maitre d', met us and with much ceremony escorted us to the most central table. He summoned several waiters to dance attendance upon us. A sommelier discussed wines with us at great length. Heating plates were brought so that everything would remain hot. We were almost embarrassed by all the attention that was showered upon us, especially as I noticed a rather short man was sitting at an empty table eating his meal on his own, without being given any attention at all.

I recognized him immediately as being Sir Ernest Oppenheimer, the head of Anglo-American Gold Mines and De Beers Diamond Corporation, certainly the richest man in the world at that time. I called Francisco over and asked him why when we got the full treatment, something similar wasn't given to Sir Ernest. He said "If we even acknowledged his presence in any special way he would never come again."

On the way out, Oppenheimer's Rolls Royce was parked in front of the hotel under a "No Parking" sign as a traffic inspector passed by without comment. We went round the corner, to get our car, only to find that we had overstayed the time limit, and had got a hefty parking ticket to boot.

Sir Ernest would not have to pay a fine, while the cost of our ticket doubled the cost of our evening out. It annoyed me to the extent that the words of the old cockney song came irritably to my mind. "It's the same the whole world over, it's the poor what gets the blame, and the rich what gets the pleasure, isn't it a bloody shame."

# 60

## *Don't Tell Susan*

***Ring-a-ding ding!*** Does the telephone really give an extra insistent ring when my family has something important to tell me? I swear it does.

"Dad." It was Janet. I thought as much by the urgency of the ringing tone. "Will you be able to take Ivan and me to the airport next Thursday? And please don't let Susan know that we are coming. It has got to be a surprise."

I knew that Janet, my daughter who lives here in San Diego, had hoped to be with her twin sister in New York on the 23rd of July to celebrate their 50th birthday. But, as she, her husband Ivan, and their three children, had since arranged to go on a visit to South Africa the following week, I thought it was out of the question. Now, however, I know differently. Not only were they still going to New York, but also Susan was not to know.

"Of course I'll take you, I would not miss it for the world." I said, thinking back to the many exciting incidents that had occurred over the years when driving the family to the airport. This time of course without the children, just Janet and Ivan, it would be a piece of cake.

We dined together the night before, to make final arrangements. Their plane was to leave at three-thirty, and they asked me to pick them up at two forty-five.

"Isn't that leaving it a bit late" I asked.

"No," Janet said looking at Ivan for confirmation. "We know you and mom always got to the airport an hour or so early, to make sure you were the first to know if the flight was delayed. But not us." Evidently this was a family joke.

By sheer luck I was home at a quarter to two next day when the phone rang again with that insistent Ring-a-Ding.

"Dad!" It was Janet sounding more time conscious than she is likely to admit. "I wonder if you can get here at 2:15 as I want to pick up my docent card at The Museum of Contemporary Art on Prospect. Perhaps, even make it a little earlier to allow us to pick up our passports at the travel

agents. They have just been stamped with South African visas."

"Passports?" "You don't need them to go to New York," I said.

"Oh, didn't we tell you that we are all going on a two night cruise ship? As it goes outside American territorial waters, passports are needed. But for goodness sake, don't tell Susan!"

I got there before two. Janet stacked the luggage into the trunk, except for one large carryall, which she put into the well of the back seat. Presumably Ivan was locking up the house. When he did arrive he sat on the back seat with the carryall between his legs.

In the meanwhile they had established that Ann their travel agent had taken their passports with her when she had gone for lunch. We got to the art museum in Prospect after being held up at every traffic light. I breathed a sigh of relief that the docent card was ready for her.

They then suggested that I go back up Silverado to Nine Two Eight where Ann often lunches. She was not there.

"Dad, there are two more coffee places that she frequents, so turn back into Fay, and after that we can try that place in Girard." This meant turning round against the traffic, not made less stressful, by the three traffic lights that were involved were against us. Ann, wasn't there either.

"Perhaps she was on a diet," I suggested.

It was then decided to my relief that we go straight to the airport and I should some-how see that the passports, get sent by Federal Express to ensure that they arrive at their hotel on Central Park South, before ten next morning. Hurrah, we were on our way. But I spoke too soon.

Just before we got to Ardath, Janet asked Ivan if he had Kim's passport (she works in Manhattan). "No," he said. "I think it must be in the locked cupboard in the bedroom."

"I did not know the children were going, too," I said.

"Well, Kim is, but don't tell Susan. It must be a complete surprise."

Jointly they decided it was imperative that we go back to the house and get it.

"Keep calm," I told myself. "We can't afford to have an accident."

We returned to the house, found Kim's passport and were about to go, when I asked if they had their tickets. "Of course!" they said in unison.

"How silly of you to ask."

Every traffic light turned red against us. At the terminal, vast holiday concentrations of cars were jostling one another to get to the skycaps on the curb; just the set up for some friendly fender bending.

"Go in there," said Janet pointing to a spot that might have been suitable for a baby Fiat. "Keep calm!" I told myself. We can't afford to have an accident. A car moved out, I slithered in, and gave Ivan the key to unlock the trunk. We had arrived just in time it seemed, but before saying goodbye I unlocked the trunk again just to make sure that they had taken out every piece of their luggage. I was taking no chances; we had had enough drama for the day.

I had a relaxing drive home. Even the traffic lights turned green as I came up to them. What is more there was a message on the answering machine that I had no need to worry about the passports, Ann, the travel agent, had arrived at the airport with them. All was well.

An hour or so later, the telephone rang. It sounded suspiciously like that urgent family Ding. It was Janet from the plane, and the first time she had used a plane phone. Trouble. They had left the carryall at the back of the car notwithstanding that Ivan had to step over it to get out of the car. Their cameras, binoculars and reading glasses were in it, none of which they can do without. Please send them by Federal Express to get to them by ten next morning. I got them off that afternoon at the cost of twenty dollars or so. Well, that is that, or so I thought.

Ten thirty that evening the phone rang. Was it that insistent family urgent tone again? It could not be, but it was. It was Janet from her hotel in Manhattan. She had been looking for her toiletries and she remembered she had put them in carryall, and in the toilet-bag was some prescription medicine that they had to have. Please could I send it off in the morning by Federal Express. I found it and sent it off at the cost of another twenty dollars. Someone has to keep these courier services going I suppose.

I telephoned Susan, Janet's twin, in Connecticut next day, to wish her a happy birthday. She said that she felt something was happening. All the family was behaving peculiarly. Her husband was insistent on taking her all the way to Manhattan for a birthday lunch, and suggested she pack some clothes for an overnight stay and even include a swim suit

"There is some big deal going on! Have you any idea what it is, Dad?"

"None at all," I said.

I fetched Ivan from the airport on the following Tuesday evening; Janet was to stay on with her sister Susan for another day or two. On getting into the car, he said, "Janet was all worked up before we left to catch the plane to New York. It was not like her to leave the carryall behind!" I did not remind him that it had been between his legs at the back seat and he had to step over it to get out. Why make trouble in the family?

Well! Well! I do not know if having two fifty-year-old daughters makes me one hundred years old, but it certainly made me feel like it.

# 61

## *Twice One Are Two*

***My wife Clare and I,*** having been favored with identical twin girls, to avoid any confusion, always dressed Susan in reddish colors and Janet in blues, not that we did not know one from the other, but to make sure that nobody else confused them. It is true that they took longer to speak than most. For a year or two they had a language of their own but after a visit to the logopedic (speech) department at the university we were assured that it was quite usual for twins to take longer to speak coherently.

The trouble began about their wanting to be recognized by their own names when they started school at Rosebank Elementary at the age of five. They both had to wear identical school uniform, a navy blue gym dress bearing the school emblem. We left them at school in the morning only to hear afterwards that when the teacher called them by their wrong names they were inconsolable. So much so that when my wife could not be reached at home, they had to send for their granny to come and fetch them. After that, we had brooches made with their names clearly legible, so they would be called by their own name in future.

One trouble was that when my wife Clare and I were in the car driving with the girls at the back their voices were so alike that we had to look back to see who was talking. It upset them if we mistook who was speaking.

In high school, after being advised by the headmistress, Susan took French and Janet took Latin. This ensured that they would be in different classes for every subject. This by no means altered their relationship with one another but it gave them a wider number of friends to share.

After school Susan studied shorthand and typing and commercial subjects and got a job as a secretary. Janet was artistic and went to art school. After a year or so she rebelled against the conventional restrictions imposed by the lecturers. So much so, that one day the Principal phoned me at my office to complain that Janet was upsetting the discipline of the school. I remember saying to him "Mr. Botha, you must have hundreds of eighteen year old girls passing through your hands over the years, whereas I have never had to deal with an eighteen year old girl before. I leave you to handle it as you must know best." We had no more trouble and Janet never mentioned it.

In those days steamships were the only connecting link between South Africa and Europe. It was usual to send one's children overseas for a year before they started on their careers. I had arranged for an American business machinery firm whose European and African Headquarters was in London, to employ them. We saw them off at the Johannesburg Railway Station on the way to Capetown to catch the Union Castle mail boat that would take them on the two-week journey to Southampton. There must have been lots of young people on the ship because they joined up with a number of them to go skiing in Austria before going to their job in London.

July is very cold at night in midwinter in Johannesburg. Our house was situated on an unpaved road on the city's outskirts. There was a long dark walkway from the entrance gate to the house. Never before has our doorbell rung at nine thirty at night. That night it rang, shaking us out of the comfort of our cozy seats on the sofa that we had pulled up to the fire.

I got up, switched the porch light on, and opened the door. A woolen-scarved, trench-coated man with a felt hat pulled over his eyes was there. He rudely put his foot forward into the passage to prevent me closing the door. He asked me if I was Mr. Herman and were my daughters' names Janet and Susan. On assuring that they were, he said he was from the Rand Daily Mail. Thrusting a cablegram at me, he said, "We are publishing this in the morning." I took it back to the fireplace to read. He followed behind me.

It read 'South African twins in the jam. Janet and Susan Herman have today been fined thirty shilling each at Bow Street Magistrates Court for stealing jam.' I said, "Surely you can't publish this until we hear their version of the story. Let me put a telephone call through to London." To my horror the operator of the overseas line assured me that overseas telephone lines closed at ten-o'clock, and it was past that time already.

I immediately phoned the Editor himself, who agreed not to publish it until I had spoken to the girls. I tried to get through to London next morning but in those days it was impossible to get an overseas call through for many hours. By two o'clock, the first edition of the Star, an evening paper, had come out with the headline "South African twins in the Jam."

It was late that afternoon when I eventually got the girls on the phone. They were surprised we had heard about it, not thinking it was that big a deal. They were staying at the overseas Visitors-Club, a favorite place for Australian and South African students. It being their twenty-first birthday, a lot of friends called in on them. Not having enough to offer these unexpected visitors, they went down to the kitchen to see what they could find. The manager of the hotel was away and there was no staff about. A closed wooden kitchen cupboard merely fastened with a small padlock on a hasp and staple was there. They opened it and took out some milk to make tea and some loaves of bread and some jam.

The temporary acting manager later that evening saw the cupboard had been forced open, called the Police. The twins were located by the noise of their birthday crowd, and charged with stealing. Nobody was more surprised than the girls to find that the media had made an international incident out of it.

South Africa was good copy for the newspapers in those days, because of the Sharpeville incident (a riot in which a number of Africans had been shot by the South African Police) the previous year. Because of it, raiding a cupboard to borrow a loaf of bread and a jar of jam by South Africans was treated as though the Tower of London had been broken into and the crown jewels had been stolen.

## 62

## *Twice One Are Two (continued)*

***People telephoned me*** from all over the country, having seen the "South African Twins in the Jam" article made much of in the newspapers. I dreaded the publicity that the expected headlines in the Sunday newspapers would bring.

A very big international sex scandal was exposed that weekend, one that involved many names not only of people of the highest rank in Britain but that of a European Ambassador as well. This made not only all the headlines but also filled most of the inside pages of the Sunday Papers as well, relegating the 'Twins in the Jam' story to a mere small paragraph on a back page.

Senior officials of the South African government with whom I was closely involved, suggested that as I intended flying to London forthwith, they would get Jacques and Company the government legal advisors in Britain, to try and get the conviction retracted.

My wife and I caught the next plane to London and sat next to Molly Weiss our neighbor, who was also our Member of Parliament. She annoyed us by saying our girls had let South Africa down, which ridiculous as it was, made us more determined than ever to get the matter righted.

The girls met us in at Heathrow and, after the joyful yet tearful greeting, we got in their diagonally parked rental car. We could not get the gear lever into reverse, however hard we tried. Nobody, including a policeman was able to do so either. Eventually with a lot of help from bystanders we lifted the car and turned it round so we could drive it to our hotel in Half Moon street where we parked it parallel to the curb. After booking in, and having lunch we went outside and found a meter maid ticketing the car. When we explained our predicament, she fortunately knew that this car's gear lever had to be lifted up, to put it into reverse. It was the first car to have this system and very few people knew about it.

Jacques and Co. meanwhile advised us not to pursue the matter in the court as it would entail a lot of publicity that would not be in our best interest. They got in touch with the hotel management, who offered to send us a letter of apology exonerating the girls. This we agreed to accept and considered the matter closed.

To get the girls to come back with us to South Africa, which they were loath to do, we bribed them by promising to take them to Italy for several weeks on the way home. But as Susan had previously arranged to do a Business Machinery course in Holland in a few weeks time and Janet was getting some commercial art experience with Walter Thompson, the advertising agents in London. We decided to spend some time in Scotland and the Lake District while waiting to eventually collect Susan in Holland before leaving on the Italian trip.

On the plane to Amsterdam we sat next to a couple who invited us to join them that evening. It appeared that the husband was a pilot on the Irish Airline who knew Amsterdam well: and had promised his wife to take her to the infamous Red Light District. She was not happy to go unless she had another woman with her, hence she asked us. We agreed, provided we could find something suitable for our two girls to do on their own. We found that there was a canal dinner trip that they could join.

The dining room in our hotel was famous for its numbered steaks. Over the years they had served millions of them and ours duly arrived decked with a small Netherlands flag on which a six-figure number was printed. A feature of the vast dining area was that on request your waiter would shout out your order to the kitchen. It was a lot of fun, if a trifle noisy.

I was surprised that several people came up to our table to compliment me on my wife and the girls' hair. Everybody rides bicycles on the flat and windy roads here, consequently most Dutch women's hair is just a windblown mess, and anybody whose hair has been done professionally, must be a film star at least.

In Amsterdam, it is evidently considered rude to close the curtains of one's living room. Consequently, Dutch family life carries on, in full view to all who pass. At night time these Dutch interiors are each a picture in themselves.

Along the canals in the port area is the Red Light district catering supposedly for sailors. Here the living room curtains are also not drawn and the girls sit at lighted open windows awaiting clients. We finished up at a cafe where the main decoration was various items of underclothing hanging on lines above us. We with many others were encouraged to sing our national songs. All very jolly, it was surprising how many nationalities were there.

When we arrived in Rome, our concierge suggested that as Roma and Lazzio, the two local soccer teams, were playing one another it would be worth our while going to watch it. He would get us tickets. It was to be played on Sunday at the magnificent stadium built by Mussolini, as a showpiece for the Olympic Games. It probably holds two hundred thousand people in complete comfort, and had a moat between the seats and the playing field. This prevents the excitable Italian crowd from rushing onto the field if they are dissatisfied with the result.

We had forgotten that traveling with two good-looking girls in Latin countries is not the same as traveling with them elsewhere. We should have remembered the trouble we had in Mozambique with Portuguese men driving around the hotel, following us wherever we went. Here, as we arrived inside the stadium, several men arrived from nowhere, lifted them up, and took them with them, god knows where, somewhere in the upper reaches. The girls did not seem to mind and we had to hope we would find them safe and sound after the match.

As for ourselves, an usherette looked at our tickets, and evidently deciding that they were not good enough, marched us to front row armchair seats above the centerline. Mussolini probably sat in them originally. Surprised at being shown such unusual consideration, we offered her evidently sufficient Lire to make her think she had not wasted her time. When the match was over, we were relieved to find our two girls waiting for us at the spot from where they had been kidnapped.

Thinking it over, two may cause double the trouble occasionally, but they certainly can cause very much more than double the pleasure.

# 63

## *Sentimental Journey*

*I was driving* LeeAnn, my granddaughter, to the San Diego airport to catch a plane to New York. She hoped to find a summer job there before she was due to start at The New York School of Fashion Technology in September. I mentioned that I was about to visit friends in Switzerland for a week, and had been offered accommodation in London at a very reasonable price, but had decided not to go there, as I did not fancy going alone.

"Why don't you take me with you?" she said "I was only six when we went skiing in Switzerland and have never been to London." It was the last thing I had thought of, and did not answer immediately. Why a am I hesitating? It will be a wonderful opportunity for her and wonderful company for me. What more could I want? Before we arrived at the airport it was all arranged, we would leave in one month's time.

We left Kennedy Airport four weeks later on the Sunday for the six and a half hour journey to Zurich. We arrived on Monday morning at seventhirty. We were met in by my friend Kurt Kaspar and drove the thirty odd miles to his recently built home in Ruti Fagswil. It was built on what had been a portion of his farm, the portion that had held the magnificent two hundred year old barn and a large number of the farm's large old cherry trees. A pity perhaps, but that was the only portion of the farm that Swiss law allowed to be used for other than agricultural purposes.

The village of Ruti was in a large farming area, comprising a wide vista of magnificently manicured landscape, dotted here and there by clumps of deep green tall trees. One could walk for miles and see only an occasional farm house and here and there a farmer doing odd chores or mowing the long grass. Now and then horse-drawn vans passed us, filled with grass cuttings that would provide hay for the winter's feed. Large piles of firewood cut into meter lengths were stacked outside every home we passed. The wood, neatly piled, was covered mostly with sheets of corrugated iron fixed firmly to the ground.

Picturesque brown Swiss cattle and fat healthy sheep were grazing contentedly in every field. They were confined to the pastures by single strands of electrified wire that was stretched between slender, roughwooden stakes set a few meters apart. The wire was wound through ceramic insulators attached to each stake. The very low voltage was obviously sufficient to keep them away. I touched the wire myself and felt only the slightest tingle.

The next day we were driven into Zurich and shopped. We had hoped to go into the Frau Munster to see its famous Chagall windows but an important funeral was being held that morning, so it was closed for viewing. However, the town's fascinating maze of narrow streets and alleys held enough cafes and shops to more than keep us busy. The Bahnhofstrasse, Zurich's main street, runs from the station to the Lake. It was there we caught the Zurich Lake Ferry, which stopped at every village bordering the lake. Consequently it was two and a half hours before we reached our destination. This was Rapperswill (Village of Roses) where we met and driven on to Ruti.

During the days that followed we explored our surroundings. One day we drove up the winding roads to two of the nearby four thousand foot hills, the Grunscherfoot Alp and the Zoo Alp where we had an excellent lunch at a restaurant at the top of Zoo Alp. Yes, to my surprise "Alp" refers to single mountain, I thought the word was always plural.

One day we drove to Lucerne and Interlaken, which meant traveling through the many winding roads and long tunnels to get through the Grunig and Gotthard passes. Just before reaching Interlaken we stopped for lunch at Ballenburg, an open air Museum of Country Crafts and Architecture.

All the villages that we passed through were dominated by tall, narrow, square church towers each with large clocks on all four sides. These were surmounted by high pointed copper steeples mostly topped with a weathercock or some such. It struck us that Swiss watches must be mostly made for export, as Swiss villagers, need only step outside their front doors to look up, and find what the time is.

On Friday we were driven to the Zurich Airport to go to London. We left at 12:15 p.m. and arrived in Heathrow, a one and three quarter-hour journey. I am ashamed to say that we were met at the Airport by a chauffeur with a private car. I was beginning to feel like royalty being taken and fetched everywhere we went. Di Venison who had insisted that she was going to meet us in London could not start her car and in desperation she phoned a limousine company to collect us. We were driven to The Royal Garden Hotel, in Kensington, where we were met with great ceremony. This was getting embarrassing; Di's son was the manager and had obviously been told by his mother to give us special treatment. I don't know how it will feel on my return to California, to be treated like an ordinary human being again.

That evening we found a likely looking restaurant down a small lane opposite the hotel and were joined by a school friend of LeeAnn who was working as an intern at the United States Embassy in Grovesnor Square for the summer.

The next day was Saturday and from just outside the hotel we took a bus to Portobello Road, famous for its antique silver, jewelry, and books and much else. Stalls line both sides of the street with further stalls on the sidewalks in front of shops that are like arcades inside, cubicles crowded on two floors with only narrow passages between them. The Victorian houses were very old, with floors and rickety staircases made from wood, no exits other than the narrow doors through which we entered. They must be a fire hazard waiting to happen. No fire regulations seemed to be in force, otherwise surely, they would be condemned.

Sunday we took an open deck tour bus that went around the main points of interest in the city. We could get off wherever we liked and catch the next bus, which run at eight-minute intervals.

We got off at St. Paul's Cathedral, where a service was in progress. This was Wren's masterpiece and can only be fully appreciated from inside. Two well-dressed men wearing a wide sash from which a large gold medallion was suspended kept us tourists from disturbing the service.

This area was my London, where I had worked as a boy and later, when I was in business in Johannesburg, it was where my London buying office was situated. We took the Tube Train to Liverpool Street station and followed the crowd to Middlesex Street to the famous Sunday market called Petticoat Lane. Stalls line the street and we had difficulty forcing our way through. I was disappointed that it did not have the same cockney atmosphere that it used to have-cockney-speaking Arabs seem to have taken over. With swarms of people everywhere, pick pocketing was rife. It used to be said that if your watch were stolen when you entered the Lane you would be able to buy it back from a stall at the other end.

Here disappointment lay ahead for me. My chief reason for going there at all was to eat at Blooms, the most famous kosher restaurant in England, known for its English-type Jewish food and the smart backchat of its cockney waiters. I had always made a point of eating there at least once during my trips to England. This time we found it had been closed some years before.

It was a grubby district and as it was Sunday everything was closed, but eventually caught a taxi, and with sudden burst of inspiration told him to take us to Simpsons in the Strand.

This is the most traditional British Temple of English food. There, surrounded by its mahogany splendor, we lunched on the most English of English food, served efficiently by male waiters trained since boyhood, supervised by gentlemen in frock coats. Heated silver dishes covered by their famous large silver meat covers hold huge joints of beef and lamb which are carved in front of you by the chefs.

I chose to start with their potted shrimp followed by lamb and roast potatoes and finished with their renowned bread and butter pudding. The starched linen tablecloths and napkins, the heavy silver cutlery, gave a regal atmosphere to the meal. There was a huge choice of every course, I chose the most British, "God save the Queen." Probably the same menu with the same flair has been served over the last one hundred and seventy years. I should not be surprised if one or two of the supervisors were descendants of the original founders.

Outside the restaurant one of the tour buses had just stopped outside, as though it was waiting for us. We rejoined it for the last lap of its journey. It enabled me to show LeeAnn many of London's landmarks, such as Trafalgar Square, commemorating Admiral Nelson, Parliament, with Big Ben its famous clock, and the historic Tower of London. We crossed the well-known Tower Bridge and arrived on the south side of the River Thames where the driver pointed out an old house that I had never seen before. It had housed Bedlam, the original lunatic asylum. The word Bedlam, indicating chaotic conditions, is in general use, but I had never given a thought to where it had been situated.

That reminded me that when I was a boy, the mental asylum of that time was at Colney Hatch. I do not know whether it is still in existence or has changed its name but it had the same sort of reputation as Bedlam.

# 64

## *Henochsberg Saga*

***When Julius Henochsberg*** married Caroline Abrahams in 1844, they gave Julius as a second name to each of their five sons, and named their only daughter Julia. Julius died in 1857 leaving Caroline and 6 children; she temporally put the boys into an orphanage until she remarried a widower, David Nathan. A much younger man, who also had five children. The Nathan children changed their name to Henochsberg, as it was awkward not having the same name as their elder stepbrothers and sister. Now with eleven children bearing the surname Henochsberg it was expected that the Henochsberg name would last for many generations.

Joseph, born in 1845, was the eldest. He was the only one I never met as he had immigrated to Australia many years before I was born.

Samuel born 1848 and Maurice born 1850 were the only ones who stayed in England. The others all eventually settled in South Africa.

But Maurice, who was my grandfather, could not resist succumbing to the family's adventurous spirit, but only for a year or two. In 1886, he took his wife and his six children to look for gold in South Africa. The 2000 ton S.S Scot took them six weeks to get to Durban. Arriving there, he left them with his brother Henry and traveled the 400 miles inland to Barberton a town in a mountainous part of Northern Transvaal where alluvial gold had been found. Not having much success, he went southward over shocking roads to the new booming mining town of Johannesburg.

In this vital exciting atmosphere, promoters were forming gold mining companies and issuing shares without knowing or caring whether the areas they owned had any gold in them or not. He bought and sold many such brightly colored dubious share certificates on the street stock exchange, which took place in a street that had been chained off, called "Between the Chains." In the newly opened Turffontein Race Course he bet on horses that nobody had ever heard of, with bookmakers who sometimes disappeared overnight. He bought plots of land and sold them at a small profit within a day or two. Eventually he went back to Durban only richer for the experience. The family returned to London where he resumed the more orderly life of art dealing.

Alfred, born in 1846 the second boy, was in business in London until he went to South Africa to wind up the affairs of his two sons who had died in German West Africa during the First World War. While there he bought a jewelry business in Johannesburg and patented a pocket watch that became the standard railway timepiece for many years.

He remembered the Great Exhibition of 1851, which took place in the newly built Crystal Palace then in Hyde Park. He was taken when only five years old to hear Dickens read chapters from his Pickwick Papers. He became an avid reader of Dickens's works for the rest of his life. He would take every opportunity to recite from one of Dickens's books, to any audience that gave him any encouragement. One evening he asked me to take him to the broadcasting studio in Bree Street. In those days the rights to broadcast were owned by the African Theater Group who welcomed anybody who would care to perform, for a very nominal fee. He was to read the court scene of the breach of promise case "Bardell versus Pickwick." I accompanied him into the studio, and was asked to shout, "How dare you sir," at a specific portion of the reading.

Samuel, the third son born in 1848, never left England. He was a woolen merchant, and with his wife and two children, Donald and Hilda, he lived in a street at the top of Hampstead Heath. It was the highest point in London and from there one could view the whole of the town. My brother Jack and I kept our toboggans there and when there was sufficient snow we could slide all the way down to the Spaniard's Inn. Donald, the son like every boy of that generation also had no son.

Henry, the fifth son, born in 1854, was trained to be a draper. He joined a Mr. Hart in an outfitting shop. As "Hart and Henochsberg" they transferred the business to Durban. They separated when Henry decided to start manufacturing locally, and Hart did not want to be involved. Henry J Henochsberg became the first clothing manufacturer in South Africa. When the Boer War ended, he moved the factory to Johannesburg. Over the years the firm specialized in manufacturing uniforms starting with school cadets, municipalities, theaters, and in course of time for the South African Railways, the Defense Force and the Police. Having supplied army uniforms for both World Wars, it was said that probably every South African man had worn something made by Henochsberg's at sometime or other. I started working in the firm on arriving from England in 1926. I stayed there for 55 years it was my life's work. Henry Henochsberg had two sons. One, Dudley, never married; the other son, Alfred, had only daughters.

Edgar Henochsberg born 1890, was the eldest of the boys whose name was originally Nathan. He became an eminent Judge and headed the Boy Scouts movement in Natal. His book on company law was authoritative and was used in law schools. He also had no sons.

When Julius and Caroline were married in 1844, all that time ago, they gave all their sons the second name of Julius. With so many sons they must have thought that the Henochsberg name would be handed down to posterity. But neither the middle name of Julius, nor the surname Henochsberg survived, because all the sons, of the generation that followed, had only daughters. It was the end of the line.

If, by a strange coincidence, an old railway time-piece known as a "Henoch's Lever," or a uniform or cap bearing the name H. J. Henochsberg, and perhaps an old copy of Henochsberg's company law, is found, they will be the only reminder that the name Henochsberg was considered of some importance in South Africa for more than one hundred years.

# PART VI

# Odds And Ends

# 65

## *African Flight*

*To our annoyance* our flight was delayed, and without being told why we sat in the plane at Heathrow for an hour. It turned out that customs were refusing to allow several rifles on board that two passengers wanted to bring with them. It took a call to the United States Ambassador before the rifles were released.

The two young American men eventually boarded the plane, and the seated passengers did not hide their feelings. My wife and I sat in the same row across the aisle from them and they apologized for the hold up. It was due to them having mislaid the form from their consulate stating South African Airways had allowed the guns to be transported, providing they were in a locked case.

They had finished their four years at college and were taking a year off, before deciding on a career. Their plans were to go Nairobi for some big game hunting before traveling through Europe.

It was 1950. We were traveling on a DC 6, a four-engine plane. It was not pressurized and the flight was often bumpy. Brown paper bags were provided for airsickness. Over the Mediterranean the Captain came to sit in an empty seat next to us. He confided that the left engine had failed and we would have to come down in Tripoli to get it replaced.

When he returned to the cockpit Clare said, "I wish this chap hadn't confided in us about something we would be better off not knowing."

We spent that night in Tripoli and most of the next day. It was quite obvious as we looked around that the airport had seen much fighting in WW II. The hangars were riddled with bullet holes. Our Captain whom I knew well had been General Smut's pilot during the war. He lunched with us next day and on learning that my son collected stamps, insisted on giving me a packet from his own collection.

When the plane lifted off we had dinner and chatted with the two young American boys. The film to be shown was the Marx Brothers in "A Night at the Opera." One of them had seen it several times and did not want to see it again. So he joined us and unburdened himself with some of his problems. His name was Pfaff and his family's business was a large brewery, which he was expected to join as a matter of course.

His trouble was that he was concerned about the very basis of a business that encouraged drinking. He had joined a group at college that had foresworn drugs and alcohol. He drank only Tonic Water during the journey. He felt guilty that he had received all the advantages that his well-to-do family were able to provide and felt strongly that his life's work should be something to help the less fortunate. Clare was very sympathetic to this way of thinking.

On the other hand I was not. As an industrialist, I pointed out that there were many aspects of a large business that he could influence. For instance, the welfare of the workers, and their health issues, I don't know whether I was making any headway, but I am sure it gave him something to think about.

On arriving at Nairobi, they got off, stumbling down the stairway to the tarmac fang over their heavy gun cases. A Safari Company probably met them and I expect there would be a lot less wild life left in Kenya, by the time they leave for Europe.

We left for Johannesburg on what was an eight-hour flight that evening. During the night the plane rose to ten thousand feet to avoid a storm. The plane was not pressurized and Clare fainted in her sleep and fell on my lap. I rang the alarm and thank goodness oxygen as given her in time.

Back in Johannesburg a group of friends wanted to hear all about our trip. We were the first people they knew, that had been back to London since the war. We met for lunch at a restaurant, and had drinks before ordering. All the men ordered a Castle, a South African beer. I ordered a Pfaff, but the waiter had never heard of it, so I changed my order to a Tonic Water. I am sure my American friend would have approved.

# 66

## *Dinner on the Plane*

***The Pan American Express*** from San Diego belies its name. It was a small plane seating perhaps thirty or forty people. It stood on the runway for twenty non-air conditioned minutes before taking off on its shaky, bumpy, very warm journey.

As I had presumed that Zurich would be very cold in December, beside an overstuffed carry-on bag, I had a heavy raincoat, a long woolen scarf that kept tripping me up and a felt hat. The rest of my luggage containing clothing suitable for the heat of a South African summer was booked right through to Johannesburg. The carry-on bag was full of everything that could be possibly needed for my few day's stay in Switzerland, but it proved to be much too heavy for the long distances in the airport.

On arriving at LAX and managing the first tier of escalators and lengthy passages with which I was confronted, I was told that by proceeding outside and bearing right, it was no distance at all to the International Terminal and Swiss Air.

After five minutes of lugging my overweight case plus separately carrying the heavy raincoat with its detachable woolen lining, my head was protesting at being confined by my very much, unused, felt hat. I eventually stopped at an information window abutting the side walk where I was informed that I still had at least a further ten minutes walk. But if I retraced my steps to a transit notice on the curb and boarded a bus marked "A" it would take me there. The bus "A" only took me partly there, just another few minutes away. Alighting and walking in the direction pointed out by the driver I found the hidden escalator that he said would lead me to the Swiss Air counter. Most of the instructions I had been given were by willing but inarticulate persons whose Spanish I hope was considerably better than their English.

To my chagrin, the young person at the Swiss Air counter not only found trouble in understanding English spoken with my particular dialect but also was unable to get her computer to acknowledge that I was booked on Flight SR 107 at all. In desperation she referred me to the airline clerk in an adjoining booth who managed, after several false starts, to encourage her computer to admit that I was indeed booked on flight SR 107. "Just make a left and you will get to Gate 104. You will be able to board in an hour."

I made a left, and at the end of what seemed an endless passage I could see Gate 104 in the distance. Since my flight was not due to leave until 9 p.m. I had taken the precaution earlier that afternoon of finding out if dinner would be served on the plane at so late an hour. "Yes," I was told by a charming female voice at the 800 number dealing with such things, but only after I was requested to press a variety of numbers if I was speaking on a touch-tone phone. "Please do not eat anything before boarding, as you will be served an excellent meal that will be spoiled if you have eaten beforehand." I took her advice.

While waiting I took a seat on a bench, with my carry-on bag by my side my raincoat and felt hat balanced precariously between my legs. I was joined by an extended family of Asiatic descent. Grandma, evidently nonEnglish speaking, sat on my left. The four small children sat on my right next to their father, pretending that their bad behavior had nothing to do with him. Notwithstanding that everybody talked to one another across me, I was too tired to move away. In any case there was not another seat in sight.

A rather appealing Buffet Kiosk beckoned to me across the way, but the risk of losing my seat, beside the probability of spoiling the excellent dinner that had been promised, forced me to remain where I was. I was now in the middle of a kindergarten form of Ju Jitsu and All-in Wrestling that was getting rougher every minute.

Endeavoring to get my mind of it, I took out my notebook and pen to record my feelings. It was not so easy because Grandma was now standing to the right of me to better talk in some far eastern language to Father on my right.

I only hoped the headache, rampaging across my forehead, would disappear when I escaped these chaotic surroundings. Horrible thought! I wondered if this extended family was going to travel on my plane? If they are. I may well decide to stay in Los Angeles overnight and return to San Diego in the morning.

Would I be brave enough to forego the "Special Dinner" and let down the very enthusiastic Swiss Miss on the 800 information number who resides in an unknown office somewhere in America? An office that can only be reached by press dialing a 2 followed by a 3 and then by a 5, if one is fortunate enough to have touch-tone telephone. Well, I might, because after all she will probably never know.

I heaved a sigh of relief when my bench companions moved on, taking their offspring with them. I was in a much happier frame of mind when I boarded my plane soon afterward. I settled into my seat with a considerable degree of pleasurable anticipation. I allowed my thoughts to wander to some of the excellent dinners I had enjoyed in the past. An immaculate white tablecloth spread before me, with several lighted candles highlighting the features of the beautiful woman sharing the meals enjoyment with me. The maître d', advising us of the chef's specialties. Attentive waiters in attendance, willing to anticipate our every need. Soft music being played in the background.

This dinner was not served until close on half past ten. I could well have eaten something beforehand without spoiling my appetite. It arrived on a partitioned tray containing the usual foil wrapped, reheated, pre-packaged offering, certainly no big deal. It got cold while I struggled to open the plastic coverings on the cutlery and condiments.

I do not blame the airways for this, they do all they can in the confined space of an aircraft cabin. I merely question the advice that the enthusiastic Swiss Miss gave me, on that 800 number somewhere in America she told me not to eat anything beforehand, because it would spoil my dinner.

# 67

## *Edinburgh Castle*

***I boarded the*** Edinburgh Castle at Capetown for the two-week journey to England. I found myself elected to the sports committee in no time, as did everyone else who admitted that this was not their first voyage. This involved arranging games every day and bullying passengers to participate in them. One of the games I was responsible for was to help a number of sailors who ran what they called horse racing. This was rather like Minaru in which five lines or tracks are marked on the deck. Each track has a different number of compartments, three, four, five, six or seven as the case may be. One end is the starting place and at the other end is the winning post. Objects representing the horses are placed at the start.

The sailor acting as a bookmaker deals one card from a pack on each of the five lines. The horse with the highest ranked card move up one place. Then more cards are dealt and again the one with the highest card moves up each time, until one reaches the winning post. The number of spaces that each horse has to move differs and that controls the odds that are paid out. It went on every day and you could bet whatever you liked up to two shillings. The game was very popular. The bookmaker paid out to the nearest shilling. Any surplus we were told, was for the benefit of the widows and orphans fund.

As the end of the voyage approached we stopped the horse racing game. One evening I met with the group of sailors who ran the game. Over a beer I was handed twenty pounds, about fifty dollars in those days, as my share of the surplus. Surprised beyond belief, I told them that I understood that any surplus was to go the widows and orphans fund. I handed the money back to them and insisted that they do the same. I was far from popular and was threatened by some of them.

Next day, the purser told me that the captain had invited me and other officers for a drink in his cabin that evening. Considering that an honor, looked forward to going. To my surprise the Captain and I were the only ones there. He handed me a drink and in a tactful way proceeded to give me a lecture. Morally my action about the surplus money would seem to be perfectly correct but, although he cannot officially condone their actions he turns a blind eye to it with one proviso, that the purser sees that the widows and orphans fund gets at least half of it.

"Look it like this, Mr. Herman the sailors pay is eight pounds (sixteen dollars) a month. It stops directly they get ashore and they don't get any pay until the ship sails again. Patting me on the shoulder he continued, "By all means give your share of the ill-gotten gains back, but in the five years I have captained the ship you are the only committee member to complain."

# 68

## *A Flying Start*

*I have before* me a copy of The Times of London published on the 26th of September 1910. What a peephole into the world of nearly a century ago it is. Stories could be written about every one of the many different subjects that are reported in it. But from my point of view almost a century later, it indicated that the world was experiencing A Flying Start.

The Court Circular from Balmoral Castle was reported in the paper as it evidently did every day. And Foreign affairs of course were covered at great length. But flying and the exploits of its intrepid pilots were the most interesting news of the day.

It reported that seven thousand people paid for admission to the first day of The Doncaster Flying Week. The majority of them stayed on until the end, although owing to the high wind there were only ten minutes of flying all day.

A one thousand pound prize offered for the first plane to fly from Paris to Brussels was not won. Neither of the only two competitors completed the course. The first was forced down by engine trouble in the Bois de Bolougne, killing a dog that got entangled in the propeller. The second man, attempting to make a halt at Saint-Quentin, landed in a tree, and could go no further.

It also reported that several French airmen crashed their planes during the week. Two of them were killed and a passenger seriously hurt.

However, it was the Trans-Alpine Flight that attracted most interest. The Times special correspondent from Milan wrote that it was impossible to describe the excitement of the people here. Crowds thronged the streets waiting for the planes to fly over the town. Only one plane accepted the challenge. The rest decided that the conditions were so unfavorable that they merely flew over the center of the city before returning to the aerodrome.

Chavez was the only pilot to continue. Over the Simplon Pass, he appeared to be flying too low. An eyewitness reported that the plane battered by high winds was unable to clear an obstacle. The pilot attempted to change course, but the strong wind caused the wings to collapse and the plane fell to the ground

Chavez was removed from the wreck murmuring; "C'est terrible; c'est terrible," and "Oh, mes amis." He was taken to hospital semi-conscious, having several broken limbs. When he came round, he was much cheered to think that he had actually crossed the Alps. He was further consoled the committee's decision to award him two thousand British pounds (four thousand dollars) of the original first prize total of two thousand eight hundred.

Well, that was Flying's Start, or was it?

I have just turned over to page three and noticed there is a column there from The Times of 1810, one hundred years earlier. Among other news of that day in September, there was an extract that made me think that my 'A Flying Start' was perhaps a century too late.

I'll give a précis of the newspaper article while trying to preserve the flavor of the language of the time.

The people of Bristol were gratified with the ascension of Mr. Sadler's balloon, from a field outside the town. The whole of the Bristol volunteers were on duty, and kept the ground. He ascended at half past one o'clock. But previously at one o'clock exactly, the signal of ascension was given by a salute by 21 guns from the artillery.

A Wm. Clayfield, a gentleman distinguished by his chemical knowledge and of great respectability, accompanied Mr. Sadler. Nothing could exceed the grandeur of the scene. The balloon ascended amidst the cheers of eighty thousand people. It was completely obscured by a heavy black cloud, soon after its ascent. However in two or three minutes the sun shone on the cloud, and the appearance of the balloon through the transparency occasioned by the sun's rays, was more beautiful than anything imagination can possibly conceive. In a half an hour the balloon was out of sight. (Four o'clock) No tidings from the astronauts.

We won't know if they ever arrived safely we would have to get the next day's paper to find out. But this 1810 Flying Start, that was so colorfully ported on, reminds me of the old song.

"It will be all the same, all the same one hundred years from now. No use a scurrying, no use a worrying, no use kicking up a row."

# 69

## *Honest*

**Edward Mirvish** is a successful Toronto character whose varied business interests range from his first as a storekeeper, then a restaurateur and now as the owner of a theater. He must have cut a few corners to deserve the appellation "Honest Ed." I must admit that the meal that I enjoyed at his Toronto restaurant was exceptionally good, but the art and the general decor that surrounded us were, in my opinion, in the worst of taste. Perhaps that was the secret of his success.

Probably influenced by his wife Anne, a singer and actress who had been thwarted by family problems from making her Broadway debut years before, he bought the Royal Alexander Theater in Toronto without knowing anything about the stage business. And he made it a payable proposition for the very first time.

A visit to London by Mrs. Mirvish may have sowed the seed that led her husband to gamble $2-1/2 million on rescuing the "Old Vic." The "Old Vic," a famous traditional theater in London, had fallen on hard times. Mirvish bought it, notwithstanding the protests of many English theater-goers.

With the alterations to the theater in full swing, Mirvish donned a hard hat emblazoned "Honest Ed" to show his wife the progress being made. Anne Mirvish coughed as the dust flew into her eyes, and asked if the builders could stop for a minute so that she could see what was being done. "No," said her husband, "They are right on schedule, I am not going to slow them down now."

A member of the press who was present asked her if she was satisfied with what was being done. "I am sure it going to be fine," she said. "But if you are going to mention my name in your paper, call me Mrs. Mirvish. I don't like being referred to as 'Honest Annie,' the name that has been used once or twice here in the London Press. I may be honest and my name is Anne, but putting the two together is merely insulting. And, I don't like honest."

# 70

# *Incidents I Would Rather Forget*

***There is no doubt*** that various incidents, in which I have been involved, have influenced my behavior in later life. For instance, for years I waged a losing battle with my wife and children when they ran around with bare feet. Warnings of the dangers did not impress them, and they carried on heedlessly without any dire consequences.

I know full well the reason for my continual nagging. It was an incident that occurred to me at the age of three. I caught scarlet fever and was put in the fever hospital. The disease must have been rampant then, because I was placed in a ward with at least twenty other children who had it. One night after supper when the ward sister had gone to the nurse's canteens for a few minutes, we all got out of bed and played on the cold floor with our slippers.

The matron, a fearsome character, in a forbidding dark blue dress fastened with dozens of buttons down the front, a starched linen matron's cap perched precariously on her gorgon locks, stormed in. Ordering us back to bed, she lectured us in the ringing tone of a sergeant major of a boot camp, the purport of which was, 'You will all catch colds and die if you run around barefoot.' I doubt whether we knew what she was talking about but it frightened the life out of me.

Many years later this fear was further entrenched when, seeing my whole family enjoying the freedom of being unfettered by shoes, I took off my own and walked across the lawn, only to stand on a bee embedded in the grass. I found I was allergic to the sting and had to be treated in a hospital. A bee sting was not one of the dangers

I had been warning them against, but it was enough for me, in fact, so much so that I refused to see the movie Barefoot in the Park.

Another incident that occurred many years ago impels me to insist my children and grandchildren drive with two hands on the steering wheel when I am in a car with them.

As a young man, four of my friends and I decided to drive down from Johannesburg to Durban overnight. As the four hundred miles of potholed and corrugated dirt road made driving tiring, we decided to take turns at the wheel driving in no more than one hour shifts. The fact that it was raining did not deter us, but it slowed us down, especially when we had to test the depth of the water by first wading across various fords before driving across some small rivers where bridges had not yet been built.

Driving at night on these two-way roads needed intense concentration, especially when blinded by the lights of oncoming cars. When it was Max Raphaely's turn to drive, he insisted on leaning back in a relaxed manner holding merely the bottom of the steering wheel with one hand. After skidding once or twice on muddy bends we asked him to be more careful, but soon after, while crossing a narrow bridge he hit a culvert, badly damaging a fender and causing the car to spin around leaving us facing the way we had come. We refused to let him continue.

This almost forgotten incident was brought back to me in a very tragic way many years later. Max died instantly when his car overturned on his way back from his honeymoon. We could only assume that he was driving with only one hand on the wheel. Unfortunately, although I still worry about it, these days I am finding it more difficult to insist that two handed driving be the rule. Car phones and Starbucks coffee are two of the main reasons causing one-handed driving. I would ban both of them if I had my way.

Another incident that I would rather forget was the first and only car race that I attended. It was to be held on the Germiston horse race track. Germiston, a gold mining and industrial town cast of Johannesburg, had a big sporting population and it was expected that car racing would be popular and draw large crowds.

It certainly drew me, and several of my friends, to its first meet. At first, our intention was to sit at the bend of the track so that we could watch the cars endeavoring to pass one another on the curve, but just before the first race started we moved nearer the finish line. The first two races went off without incident and provided close finishes. It was in the third race, however, that tragedy struck. Thank goodness we had moved from the bend, because two cars collided and both mounted the six-foot concrete wall and literally flew straight into the crowd sitting there. It was chaotic. How many people died or were hurt I do not know. Racing was stopped, and considerable alterations had to be made to the track before car racing was ever allowed there again.

Now, if Daytona or any other car-racing venue is mentioned it meets with no response from me. I confine my sporting conversations to such mundane questions and answers as, 'Do you play tennis, Dennis?' 'No, I play golf, Rudolf.'

# 71

## *The Insect World*

***March is a wonderful*** month in Capetown. The intense heat of December and January has passed. Holidaymakers have gone home and the Cape's many attractions are at their best.

That March, I was to attend a meeting on Monday in Capetown. Clare came with me saying that it would be an opportunity to visit Kirstenbosch, the National Botanical Gardens.

We arrived on Friday evening and next day, Saturday, we went to Maskew Miller's bookshop and asked if Professor Skaife's new book on entomology was out yet. They said "No, but why don't you phone and ask him yourself? He would love that."

They gave us his number and we telephoned. The professor said it was nearly finished, and we were surprised when he asked us if we would liked to go there, and talk about it that very afternoon. His home stood on the mountainside overlooking Hout Bay. Mrs. Skaife insisted on our having tea and some of her homemade cake while the Professor talked about his book.

Skaife said the book was practically ready for publication, only waiting for the photographic illustrations he was still working on. He showed us a lot of miniaturized photographs of his grandchildren, and some enlarged pictures of various insects and grasses.

He intended to combine the photographs in such a way that the children would look as though they were walking through a jungle inhabited by huge insects much larger than themselves. The story would bring the insect world into a greater perspective and emphasize its importance in nature, especially to children.

Accompanied by his per blue crane, he led us up the narrow path to his laboratory, which was in a separate cottage a good distance above the house. Before we entered the cottage, he formally introduced us to Sally his pet and constant companion. She had a broken wing that prevented her from flying, but followed him everywhere.

He told us that during the war he had been called in to investigate small leaves that were being found in the jet engines of several planes. It was only happening at the military aerodrome in Capetown and there had been no explanation as to the cause. On examining the engines, he found their blades covered by cleanly cut small portions of leaves. He immediately recognized what was causing trouble. They were being carried into the engines by the tiny leaf cutting ants that abounded in the local foliage probably attracted by the warmth of the engine mounting.

Since retiring, he found time to explore Table Mountain, and found it housed many unique specimens: flora, fauna and entomological that are not found elsewhere. For instance he showed us several of the narrow spear shaped velvety silver leaves that grow only on Table Mountain. Also, he had discovered on the mountain a peripitus, accepted as being the missing link between the worm and the insect world. Visiting scientists come from afar to personally examine it.

We were particularly interested in one of the major studies he was conducting that day. It was of ants. He had set up a table that had single elecric globe suspended on a pulley over its center. At each corner was an ant's nest. When the light was switched on, ants brought their eggs to a place where the temperature was exactly sixty degrees. When the globe was aised or lowered, the ants came back and moved only their own eggs to a new position that was now sixty degrees.

He then showed us how solitary bees and wasps had made nests in small glass tubes that lay horizontally in pigeonholes in a wooden crate on his stoup. This enabled him from time to time, to take up a tube and inspect what was happening inside.

Returning inside, he showed us work he was doing with queen bees. He as particularly interested in how the nourishment of the jelly she produces is powerful enough to feed her whole swarm. He was exchanging notes with a German scientist on this matter. In fact he had just received some samples of jelly from Germany, extracted from a very fertile queen bee.

We asked him what he intended to do with it. He said he was going to get Mrs. Skaife to take a spoonful three times a day to see if it improved her health. I asked Clare if she would like to try it too. She said, "Let's wait until we come back next year and see if Mrs. Skaife is still alive."

# 72

## *A Lone Voice*

***Notifying me of*** the death of my cousin Lewis Ronald Dison, his widow Naomi, enclosed speeches made by his colleagues at the Bar, when the Cape Provincial Division assembled after his funeral.

Two quotes from these speeches summarize the essence of the man.

*The first,*

*"In his days at the Johannesburg Bar, he was the bête noire of every municipal council on the reef. Like a knight of old bearing a banner, not of 'Excelsior' but 'Ultra vires', he waged litigious warfare against the forces of bureaucracy, usually successfully. His career at the Johannesburg bar was marked by a dogged tenacity in defense of the underdog at a time when he was a lone voice in the fight against repressive regulations."*

*The second,*

*"A devoutly religious man, he had a deep spiritual feeling that he not only preached but practiced. A private person, softly spoken, and self-effacing. Of him Chaucer's words are very apt; he was 'A parfait gentle knight'."*

As a mark of respect the Court adjourned from 10:20 to a quarter to eleven. Justice in the Cape was put on hold for twenty-five minutes, in his memory.

Relation may be God-given; usually the less said about them the better. My cousin Lewis, however, was so different, and certainly more interesting than the usual run of cousins. Having had to admit my relationship to him to so many people, so often, I feel duty bound to put down the Lewis story, as I know it.

Born in Johannesburg, he was taken to London by his parents when he was about nine years old. There, as his mother was having a series of medical treatments, Lewis was placed as a day boy in a prep school and left very much to his own resources. Most of his free time was spent browsing among the many and various second hand bookshops that abounded then in Charring Cross Road.

Some time after their arrival, his father was awakened, late one evening by an Indian university lecturer wanting to see the first edition of an out of print book that was advertised in the Daily Telegraph.

"I am afraid you have made a mistake," said an annoyed Mr. Dison, still fiddling with the cord of his dressing gown.

"That's alright dad," shouted young Lewis from the second floor landing. "It's for me." This was the start of a steady stream of earnest collectors who would arrive at the St. John's Wood apartment at all hours to purchase difficult to obtain books.

His mother, my mother's youngest sister, died soon after their return to South Africa, so Lewis was placed as a boarder at St. John's College, the premier boys' high school in Johannesburg. During the next few years I saw very little of him, but he brought himself forcibly to our attention after entering the Witwatersrand University to study law.

It did not take long for him to be the talk of the college, and achieve a considerable degree of fame/notoriety.

It started when he was summonsed to appear in court for non-payment of a bus fare while traveling to lectures. He appeared in his own defense, accompanied by a large number of his fellow students, who had made sure that several members of the press were present. The charge was, that he had been unable to produce his bus ticket when asked to do so by a ticket inspector, and, further, for publicly accusing the inspector of being drunk.

Spiritedly answering the case for the prosecution, Lewis produced the pulpy mess of a chewed up ticket that the inspector refused to accept. Under cross-examination, the unwilling bus conductor, whom he had subpoenaed, admitted that he had sold Lewis a ticket. Then Lewis dramatically producing ancient leather bound tome, quoted the obscure case of Liverpool Tramways versus O'Brien early in the century. The ruling in that case established that the production of a legible ticket was not necessarily the only proof of payment. After this the magistrate asked the prosecution to drop the charge, the accusation of drunkenness was conveniently forgotten.

Lewis suing a girl who had thrown a snowball at him, charging that she had made an unproved attack with a dangerous weapon followed this. To prove it, he produced the remains of the snowball, he had carefully preserved in a freezer, as well as his spectacles with one lens cracked. Several other such incidents ended this hilarious first year.

During the three months break before the start of the second year at college, he rented a small furnished office in town and put in advertisements offering advice to school leavers about to enter college, which subjects required less swatting and which lecturers should be avoided. He was hard put to deal with the tremendous number of parents and students who consulted him. The University however, was not so enthusiastic when there was a tremendous increase in the number of students wanting to take Italian that year.

During the next few years, while working for a law firm and studying for his LLB degree, he kept a low profile. After qualifying as barrister in 1941, he was accepted into the army as a Jewish Chaplain with the rank of Captain. This surprised us as his schooling as a boy had been at Church of England private schools. Obviously, over the years he must have acquired the necessary religious qualifications and been sponsored by the Rabbinate.

His army career took him to Egypt and Italy. The next time I saw him was in Durban just after the war ended. He had lost weight and looked almost transparently frail. He had just been discharged from hospital after a bout of amoebic dysentery contracted in North Africa. He was now awaiting his discharge from the forces.

My wife and I attended a High Holiday service he was conducting for servicemen and holidaymakers in the large hall attached to our hotel. His sermon, delivered with obvious conviction and dramatic flair, held the congregation spellbound. But still obviously weak, standing at the podium his tall spare frame slightly bent over, an occasional wince of pain appearing on his lips, the heart of every woman present went out to him. Once again, having been forced to admit to our relationship, I had to fight off several mothers demanding that I introduce their daughters to him.

With the advent of the Nationalist Party getting into power in 1948, restricting laws affecting the relationship of the various racial groups were imposed. Laws such as Job Reservation, The Group Areas Act, The Mixed Marriage Act and others, created much hardship and contention.

Now, Lewis's inborn adversarial mentality, his flair for discovering faulty drafting of the regulations, his unrivalled ability to ferret out old decisions that ran counter to the government's thinking made him the counsel of first choice in the myriad of cases brought before the courts. Time and again he took points that caused the cases to be withdrawn, until the wording of the legislation was amended.

For several years he successfully defended people of all races charged with contravention of these acts, causing the State Attorney's office continual annoyance and aggravation. It was stated that the police had investigated and reinvestigated him, hoping to find that he was communist or had some tie to the A.N.C. that would give them cause to ban him, without avail. In court, he also used his knowledge of the Talmud to use rabbinical logical methods of redefining the case. It was suggested, probably without foundation, that the Minister of Justice at the time was reported to have said, "Who will rid me of this Turbulent Priest?"

Eventually he decided that he was being typed, and only offered one sort of brief. So, packing up his family, he journeyed the one thousand miles to Capetown to start afresh and attempt to build a more conventional commercial practice.

This did not mean that he stopped tilting his lance against Apartheid windmills. Always prepared to enter uncharted territory he often ventured where his colleagues feared to tread. He accepted one case opposing an administrative decree that was considered above the law. First losing before one judge, then losing again before a full bench of five judges he continued against all advice, until he finally succeeded by a majority vote in the Appellate division. This victory maintained the right of judicial review over government sponsored administrative regulations.

The case was written up in The Law Journal entitled "Twas a Famous Victory."

# 73

## *The Missing Link*

***It invariably happens*** that if any scientist makes claim that he has discovered something that differs from a previously held theory, he is immediately derided as a charlatan or worse.

In 1912 a skeleton was unearthed in Britain that was said to prove Darwin's theory, that man and apes had a common ancestor. It was discovered at Piltdown, and was something between a bipedal man and a knuckle-walking ape, with a normal size cranium. To the English it was logical that the first man on earth had been a big-brained Englishman.

In 1924 Dr. Raymond Dart, the professor of anatomy at the University of the Witwatersrand, examined a one million year old, small brained skull and realized to his surprise that it was undoubtedly a hominid and had walked upright. It was neither ape nor man but something in between. He called it the Taungs Skull and said it must definitely be a Missing Link. Sir Arthur Smith Woodward, whose huge reputation vested on his discovery of the Piltdown skull twelve years earlier, was almost venomously scathing in denouncing Dart's claim. Dart's find was merely the skull of a chimpanzee, he said.

A decade later when a second specimen of an adult man-ape was discovered near Johannesburg, the Old Guard in Britain still refused acknowledgement. However, in 1950, came the bombshell that Woodward's Piltdown skull was a complete fraud, a student hoax. Only then was it accepted that Africa was the birthplace of modern man. Dr. Leakey was unearthing new finds confirming it in Kenya.

Dr. Dart retired and remained in an Emeritus capacity. His most outstanding student, Professor Philip Tobias took his place as head of the Department of Anatomy. Together they founded "The Society for Study of Man in Africa." Tobias was a charismatic speaker and the society attracted members from all over the world.

Clare and I were members from its inception. Besides attending the lectures that were held monthly in the large hall of the medical school, we invariably went the society's tours to the Sterkfontein and Makapansgat caves where many prehistoric bones were being found.

Scientists from all over the world considered it a privilege to be invited to be the guest speaker at its annual Raymond Dart lecture. Noted speakers included Aldous Huxley and Dr. Leakey, amongst others.

Dart was delighted the year he was able to persuade Professor Heinz, the famous German paleontologist, to be the guest speaker. Before a large, expectant audience, Dr. Dart introduced the guest in a flowery speech of welcome, listing the professor's many achievements in the scientific world.

Professor Heinz came to the podium and after adjusting the microphone, thanked Dr. Dart for his welcoming remarks. He said what a pleasure it was to come to South Africa, a place he always wanted to visit. His opening remarks were well delivered. They must have been memorized and well-rehearsed, because later it became apparent that he was uncomfortable speaking English. Hunched over his notes, he began to read them with difficulty. He mispronounced and stumbled over words, which together with bad phrasing and spoken with a heavy accent rendered his speech practically incomprehensible.

We sat in embarrassed silence for three quarters of an hour struggling to get something out of it, with very little success. It was a relief when he finished and Dart got up to the give a vote of thanks. He thanked the speaker and made the usual complimentary remarks. But still badly shaken, he tried to put the speaker at ease stammering, "I wish I could speak German like the professor speaks English."

Professor Philip Tobias, whose sense of humor was legendary, was heard to remark when he was well away both from Dart and Heinz, "What you have just heard may well be 'The Missing Link' between two great European languages."

# 74

## *Money for Jam*

*Various credit cards* are offered me for pre-approved large amounts, stating that, if required, a higher amount will be readily granted. One such is Chase Gold Visa that says in the event of my death they will pay any outstanding balance owing at that date up to ten thousand dollars. It should certainly be sufficient for my expenses, unless I am given a State Funeral.

As generous as all these offers are, I don't think they total much more than a million or so. Which is an insignificant amount compared to the five million Reader's Digest is imploring Clare Herman, my late wife, to take. The fact that she has been in heaven for over five years now does not seem to put them off. I suppose they think that there is a heavenly Rodeo Drive where five million dollars will not go that far.

Anne Milford, the sweepstakes manager for Reader's Digest revealed something that she says has only told to very few, that by placing the gold confirmation seal on the entry form Clare will be entitled to a further one hundred thousand dollars. The deadline for returning this entry form was August 17th.

Another important looking entry form arrived stating that the first installment of 167,000 dollars would be drawn on Citizen's State bank for deposit in Clare's bank account in La Jolla. The date for returning this entry form was now August 24th.

Ten further letters arrived over the next month or two, most of them enclosing different colored seals, which if attached, to the entry form, would entitle her to win various other prizes, all assuring her that because of this or that reason, her chances of winning the big prize was practically guaranteed.

In every letter, the deadline for her entry was extended. The original deadline was August 17th then the 24th. It was then extended to October 5th followed by November the 6th and then November the 9th.

A further advice has just come giving Clare a confidential security code number. The closing date now has been extended to December 26th, but they say if she mails her entry by December 16th she will win $5,120,000 but if she delays it until the 26th she will only be entitled to the $5,000,000.

The Citizen State Bank has now stated that they will definitely pay the first installment of $167,000. But, a Jeffrey Berghuis of the First Monetary Corporation has also guaranteed a payment of $167,000. What is more, a limousine no less, will pick her up at her house and take her to the airport, for an expense-paid weekend in New York, as well.

It has put me in a quandary. If I am allowed to collect these monies on Clare's behalf when she wins, do I keep both of these guaranteed amounts and not say anything about it? Or shall I return one of these sums of $167,000 to Reader's Digest pointing out the mistake.

How silly of me, seeing that the prize has got to get to heaven.

Of course I must return one of the checks, otherwise it would ensure me of getting a one-way ticket to Hell.

A prominent medium with whom I discussed the matter told me that. while there is some form of a financial institution on Cloud Nine, I should not bank on it. However, recently she has been in touch with a wellknown philanthropist who passed over. He gave her the impression that he is not without means up there, but no interest is payable on his capital. He did infer, though, that from time to time the capital might be allowed a cost of dying increase.

Getting the winning cash past Peter at the Pearly Gates is a problem have not faced up to yet. But, I should think that the Reader's Digest is in heaven's good books, and the money will be allowed in, probably shown as celestial credit in their accounts.

# 75

## *Order Please*
## *A lighthearted look at the eating scene*

***Overeating has probably*** killed off more people than starvation if the truth be known. But food and its preparation is a popular subject of conversation everywhere in the world. "Can I have the recipe?" is a question women ask more often than any other.

When traveling abroad one seldom has the opportunity of dining in private homes, so any observation can only be based on the experience of eating in hotels or restaurants. Because of climate and customs the type of food eaten varies considerably. To a great extent the temperament and personality of a nation is reflected not only in the food itself but also how it is prepared and served.

In England they start with the terrific advantage that in the pubs at least the bill of fare is written in English. With the disadvantage, however, if you try the roast beef and two veg. you may never recover. Steak and kidney pie is usually good, but bear in mind that the complicated liquor licensing laws are such that you may have to eat your food faster than you intended. "Hurry up and eat it duck, the bar is about to close."

"God save the Queen."

In Germany you tuck a king-size linen napkin into your collar and get right down to a heaped platter of good solid food. Improved no end by a tankard or two of lager.

"Danke schoen."

However more important than the food itself, Der Oberkellner will be watching to see if the plates are piping hot. Heaven help your waiter if they are not.

"Donner und blitzen."

In Switzerland however it is the food that must be hot. "Nein! Half of it is kept back and placed in a warming oven close by. Then just as you finish, thinking you have eaten more than enough, the waiter whips your plate away, and replaces it with another equally hot portion. With a look that seems to say...

"Don't let it get cold......Ja."

In Italy eating is a favorite national pastime, opera coming a bad second. While serving your meal the waiter will probably stand by and savour your enjoyment. Pasta with a bottle of Chianti will be merely the start of a long, long session. He won't worry if the soup is cold, but his eyes will glisten with pleasure if you are enjoying the food. In Rome at least, Fettuccine Alfredo is served to you with the same golden spoon treatment that has been given to Presidents and film stars, with such flair and flourish that you fully expect a fanfare to be sounded as you eat it.

*"Bravo!"*

*In France food is taken very seriously indeed, almost a religion. After all Haute Cuisine is internationally recognized as an art form. Words like Hors d'oeuvres and Entrees are in general use worldwide. Even people other than the French now eat escargot on occasion. Their wines are universally acclaimed, and if Maurice Chevalier is to be believed, they invented champagne in one night.*

*"Bon Appetit!"*

*However it is no secret that the Italians have influenced French cooking to a greater extent than most master chefs would be prepared to admit. What is more, one was a woman. "Sacre Dieu!" It was the Duchess of Estrees, an Italian, who personally chose and supervised the cooking and preparation of the food at the Court of Louis XIV. To honor her great skill and talent she was awarded the Order of the now-famous "Cordon Bleu."*

*"Molte Grazie!"*

*In America great care and preparation are given to the cooking of the turkey and traditional side dishes eaten throughout the nation to celebrate a national holiday. But it is their timely invention of Fast Food that has earned them international acclaim. The hamburger on a soggy bun, the not-so-hot hotdog followed by copious drafts of Coke or Pepsi are now found all round the world, even in Moscow.*

*"Have a nice day!"*

# 76

## *Out of Touch*

Harry Emdon, a Johannesburg stockbroker who years later became my father in-law was often offered shares at nominal prices in gold mining companies about to be formed. He usually bought some of these initial shares as a gamble for himself and for several of his clients. After a shaft was sunk, the content of gold ore found in a sample of rock would decide whether it warranted a mine being established or not.

His elder brother Alfred, a bachelor, came to Johannesburg from London for a family function. He decided to settle here in a year or so after selling his house and settling his considerable other affairs in London. Before going back to England, he bought a few thousand shares at these minimal prices as recommended by his brother. The shares were in gold mining companies about to be formed.

Initial results of test drillings were usually unsatisfactory and the companies went no further. One however, Harmony Gold Mining company, found that the rock brought up in the first instance showed enough gold content to warrant them proceeding. The next alloy report unfortunately showed no gold content at all. Harry Emdon the stockbroker quickly sold his shares and recommended that all his clients do the same.

Unfortunately Alfred had already gone back to England and taken the share certificates with him. There were no overseas telephone lines in those days and letters took three weeks to get to England. Alfred, on arrival in London, had gone traveling to the Continent with his great friend Harry Jacobs. They went for an unspecified time and left no address. Wealthy bachelors and gourmets, they intended to savor the offerings of all the most famous restaurants and visit all the well-known opera houses in Europe. Time was of no object to either of them.

In the meantime Harmony after sinking the shaft deeper struck a reef that indicated that it might contain the largest gold content, of any mine yet discovered. The Rand Mining Corporation which owned considerable gold mining interests, offered twenty pounds each, for the five shilling shares. They intended to develop the property, backed by their unlimited resources and their past experience of deep level mining.

After further exploration it was found that the reef was much wider than previously thought. On this information the shares started to trade rapidly upwards, eventually reaching almost ninety pounds each. Letters and cablegrams imploring Alfred to get in touch with them, remained unanswered.

It was six months before Alfred and Harry got back to London and demanded to know what the fuss was about. Being told the present Harmony Gold Mine price, Alfred said he did not know whether or not that he had invested in Harmony. But he would look in his bank locker to see what certificates he had placed there.

At the bank, he was surprised to find that he had two thousand Harmony shares. He cabled Johannesburg to let them know that he had found the share certificates and would bring them back to Johannesburg when he came in December.

It is said that "Absence make the heart grow fonder," but Alfred's brother the stockbroker's feelings were far from fond. In his experience stocks that went up too quickly, usually dropped to a more reasonable level later on. He would have sold them at a much lesser price on their way up.

Alfred being out of touch during the whole of this critical period, showed that in this case "Ignorance was bliss and it would have been folly to be wise."

# 77

## *The Pictures on My Wall*

***I draw great comfort*** from the pictures that surround me on the walls of my home, here in San Diego. They are paintings, sketches and lithographs that my wife and I brought here from South Africa. Each has a tale to tell.

No one can forget Madame Haengi, an art dealer, who in her improba ble mid-European accent used to kill off artists before their time. 'Battis (A well known South African artist) is very ill', she would say, 'Get in now because his pictures will treble in price after his death. But Battis's carly demise and similar predictions concerning other artists were greatly exag gerated.

The 'Battis' we bought from her before the price went up, we later exchanged for a 'Domsaitis,' an exciting study of the Karroo. She warned us not to buy a 'Domsaitis' from any one else but her, as she expected that his widow was forging his signature on her own paintings. However Madame's knowledgeable enthusiasm about the art she had for sale was such that we bought our Van Esche and probably the 'Lipkin' as well. from her, despite any wild predictions about their health she may have made.

One painting that we own she did not sell us was the 'Alex Preller' entitled 'Image of the Sun,' a reflection of a melting sun in an impasto of shades of reds and black laid over gold leaf that filters through. Now in sole possession of one wall, it has given us much joy over the years. At a showing of Prellers' work in Pretoria, both Clare and I had no hesitation in selecting it, then waited until it was marked sold before going around the rest of the exhibition.

On our return a half hour later, we found Mrs, Vorster, the wife of the Prime Minister, demanding to buy it. Preller, a sensitive soul, looked at us pleadingly, hoping we would agree to give it up and save him from a most embarrassing situation.

With as much grace as we could muster we politely refused. By the look Mrs. Vorster gave us, it was obvious that she would recommend to her husband that under no circumstances was he to confer the ambassadorship to Switzerland or any other such honor, that he might have had in mind for us.

After the exhibition closed, Preller delivered it to our home himself. He had re-framed it with a four-inch bright copper surround that he assured us that with time would achieve a dark greenish-bronze patina a setting he had originally envisioned for it. He agreed that the wall over the fireplace was a suitable position for it, as it would catch the setting sun, but he disliked the black-slate mantelpiece. He took the painting away with him, and only brought it back after we had replaced the black slate with white marble. He then brought it back and hung it himself, to his satisfaction.

Preller invited us to his farm in Brits to discuss the intaglio work with which he was experimenting. He was in his impressive marble floored studio when we arrived. It had been extended to its fifty-foot length when he had been commissioned to paint the ten by forty foot mural that now graces the conference room of the Transvaal Provincial Building in Pretoria.

We found his lifestyle to be as experimental as his art. He lived at a uniquely low level. His bed and all the chairs were only inches above the floor, and several abstract paintings (not his own) hung a mere four inches up the white washed walls. His bathroom was open to an enclosed courtyard graced by peacocks.

The attractive young man who acted as his secretary came in with messages from time to time. It was obvious their relationship was more than close. Preller died soon after from cancer, having left all his possessions to his young friend. After the funeral the young man went off in Preller's Jaguar and drove over a cliff.

It is said that a picture is better than a thousand words, but it might take more than a thousand words to tell the whole story of a picture.

# 78

## *Silence*

*My children and grandchildren* sent me as a gift, a copy of the New York Times dated 26 September 1910, the date of my birth. It was copy, numbered 21885, authenticated by the Historic Newspaper Archives in Washington DC.

A column on the front page, given full prominence was headed WEST POINT CADETS ALL UNDER ARREST. The Military Academy announced that it was because of "A Remarkable Act of Insubordination."

Captain Jordan, a newly appointed officer charged that he had been given the Silent Treatment. Not a Cadet Spoke, or ate a mouthful when assembled at dinner and the silence was repeated at breakfast.

The regulations of the United States Military Academy Article 129 provides severe punishments for such acts of insubordination. The senior class-men who sit at the end of each table are responsible for everybody at their table. Punishment for such behavior can be either.

1. Reprimand.
2. Deprivation of recreational facilities, which may include restriction in prison.
3. Or, public dismissal.

One of the cadets involved was the only grandson of Stonewall Jackson. the Confederate General, and another was the son of Colonel William Larned, one of the best-known members of the academic staff at West Point. As yet, which punishment and to whom it will be administered, has not been decided.

The paper also recorded a previous "silence" had taken place at Annapolis, where a Lieutenant Berthalf U.S.N. was similarly treated. What punishment was administered then, was not recorded, but penalties for obstreperous cadets have been much modified in recent years.

As a boy, I immersed myself in the many books by Captain Marriot dealing with the adventures of Mr. Midshipman Easy. My life's ambition at that time was to serve before the mast, and travel the world, as he did. As Midshipman Easy, I would confide any troubles to the elderly bos'n, who in the book solved every problem by saying "Mr. Easy, its merely zeal just zeal.

While zeal may solve the cadets' problems in West Point and Annapolis, it certainly was hardly zeal that troubled the cadets of St. Cyr in France as recorded by Dorothy Parker.

It was commonly accepted that the toast of Paris was Madam Le Blanc. Undeniably she was the most attractive woman in the whole of France, famed as a courtesan, whose favors though costly, had been granted to visiting princes, and to many of the most powerful politicians in the land.

The cadets of the military academy of St. Cyr having heard that for the sum of twelve thousand francs she might possibly be available, decided collectively, that six hundred of them should each put in twenty francs and draw lots to decide the winner. A handsome lad, some twenty years old, was nervously surprised at his good fortune.

He placed the money in a brief case and went to an intermediary to effect an introduction. His youth and good looks besides having the ready cash available were sufficient to get him an appointment that very evening.

Next morning after a blissful night he was asked how it had come about that he could afford such an expensive evening. On telling her how six hundred of them had put twenty francs in a pool.

She expressed alarm and insisted that the evening should not cost a cent. Delighted, he thanked her. Now he would have the pleasure of taking the sixteen thousand francs back to the boys at St. Cyr. Instead she opened her purse and handed him his twenty francs while kissing him goodbye.

# 79

## *Smoke and Mirrors*

***"What's the use of worrying,*** it never was worth while. So, while there's a Lucifer to light your fag, smile, smile, smile!"

This was a song from the First World War when cigarettes were

included in most tuck boxes sent to the soldiers fighting in the trenches in France. They were the item they mostly requested. Lighting a cigarette and puffing on it saved them from utter boredom. What else was there to do?

I emigrated to South Africa in the nineteen twenties. At that time a packet of fifty Springbok cigarettes cost only shilling, and were commonly known as coffin nails. This appellation did not stop people from buying them. That they might be the nails in their own coffin was never given a thought. Death was a thing that happened only to other people. Smoking was a social thing. It was polite to offer cigarettes to one another. Fancy cigarette cases and elaborate lighters were the height of fashion.

It was lucky that I never enjoyed smoking cigarettes. I had tried Turkish and Virginia types as well as some with fancy advertised brand names, but none of them appealed to me.

A group of us, aged about 18 or 19, played bridge and smoked cigarettes all night long, just for the hell of it. It was an experience that not one of us wished to continue.

In the early nineteen thirties, before sailing on a trip back to spend a month in England, my brother gave me as a parting gift a brier pipe, a full tobacco pouch and some matches. By the time I got back to Johannesburg, I was a confirmed pipe smoker.

Over the next many years I enjoyed every minute of it. Even the ritual of filling my pipe and tapping the tobacco into the bowl to ensure that it was not too compressed. Getting our the matches, lighting up and shielding the flame with my hand to allow the tobacco to catch alight, and letring the smoke spiral to the ceiling, was soothing.

All this preparation took time, time that stopped me from acting too hurriedly. Faced with a problem at home, in the office, or at a meeting, I used the time it took between taking out my pipe, lighting up, and then slowly puffing on the stem to consider and reconsider my answer before pronouncing it.

I was completely unaware that I was being inconsiderate of other people's feelings. I lit my pipe after breakfast, and only put it away when going to bed. I smoked while at the movies, and theaters. When dining out, I puffed happily on a Havana cigar after the meal. Then the world was very considerate of such behavior-ashtrays were provided in every house.

Many famous people including James Barry, the author of Peter Pan, wrote books on the joys of pipe smoking. Stanley Baldwin, the first British Prime Minister to ever speak on the radio, smoked a pipe. I felt I was in good company with men like that. On the whole it was generally considered that a pipe smoker was a responsible person who could be trusted.

My pipe smoking only became a problem when I was bothered by continual phlegm. There and then I decided to stop. It was not as easy to stop as it had been to start. I stopped and battled the cravings that beset me. Unfortunately, when visiting a friend's sheep farm in Cradock, I stood on a scale in his sheering shed. To my horror I found that it registered my weight as 180 pounds. This alarmingly was 20 pounds heavier than I had ever been.

On arriving home I rescued a pipe from my desk drawer and started smoking again. I was certainly more relaxed and had lost weight, but after a bout of coughing my doctor advised me to give up smoking for good.

I stopped, but one evening a friend came in to chat, he took out a cigar case and offered me a Havana cigar. I took one and smoked it with him. Next day, my pipe was in my mouth and I was smoking once more.

Good intentions were not sufficient to prevent all the stopping and starting that ensued over the next few years, until being taken ill at a barbeque one night, I was rushed to the Brenthurst Clinic. The surgeon who operated on me found I had swallowed an exceptionally large bone. It was a major operation and I was very ill indeed. A team of physical therapists prodded and pummeled my lungs every day, frightening me to the extent, that I promised my wife that if I ever got out of hospital alive, I would never smoke again.

To my surprise, the day before I was released, the head of the therapist group came to see me. She told me that my condition had been such that it was lucky that I was a non-smoker. I did not dare tell her that I had smoked a pipe almost continuously for fifty years.

A month or two later I went to Capetown on a Sunday to attend a meeting that was to take place on the Monday. After dinner there was nothing to do, without even a television in the bedroom, and as no shops were open on a Sunday evening, I remembered that there was a kiosk in the lobby where perhaps I could get a magazine. I took the elevator down to the ground floor and found that it was not only a news stand but sold tobacco as well.

Well! No one was with me. If I smoked just one more time, no one would ever know. I bought a pipe, a packet of tobacco and a box of matches. Taking them back to my room I opened the packet of tobacco and put some in the bowl of the pipe, to make sure it was not too tightly packed. Then I took out a match and was ready to light up.

Sitting in front the mirror, I hesitated; it struck me that I did not really want to smoke. If I actually did light it up, it was possible that the smoke would cloud my mind, and I would continue smoking.

There and then, I collected up all the smoking paraphernalia I had just bought and took it all the way downstairs to throw it away. I did not want it in the room with me any longer. That was in Nineteen Seventy-Four, and I have not smoked since.

# 80

## *Tangled Emotions*

**Bert Barker was inclined** to be assertive in manner, probably to make up for his short stature. Unusually efficient, he had a varied background having been a bank manager before becoming the secretary of the Cape Province Clothing Association. We found his past experience invaluable when he served as secretary to the executive of the Transvaal Clothing Industry.

His knowledge of Government regulations was of the greatest help when we negotiated new agreements with the powerful clothing workers union, whose leaders were avowed communists and had been trained in Moscow.

His banking background had enabled him to write the book on International Banking that was accepted as the standard work on the subject. His published history of the South African Clothing Industry covered its shaky beginnings in the early 1880s until its present-day efficient manufacturing methods and modern machinery.

We invited him and his charming wife Nora with her daughter Claudia aged eleven, a child of her first marriage, to dinner occasionally. During the year that I served as President of the Clothing Industry Clare, my wife, and I got on very well with both of them.

One day he invited me to lunch with him at the Langham Hotel. Over lunch he had a sorry tale to tell. "My wife is trying to poison me," he declared. I was aghast and said, "I can't believe it." He continued by giving me chapter and verse of incidents to show how he had come to that conclusion. In fear of his life he was determined to get divorced and asked me how to set about it. I had no experience in such matters but on being pressed, I eventually suggested he should go and chat with my brother-in-law, Louis Trevor, a lawyer. I did not tell Clare about the conversation. Bett had insisted that I do not mention it to a soul.

A few days later Clare told me that she had lunch with Nora who complained how peculiarly Bert had been behaving recently. He finds fault with everything she does and has been exceptionally difficult with Claudia, her daughter. Apart from that, he lifts the plates containing the food she puts before him and smells it before touching it. It is driving her mad. When she asks him "Why are you are behaving in such a peculiar manner?" He maintains a stony silence. What is she to do? She can't go on living like this. To my horror, Clare told me that she had suggested she should go and see Louis Trevor, a lawyer and ask his advice. It was the same man that I had sent Bert, her husband, too. What a foolish coincidence landing Louis, with having to deal with both sides of an impossible situation.

Lawyers under no circumstances discuss their client's affairs, so we will never know what he said or did. But we eventually found out that they got divorced. Nora got a big settlement, as Bert could not supply any reliable proof of her attempting to poison him.

We did hear however, that Bert married a very wealthy American woman, whom he had been seeing for a considerable time.

We know that in our attempt to solve a trauma, we succeeded, but doubt that we had untangled the problems involved in this emotional conflict.

# 81

## *Uncertain Times*

***After the leaders*** of this country continually exposed us to statements that it was essential to invade Iraq to get rid of weapons of destruction, and to dethrone the most wicked and dangerous man in the world, Saddam Hussein, it is doubtful if what they said is true.

Having been forced to listen daily to Zeeson, the German propaganda broadcasts, for many years during World War II, we know now that if anything is repeated often enough it will make people believe it to be the truth.

Despite members of the United Nations having been solidly against it, we have been told that our own weapons are so superior that we can blithely go forward alone. Obviously, it would be very embarrassing to bring everybody back now, once we have sent them there. The United Nations was a body formed to ensure peace. We are now told that it has proved to be an ineffective body, because it refused to aid our war efforts.

With most countries refusing to accept bribes and other arm-twisting efforts to vote for us, we have labeled them as traitors to the United States. Turkey, by not allowing our troops to use their country as a springboard to attack Iraq, surprised us by turning down an offer that we thought they could not refuse.

What has surprised me is the extent that people have accepted the concept that it is in their interest to leave their jobs and families, to save themselves, by fighting for *Iraqi Freedom*. But then of course they should remember how McCarthy managed to convince people to believe that their very neighbors might be dangerous communists.

Economically it is a disaster. This war commenced when our deficit was the largest in its history. How much the cost of *Saving America* will eventually be, no one has dared question.

I am bothered and bewildered to think of its effect on future generations. Obviously it is furthest from the thoughts of the White House at the moment. If Iraq is left in ruins and everybody is killed, we will have saved America. God bless us.

We will do without French fries, not buy German cars or have Turkish baths. That will teach them.

# 82

## *The Wedding Present*

***If having an artistic*** temperament meant being indifferent to the squalor of his living quarters and painting only between bouts of heavy drinking and rowdy brawling, then Arnold Frey's temperament was artistic. He lived in Greenwich Village and shared a communal studio where constant argument and loud music prevailed. But when the urge to paint came over him, he blocked all else from his mind and painted furiously for days. His work featured erotic subjects depicted in violent colors applied with sweeping brush strokes.

There was certainly no market for the undisciplined pictures he produced. He lived mainly on the earnings of whatever woman he was living with at the time. Sometimes, he was even forced to overcome his disapproval of his parents' middle-class values, and get his mother to lend him cash on the security of some of his paintings. She invariably put them straight up into the attic so that nobody would laugh at or criticize what she considered terrible. In any case, it was essential to keep him out of the house to avoid the constant conflict between him and his father.

Arnold kept in touch with his elder brother Benjamin who was a lawyer. When Ben married Pauline, Arnold arrived at the church unshaven and rolling drunk but coherent enough to say that he had left a gift in the study of their newly built home. When Ben and Pauline went to their house after the reception, they were horrified to find the study in complete disorder with one of the paneled walls covered with a mural depicting a group of wild, nude, female figures dancing on a river bank to music played by a leering Pan!

The subject matter, as well as its garish coloring, was completely out of keeping with the leather-bound legal tomes filling their handsome bookcases. After much argument, Pauline eventually suggested they cover it with a curtain that could be drawn apart when Arnold came to visit them. "After all, it's a wedding present and we can't hurt Arnold's feelings." The mural became the talk of the neighborhood, and people who would not normally have visited them, arrived in droves just to be able to say that they had seen it.

After Arnold, in a drunken frenzy, attacked the front door of his girlfriend's house with an axe in an effort to get her to return to him, his family decided to ship him off to Paris as soon as possible. To help pay his fare and finance a monthly remittance, they arranged a public showing of his paintings. The paintings from the attic, together with those from his studio, totaled more than fifty. They were displayed at this parents' home over a weekend.

This first showing at the official opening on Friday evening, was to an invited group. The general consensus was that the paintings were appalling! The comments heard on all sides included, "pornographic," "bad technique," "no color sense," and worse. Not one was sold. It was apparent that most of the guests considered the paintings to be an affront to accepted artistic values.

On Sunday evening, Hiram Zulberg, a Madison Avenue art dealer, returned to chat with Arnold and his parents and said it was his conviction that most artists must be encouraged. To this end, he offered to take the entire collection for the total of one thousand dollars, with the assurance that he was doing it only for "art's sake." The family accepted this philanthropic gesture gratefully.

Life on the Left Bank was even more uninhibited than it had been in Greenwich Village. Friends who visited him came back with reports that his output was considerable, and that he was well thought of by his fellow artists. After several years, Frey moved to a studio in Montparnasse, where he met many prominent artists of the day.

Through these contacts, an art dealer in Fauberg Rue Saint Honore, took several of his paintings and asked to have first purchase rights of anything he painted in the future.

Although now in bad health, he was being acknowledged as a leader of an avant-garde school of Parisian artists. An art journal referred to their work as an important new style that might lead art into the twenty-first century. A few years later, two of his paintings were nominated to be the official French entry in a major international exhibition. They won a top award.

Arnold's sudden death at this time prevented him from benefiting from this public recognition of his talent. Overnight, the value of his paintings increased tenfold. Art critics, not knowing that he was an American, wrote reams about the tragedy of the early demise of this newly found French genius.

In New York, Zulberg had preserved the early paintings intact. He now showed them for the first time, declaring that he had recognized the importance of Frey's work when he first saw them. The fact that he had acquired them merely for "art's sake" w was forgotten.

That an American artist was being claimed by the French as one of their own was good publicity. His work was now lauded for "the great social significance of his subject matter," "his revolutionary technique," and "dramatic use of color."

The New York Times, in reporting on the exhibition, said, "The most exciting exhibition of a hitherto unknown American artist in a decade. A must-see!" Leading collectors showed great interest, and art galleries vied with one another to include his works in their collections.

In the meantime, his brother and sister-in-law, who now lived in

Westchester, were wondering how to take advantage of the late Arnold's newfound fame. They then remembered the mural in their old house. They contacted the owners and found that the panel had been painted over some years before, but a friend thought it would be no trouble to remove the water-based paint that covered it.

Then and there, they offered to repaint the room if they could have the paneling. "Just a matter of sentiment," was the reason they gave. The owners, who had never liked the paneled wall anyway, willingly accepted.

The Museum of Twentieth Century Art as delighted to be offered an Arnold Frey mural. They had a wealthy patron willing to finance the purchase, subject to its restoration. It was thought the mural might be the major attraction at the opening at the museum's new wing in the fall. Ben was overjoyed saying, "I always liked it."

Pauline objected, "No, you didn't. I had to hang a drape over it to stop you from covering it with wallpaper."

When the director of the museum telephoned to ask them to come and see him, they went right away. In the train, they argued over what price to ask. At Grand Central Station they hailed a taxi to take them to the museum, and gave the cab driver a handsome tip on arrival.

They strode confidently into the director's office where they were greeted warmly, but then tactfully told that the restoration had proved unsuccessful. The original had been rubbed down with sandpaper before it was painted over and scarcely any of it remained.

Sadly, they came out of the museum into a world that had looked so much brighter such a short time before. They spurned a hopeful taxi driver who pulled up beside them and joined a line of commuters waiting for a bus.

"You know," said Ben grimly, "I never liked it."

"Neither did I," said Pauline.

# 83

## *Spiders and Achilles*

*March is a wonderful* month to visit Capetown, the intense heat of December and January has passed. Holiday makers have gone home and all the Cape's many attractions are at the their best.

That March I had to attend some meetings of the clothing industry and the South African Chamber of Industry. Clare came with me saying that it would be an opportunity to go to Kirstenbosh, the National Horticultural Gardens at that time of the year. She even said that she might go to some of the wives of the delegate's entertainments, something she never does, if she could fit them in. We arrived on the Friday evening before the Monday's meeting commenced. Together we went into Maskew Millers bookshop Saturday morning to enquire if the new book on entomology by Professor Skaife was out yet.

To our surprise they said "No, not yet." but why don't you phone and ask him yourself? He'd love that. "They gave us his number and phoned.

He said it was nearly finished, and we were very surprised when he asked us if we liked to go there, to talk about it that very afternoon. His home stood on a vast area on the mountainside overlooking Hout Bay. Mrs. Skaife insisted on our having tea and some of her homemade cake while the Professor talked about his book.

Skaife said the book was practically ready for publication, except for the photographic illustrations he was still working on. He showed us a lot of miniaturized photographs of his grandchildren and enlarged pictures of various insects and grasses that after he has put them together, will give the impression of children walking through a jungle inhabited by huge insects much larger than them. The story he hoped would bring the insect world into a greater perspective of its importance in nature, especially to children.

He then took us up to his laboratory, in a separate cottage, a good distance above the house. He showed us some of the various experiments that he was working on. Clare, as founder of the South African Spider Society was particularly interested in the work he was doing with arachnids. Very interested to hear that she was founding member of the South African Spider society, He promised to let her have a signed copy of the book directly it was in print.

My meetings were well attended but one afternoon the subject being discussed was of little interest to us in the clothing business. A competitor of mine Everard Savage from Durban asked me to accompany him to town to look for a book, which had been strongly recommended to him. So far, although he had been to several shops he had not been able to find it. We went to one or two more bookshops asking for "The Achilles Heel" the title of the book he had been recommended without any success.

Eventually I suggested that we try Maskew Miller the bookshop that had put me on to Dr. Skaife. They asked him who the Author was but he had no idea. He then suggested that it might have been "Hercules Elbow." They had never heard of either of them. They then looked through their records recently published books, and said could it possibly be the "The Five Fingers of Cicero," a book that had recently come out.

"That's it!" said Everard. "I had the title wrong. I knew it was something to do with an old Greek."

# 84

## *You Can't Alter Malta*

*As a manufacturer* of government uniforms I often had need to refer to the dress regulations of the military forces. These regulations govern the details of each item of the wearers clothing to be worn at any particular place and under any special circumstance.

As you can imagine it would seem difficult to find much humor in such details, but I would love to know the history of why some of them came to be enacted.

For instance why are naval officers of the British Forces forbidden to wear fancy dress at any Ball except those given by the Governor of Malta? I am sure that the reason for it is steeped some quirk of tradition but we will never know.

Owing to its geographical position at the entrance to the Mediterranean, it has long featured in world history. From the time Knights Templar built powerful fortresses there to oppose the Turks, to the constant bombing it endured by the Germans, in World War II. Britain duly recognized its steadfastness by awarding the whole population with suitable medals.

But Malta still comes into the news from time to time. Such as recently the British forces stationed in Malta performed a large involved military exercise before it was found they were on Spanish territory. Britain was most embarrassed and had to apologize profusely to avoid it being an international incident.

One of the most bizarre enactments of the government there has been the order that all chauffeur-driven cars on the island be black, although there are a number of lighter colored Rolls Royce's that were previously used for weddings and such. Brides now have to be taken to the altar in funeral like transport. No explanation has been given for such an extraordinary ruling.

Ordinary you can't alter Malta.

# 85

## *Go to Blazes*

*I suppose the term* "go to blazes" is a descriptive way of saying, "go to hell." Marco Polo must have thought he had arrived there, when he first saw people walking unburned through fire.

Many hundreds of years ago the Chinese discovered the fireproof property of asbestos. The use of asbestos in buildings and lagging (covering with insulating material) of pipes, is now prohibited because it is a health hazard.

On my very first morning in London one year, I opened the Daily Express and turned to the sports page. To my horror a picture of a racing driver enveloped in flames confronted me. He had been hauled out of his car at Brandon Hatch Race Track the day before. The article gave the driver's name and the hospital to which he had been taken.

As a supplier of protective clothing for firemen, I was extremely interested. We had traditionally used woolen garments for firefighting but realized that wool had many disadvantages. The garments made of wool were warm, bulky and became sodden and heavy when wet. Deciding to pursue the matter, I telephoned the editor of the newspaper. He knew nothing about it, and put me on to others on his staff. I eventually was able to speak to the reporter who had been on the scene.

"No, he wasn't badly burned, he was wearing a fire resistant overall, I

suppose."

"What material was it made from? "I asked.

"I have no idea, I never thought to ask, but if you are interested why don't you ask him yourself?"

"Will the hospital allow me to talk to him?"

The reporter laughed and said he was fairly sure the driver would be back at work in his garage which was somewhere near Leeds in Yorkshire.

I had no trouble in locating the man; he was very pleased to speak about it. He told me that his racing driver's overall was a standard type made from Dupont's Nomex fiber, and he had worn it over Nomex underwear, which gives the added protection of a second fire resistant layer of material as well as creating a protective barrier of air.

We used the photograph when we introduced our new line of fire-resistant protective clothing in South Africa soon afterwards. We got fire brigades throughout the country to accept the product despite considerable opposition from The Wool Board. The Board, an influential body subsidized by the wool producing countries, automatically discourages anything that replaces the traditional use of wool.

If Marco Polo were alive today he probably would find that firefighters are not wearing asbestos, but a similar synthetic to Nomex when they Go to Blazes.

# 86

## *Neighbors*

***Our first child*** was born at home. Clare's doctor Rose Baranov had arrived with a nurse and all her equipment, including oxygen if needed, and went up to the bedroom. Giving birth was a private affair in those days; I stayed downstairs in the study with Sheila, her sister.

A baby's cry announced its arrival and Sheila and I sat expectantly anxious until the doctor came down and announced all was well, a boy had arrived on the scene. Rushing upstairs we found a smiling Clare holding the baby being attended to by Sister James our own maternity nurse who was to stay with us for a month. We also had a black nanny waiting in the kitchen who would be washing the napkins etcetera.

A nursery with a cot, brightly colored walls and a cork floor that we had been advised to put down, was ready. This was not a royal baby's entry into Buckingham Palace, but the way it was expected to be done by ordinary families having a baby in Johannesburg in the nineteen forties. All very civilized, something my granddaughters don't have so comfortably, when turned out of American hospitals after giving birth, the very next day, then having to manage on their own.

Immediate news of its arrival was transmitted by our African maids to other maids in the street faster than any telephone or telegraph could have done. Some of them had been probably in our kitchen, waiting for it to happen. Although we had not yet notified our next-door neighbor Mrs. Rouse of the baby's arrival, we were not surprised when little Duggie Rouse aged two and a half arrived early next day to play football with the new boy he had been told about.

This was the start of contact with the Rouse family, our next-door neighbors for over thirty years. Dudley and Audrey with their son Dudley known as Duggie lived next door. Audrey's father, Mr. Carwell, who actually owned the house, lived with them. He was the senior math teacher at King Edwards Boys High School. I had known him for some time because he was in charge of the school cadets for whom we made uniforms. Most of my friends had attended that school, knew him by his nickname Crappy Carwell. He was a good teacher but a very strict disciplinarian.

We lived in North Road, which marked the boundary of Johannesburg. Beyond us, apart from a few homes on five acres or so there were only dairy farms here and there. It meant there were plenty of mosquitoes and flies and we had to sleep under mosquito nets, at least until the area now called Hyde Park, became a built-up suburb, forcing the farms to move further afield.

They also had a baby daughter named Valerie, eighteen months younger than Duggie, whom they left with us occasionally when Audrey had to do some shopping in Rosebank.

Dudley the father, at the outbreak of war in 1939, joined the National Volunteer Brigade with me but later served in North Africa with the South African Air Force as a mechanic. All the children both theirs and ours went to Rosebank Elementary the only junior school in the area. Strictly Church of England themselves, they surprisingly sent Valerie to the Rosebank Convent for her high school years. Probably because the nuns who taught there had an excellent reputation.

Duggie, the son, had learning problems and was sent to St. Johns College, the premier Church of England high school where he was able to get individual tuition. He was a likeable boy with an engaging smile, but definitely seemed to be accident-prone. From time to time he broke various limbs and one day when climbing over an iron fence he landed heavily on a pointed prong. It pierced his behind and he was seriously injured. At college he completely smashed two Volkswagen Beetles, landing up in hospital each time. He failed his pharmacy final exams several times, before eventually passing with minimal grades.

Now a qualified Pharmacist he joined a large International drug company to promote their products to doctors. Eventually he was transferred to their head office in England. A bad correspondent he evidentially did not bother to write home. When Clare mentioned casually to the Rouses that I was going to Manchester on business, they immediately asked if I would get in touch with Duggie when there. They gave me his telephone number in Macclesfield, which was near Manchester, and of course I said that I would do so.

On reaching my hotel in Manchester before lunch, I phoned the Macclesfield number, and was surprised that Duggie was there and answered himself. He was delighted to hear from me, and said, "It was a miracle that I had come, because he needed advice on an important matter that he had to decide on in a day or two. Can he come to my hotel this evening?" "Of course" I said, "Come for dinner." Wondering what could possibly be so urgent.

Over dinner he told me his problem. His firm had offered him the position in Iran to sell their agricultural products to the Iranian government. They would double his present salary payable in the U.K. and hold it for him. In the meantime he would earn several thousand pounds a year, payable there, plus all his expenses. It sounded like a wonderful opportunity. Yesterday he had gone to see the man who had just returned from Iran to know more about it.

"Now," Duggie said, "I have some doubts about the position, and have no one here to advise me." He was told that the Minister of Agriculture, the King's Uncle, demands fifteen percent commission on all orders placed, plus other benefits. What is more, the U.K. firm offering him the job did not want to know anything about the Minister's demands and would deny that any payment has been made. They also would take no responsibility whatever for anything that may happen to me, or any of their employees, over there. "Luckily," the man went on, "I got back here safely to a large sum of back payments, but I won't guarantee that it will always be the case. You are very much on your own over there." Over dessert and coffee, I asked, "Do you still want my advice?" "Of course," he said. "Well, I would not touch it with a pitchfork. Don't take it."

I reported that I had met Duggie in Manchester but did not tell them the details of his quandary, which was something that he could tell them himself if he wanted to.

Duggie came back to Johannesburg and resumed his old sales promotion job. Within a year he met a divorced woman and lived with her for a while. He told his parents he was about to marry her. They were absolutely against it, she was a year older than him, divorced with a child, but what was worse she was a Catholic. They would not go to the wedding and as far as I know they never saw them again. Clare and I went to the wedding and found his wife to be a sensible person with a strong personality, just the sort of woman Duggie needed.

# 87

## *Next-Door Neighbors*

*We lived in North Road,* Dunkeld West, Johannesburg, five miles from the center of town. North road marked the northern border of the city. After some years we changed the name of the house to Witsend, which we felt better expressed the vicissitudes of our family life during wartime. Our neighbors were Dudley and Audrey Rouse.

We first became friendly with the Rouses just after our first child was born. We made an initial visit next door to introduce ourselves and tell Audrey Rouse as she became known to us, how her little boy had arrived yesterday morning to play football with our new born baby, not realizing it would be a year or two before he would be old enough to play. We had a good laugh about it, and told her not to hesitate to call upon us at any time for anything at all. She brought in her one year old little girl, Valerie and introduced us to their pet cat, Dizzie, a major part of the family who slept in bed with them.

Over the years apart from being neighborly friendly in so many ways, it became a custom to visit them on Christmas Day with presents for them all. Dudley, Audrey's husband, was mechanically minded and often assisted us when we had minor car troubles. Audrey's father who lived with them owned the house. When he died he left the house to them, much to the annoyance of Mrs. Sutton, Audrey' sister who after all, had seldom visited him.

Duggie their son had left home, having married a woman of whom they disapproved, and as far as I knew they never saw him again. The Suttons took umbrage at not being left anything from their father also completely fell out with them. Dudley, Mr. Rouse, appeared to have no family of his own, so their whole existence was bound up with their daughter Valerie.

Though practicing members of the Church of England, they surprisingly made no serious objection to Valerie getting engaged to Jan Opperman, an Afrikaner. He was a presentable, attractive young man who had been taking Valerie out for some time. Jan was in public relations with the film company. It was obvious that he and Valerie were very much in love.

Like most Afrikaners, Jan had been brought up on a farm and was a natural farmer. He had been left a plot of fifty acres near Bryanston, just north of the town, which he intended to develop in due course. There was already an old farmhouse on the land, which he and Valerie moved into after they married. It was only twelve miles from the city, they drove in and out every day. With African staff to do the housework and keep the plot clear, Jan spent every weekend driving the tractor and supervising the planting, etc.

Over time, Valerie and Jan had two sons who, when they were old enough, attended schools that taught only in English. Nevertheless, they were completely bilingual, speaking as they did to the African staff and their father in Afrikaans, and to their mother in English.

Dudley and Audrey spent a lot of time visiting Valerie and their grandsons at the farm. Dudley, a retired electrical engineer with plenty of time on his hands, decided to build a house on his own on a portion of his son-in-law's farm land. A friend of his put down a concrete slab for the foundation. And sufficient bricks to build the house were delivered to the site. He rented a concrete mixer to make the mortar and literally laid the bricks and did all the plumbing and electrical work himself.

Occasionally, on a Sunday, we would take our own grandchildren for a drive out to the farm. They enjoyed the easy-going life there, but their biggest thrill was when they were driven around the farm on the tractor. This happy existence continued for some years. Valerie was involved with various charities initiated by the local church. The boys were now in high school and Jan was happily at work in the filming business and doing some farming over the weekends.

Events clouded the scene after Jan was promoted to direct film propaganda and sent to Metro Goldwyn Mayer's head office in Los Angeles. He had to spend most of his time in the states, being present at film openings, escorting film stars and attending the Oscars. He was a good looking fellow and became completely integrated into the Hollywood scene. He seldom came home and it was obvious his affairs became so involved that a divorce was inevitable.

The farm was sold. Only then did Dudley and Audrey realize that they had made a mistake of building on land that did not belong to them. When the farm sold their house went with it!

Fortunately, they still had money left over from the sale of the North Road house. This enabled them to build another house, but of course on a much smaller stand. Valerie and the boys stayed with them. By this time we had emigrated to America, but after a year or two we went back to Johannesburg to fix up some financial affairs.

We visited the Rouse family in their new home. Both Valerie's boys had joined the South African Police and been transferred to Pretoria and seldom came home. Dudley and Audrey were coping but were still annoyed about Valerie's divorce. They were convinced the Valerie had been done down, in not getting her full share in the settlement, and never stopped talking about it.

When we left, Valerie came to the car to see us off. Well away from the house, she told us that she had wished her parents had not built the house on the farm next to hers. They had interfered all the time and Jan had never been happy about it either. Now that she was on her own, they were more than ever critical of her every move.

Consequently, although she had not told them yet, she was moving in with a divorced male friend whose house was on the other side of town. She definitely did not want her parents living next door.

# 88

## *Prejudice*

**Harry Jacobs** head of Harrows, the largest firm of furniture stores in Britain, was a member of the Conservative Club. The clubs governing committee allowed for only a very limited number of Jewish people to be members, and definitely no women.

Jacobs, was a big contributor to the Conservative Party and long time chairman of a small selection committee responsible for checking the desirability of any Jewish applicant for membership. Only a very small percentage of Jews was allowed to be accepted.

On inviting my wife and me for lunch there, he explained that she would have to eat with other wives, if any, in the basement. We would join her after he and I had lunch in the dining room upstairs. He told me that he particularly want me to see this bastion of British "Old School" traditionalism.

It was all that I had expected, a vast carpeted mahogany entrance hall, a wide imposing staircase, with a magnificent oil-painted portrait of Winston Churchill facing the entrance. Over lunch he told me that his committee had turned down Lord something-or-other's application for membership, one of the richest and most respected Jewish businessmen in Britain, because their quota of Jewish members had been reached.

Before going down to Clare, who had been isolated in the basement, we went into the huge lounge and saw hordes of elderly gentlemen snoozing in high-backed armchairs looking as though they had not moved for years. The scene was like a caricature of a British club in Punch. I was not impressed.

At that time, it was soon after the Sharpeville incident, it was not popular to be a South African anywhere in England. Pictures of the South African policemen shooting a crowd of black people were being shown on television all day, every day. My daughter Susan, who was an Akaila head of a Brownie troop, the junior Girl Scouts, had been invited to speak on South African Scouting, at a lunch in her honor at Baden Powell House. She was shouted down because she said there were no black children in the group. Lady Baden Powell had to interfere on her behalf, before she could go on.

Funnily enough the only place where we were welcomed with open arms, was in Wales. The people in Wales are mad about Rugby, which is South Africa's main sport, and there everybody could not do enough for us.

Back in South Africa at that time Jewish people were not welcome at many golf or social clubs. The Rand Club a very private and important social center for the mining and industrial leaders had no Jewish members. My friend Charles Nathan was a well-known barrister. His late father, Justice Manfred Nathan, had been the only Jewish member in the early days.

Charles was approached by Judge Blackwood, now a cabinet minister, saying I will sponsor your application for membership if you will apply. Charles had no intention of being a member and said, "Why should I have the ignominy of being turned down?" I have heard that when membership is applied for, every member can signify his willingness to accept the applicant or not, by placing a small white or black ball into a box at the entrance. Just one black ball, denies the application. Justice Blackwood insisted that he apply, for his late father's sake. On giving in, against his will, the judge stood at the entrance all day long, and nobody had the nerve to put in a black ball in his presence. Now they had another Jewish member, but apart from joining Justice Blackwood for dinner there that night he never bothered to go there again.

A black scholarship student of Clare's was in Bristol at the time on a science related research project. We invited him for dinner that night. It was a rather high-class hotel set back on a large estate. We had had to park our very inferior looking rented car, in the driveway surrounded by chauffeurdriven Rolls Royces and vast continental cars whose names we had never heard of.

He did not turn up at the appointed time and so we went in for dinner without him. While we were eating our smartly uniformed waitress, told us that a person was at the door asking for us. "Yes," we said, "we were expecting him. Send him in." Looking at us with amazement, she said, "But he is black." When he joined us for dinner, everybody in the dining room looked at us askance, and finished their meal as quickly as possible.

At that time in the late 1960s if you were South African, Jewish or Black you were isolated from many areas.

# 89

## *The All Blacks*

***On arriving in South Africa*** from London in 1926, I discovered that Rugby football was the national sport. Its team known as "The Springboks" was much revered.

The following year 1927, New Zealand, the rugby champion of the British Empire, were coming here for the first time. This was acclaimed as a major happening, because it would put our "Springbok" team on the world scene, recognized as a major player.

The South African Government however, immediately caused an international incident by declaring that the New Zealand team could not play here if they bought Nepia, their Maori star fullback, with them. He was considered to be black and South Africans could not play if any black person was in the team.

There was a large population of black people here, and the government thinking was, that if one black person was allowed to play, others would insist on playing too, unheard of. South Africa's large population of black people although many work in the towns, are domiciled in their tribal areas, and were not considered eligible for national status.

Notwithstanding the ban on Nepia, the New Zealand team, incidentally called the "All Blacks," agreed to come. They were confident that even without their most well-known player, they could beat us. The first Test match against the South African team was to be played in Ellis Park, the new stadium built to hold 90,000 people. Tickets to see the match were sold out in no time.

The first aid personnel of the chamber of mines normally dealt with phthisis, a lung condition brought on by inhaling mine dust caused by blasting the rocks in the underground gold mines. Every mineworker had to be X-rayed at the miner's phthisis bureau every six months. The Transvaal Rugby authorities asked them to deal with the first aid problems of this international match.

Neither the St. John Ambulance nor the Red Cross, who usually dealt with sporting events were invited. Fortunately for me the firm I worked for, H. J. Henochsberg Pty Ltd, were to make the blazers to be worn as identification by the rugby union's own first aid personnel. The blazers were to be royal blue, with large gold embroidered letters TRFU (Transvaal Rugby Football Union) on the pocket.

While they were making them, I got one made to fit me. Wearing it, I pushed my way confidently through the jostling crowd into the stadium. Dressed in my magic jacket, I was allowed in without being questioned. Inside a T. R. F U. official not knowing who I was, told me to go the top level on the right hand side, to deal with any first aid problem that may be needed in the mass of people sitting there. I was delighted that from this excellent vantage point I was to see the match. I congratulated myself on my luck. But not for long. Just a few rows below mine, a woman under pressure from the crowd, fainted. Knowing nothing about first aid, what could I do? I must make myself invisible. I crouched down, took off my blazer and rolled it inside out.

Hoping no one had seen me 1 slunk across the stairway and hid behind the people in the top row the other side of the aisle. It was a bitterly cold day and I could not stay there very long in my shirtsleeves. Putting my jacket inside out, with its black satin lining on the outside. I stood up, now looking very all black myself and cheered the New Zealand team on. The (All White) "All Blacks," won even without their black star player. But to this day I regret that

I never saw Nepia, generally acknowledged as the best fullback in the world, play.

www.ingramcontent.com/pod-product-compliance
Lightning Source LLC
LaVergne TN
LVHW021757060526
838201LV00058B/3139